DEFENDING AND PARENTING CHILDREN WHO LEARN DIFFERENTLY

DEFENDING AND PARENTING CHILDREN WHO LEARN DIFFERENTLY

Lessons from Edison's Mother

SCOTT TEEL

Foreword by Vincent Monastra, M.D.

The Praeger Series on Contemporary Health and Living
Julie Silver, Series Editor

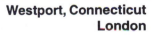

Westport, Connecticut
London

Library of Congress Cataloging-in-Publication Data

Teel, Scott.
Defending and parenting children who learn differently : lessons from Edison's mother / Scott
Teel ; foreword by Vincent Monastra.
     p. cm. — (The praeger series on contemporary health and living, ISSN 1932–8079)
    Includes bibliographical references and index.
    ISBN 978–0–275–99248–4 (alk. paper)
    1. Special education.   2. Exceptional children—Family relationships.   3. Edison, Thomas
    A. (Thomas Alva), 1847–1931—Childhood and youth.   4. Teel, Scott.   5. Dyslexics
    children—Education.   I. Title.
  LC3965.T44   2007
  371.9–dc22   2007006585

British Library Cataloguing in Publication Data is available.

Library of Congress Catalog Card Number: 2007006585
ISBN-13: 978–0–275–99248–4
ISBN-10: 0–275–99248–9
ISSN: 1932–8079

First published in 2007

Praeger Publishers, 88 Post Road West, Westport, CT 06881
An imprint of Greenwood Publishing Group, Inc.
www.praeger.com

Printed in the United States of America

The paper used in this book complies with the
Permanent Paper Standard issued by the National
Information Standards Organization (Z39.48–1984).

10 9 8 7 6 5 4 3 2 1

This book is for general information only. No book can ever substitute for the judgment of a
medical professional. If you have worries or concerns, contact your doctor.

Some of the names and details of individual discussed in this book have been changed to protect
the patients' identities. Some of the stories may be composites of patient interactions created for
illustrative purposes.

CONTENTS

FOREWORD

Great nations prosper through a willingness to recognize and benefit from the diversity of abilities in people. Societies are enriched by the contributions of the plumber, as well as the poet and preacher; by the talents of the mason and machinist, as well as the mathematician; by the contributions of the carpenter and cattleman, as well as the chemist; by the gifts of the baker, as well as the banker; by the toils of the laborer, as well as the lawyer; and by the efforts of the artist, as well as the architect. Throughout our early history as a nation, the value of such contributions was recognized. Our nation grew and our people thrived.

During the past century, as our population grew, a shift occurred in the process of educating our children. We transitioned from a society in which children learned job skills primarily from their parents and neighbors to a context in which education became the domain of governmental agencies. With this transition came a subtle but significant shift in the valuation of skills. The three R's (readin', ritin', and 'rithmetic) became the central theme of education, and other skills (e.g., culinary arts, cosmetology, fine arts, music, farming, and the construction trades) were largely devalued and removed from *mainstream* education. Over the years, the emphasis on language arts and mathematics has dominated educational centers, culminating in the present federal policy (No Child Left Behind), in which children must demonstrate mastery of English, science, social studies, and mathematics in order to attain a high school diploma.

The impact of such policy on children, whose *gift* lies not so much in putting ideas on paper but in translating ideas into the creation of the physical world in which we live, is well documented. We now live in a society in which children whose attention is not drawn to the world of books are diagnosed with an attention deficit disorder. Children whose brains were built to invent and design are labeled as *disabled* in the areas of reading, writing, and mathematics, rather than identified as *gifted* for their creativity and innovation. Without the support and collaboration of educators and parent-advocates, these children are at increased risk to "drop out of school," engage in criminal activities, become addicted to drugs and alcohol, engage in a variety of high-risk activities, and live with a sense of inadequacy and incompetence, because they struggled to learn how to read, write, and learn advanced mathematics.

In *Defending and Parenting Children Who Learn Differently: Lessons from Edison's Mother*, Scott Teel provides a guide for parents who are seeking ways to protect their children from the daily attacks on self-esteem generated by an educational system that devalues the talents of these children. Although our society holds in high esteem the contributions of the Albert Einstein's and Thomas Edison's of our nation, we seem to do little to promote their development or encourage them in the process of making the discoveries that enhance our lives. Instead, the Einsteins and Edisons of our nation thrive because of a parent or other caretaker who recognized their child's special gifts, and created a nurturing environment that encouraged learning and self-expression.

Scott Teel draws from the story of Thomas Edison and his mother, incorporates findings from leading researchers in psychology, medicine, and education, and creates a book with dozens of practical ideas for creating an environment in which children who are *differently abled* can thrive. In addition, he provides an extensive resource list to direct parents to specialists who can support them in their efforts to lead their children through the troubled and confusing years from kindergarten through high school. I often tell parents that students who struggle to attend to instruction and master reading, writing, and mathematics need to find a way through high school, with their self-confidence intact. Once they make it through those difficult years, *they* can choose to follow an educational and career path that matches their abilities. Until such a time as our educational systems begin to value skills other than reading, writing, arithmetic, and the retention of scientific and historical facts, parents would do well to learn from the lessons of Edison's mother, and help their children cherish the unique gifts they inherited.

Vincent Monastra, M.D.

SERIES FOREWORD

Over the past hundred years, there have been incredible medical break-throughs that have prevented or cured illness in billions of people and helped many more improve their health while living with chronic conditions. A few of the most important twentieth-century discoveries include antibiotics, organ transplants, and vaccines. The twenty-first century has already heralded important new treatments including such things as a vaccine to prevent human papillomavirus from infecting and potentially leading to cervical cancer in women. Polio is on the verge of being eradicated worldwide, making it only the second infectious disease behind smallpox to ever be erased as a human health threat.

In this series, experts from many disciplines share with readers important and updated medical knowledge. All aspects of health are considered including subjects that are disease-specific and preventive medical care. Disseminating this information will help individuals to improve their health as well as researchers to determine where there are gaps in our current knowledge and policymakers to assess the most pressing needs in health care.

Series Editor Julie Silver, M.D.
Assistant Professor
Harvard Medical School
Department of Physical Medicine and Rehabiliation

INTRODUCTION

Every child who learns differently needs an advocate, someone who believes in him or her and his or her ability to learn. In a perfect world, every child with a learning difference would have an entire support system of advocates—teachers, professionals, and family members who understand the child and help him or her fulfill his or her potential. Sadly, this is often not the case. Many talented and well-intentioned teachers have so many tasks to accomplish with so many students that they cannot give each child the individual attention he or she needs. As a recent Presidential Commission on Excellence in Special Education observed, the "system is driven by complex regulations, excessive paperwork and ever-increasing demands at all levels."[1] Other professionals and support persons are often underutilized or, all too frequently, never even consulted. Parents, guardians, and other family members are usually the child's last line of defense, and it is therefore imperative that at least one family member accept responsibility as the primary advocate for the child, defending and parenting him or her throughout his or her school years.

I know firsthand how it feels to be a child with a learning difference. I was a late talker, rarely speaking before I was 4 or 5 years old. Most people could barely understand my speech until I was in the third grade. I attended speech therapy classes with the other *slow* kids in elementary school. (Actually, several of my cohorts in speech therapy turned out to be very intelligent. Yet, we sounded *stupid* and were therefore labeled as such in elementary school.)

I was easily distracted and bored in school, causing me to suspect now that I had some measure of attention deficit hyperactivity disorder. I often *spaced out* through entire lessons. Of course, I did not understand the ensuing homework assignment, and therefore decided most nights to skip homework by telling my parents that I did all my work at school. My grades predictably suffered, although I always scored at the top of my class during the annual school tests.

I attended elementary school in the 1960s, before many learning differences began to be identified or widely acknowledged. My learning difficulties therefore made me somewhat of an enigma to most of my teachers. They suspected that I was smarter than my schoolwork demonstrated, yet they could not understand why I did so poorly in many subjects.

Fortunately, one educator stepped in and acted as my advocate in school. My fourth-grade teacher, Mary Lou Holmes, rekindled my love for learning (a trait that had been nearly extinguished by my first three years in school). She saw through my learning difficulties and realized that I *would* and *could* concentrate when material was presented to me in a compelling fashion. She steered me toward performing *hands-on* science experiments. She allowed me to put some of my excess energies into extracurricular projects, such as starting a weekly school newspaper and producing plays and musical performances. In short, she realized that a standard "sit at your desk and listen" education would not work on me, and she altered her teaching enough to make an impact on my life. I will always be in her debt.

Of course, the most important contribution came from my mother. She steadfastly believed in my ability to learn, and she fought for my educational rights long before significant legislation existed that guaranteed an equal education to children with learning differences. She talked my father into purchasing encyclopedias, chemistry sets, microscopes, and musical instruments for me. She talked the family physician into taking me to the hospital laboratory to use their microscopes and talk to the laboratory technicians. She bought a seemingly endless list of supplies for my science projects (petri dishes, test tubes, agar, alcohol lamps, etc.), and complained only when some of my experiments got truly out of hand (such as when I caught my *laboratory* on fire or brought a live brown bat into the house).

Even the great inventor Thomas Edison needed an advocate during his childhood to help him through his learning difficulties and problems in school. His mother, Nancy Elliot Edison, turned out to be a wonderful advocate. She was a strong, independent, and capable woman who never stopped believing in her son.

While many of Edison's exploits are well known (perhaps even to the point of being American folklore), many people do not realize the important role his mother played in developing his genius. Without her support, Young Thomas Edison (or *Al*, as they called him) could have turned into a dismal failure instead of a huge success. In fact, he was such a poor student that many considered him incapable of learning. Al was so careless that he endangered not only his own life several times but also inadvertently threatened the lives of many others through his recklessness. In addition, he was a sickly child who suffered health problems all through his youth.

With all these handicaps, it is easy to imagine why so many people, including his father, might have felt that young Al had no future in life.

Despite the negative expectations of everyone else, his mother continued to be an unwavering beacon of hope for Al throughout her life. She steadfastly refused to give up on her youngest child, constantly believing that he could overcome all of life's many obstacles and difficulties to become a great man.

This book will tell you the wonderful story of Al and Nancy Edison, and explain how parents of children who learn differently can emulate her today—defending, encouraging, teaching, and parenting their children as she did more than 150 years ago.

1

NANCY EDISON'S MIRACLE

My mother cast over me an influence that has lasted all my life. I was always a careless boy, and with a mother of different mental caliber I should have turned out badly. But her firmness, her sweetness, her goodness; they were potent powers to keep me on the right path. She was the making of me. She was so true, so sure of me. I felt I had someone to live for, someone I must not disappoint.

—Thomas Alva Edison

Thomas Edison always spoke of his mother Nancy Elliott Edison in quiet, reverent tones. He was fully aware that so many of his great achievements might not have been possible if not for the love, determination, and skill she displayed in raising and educating him.

Although Edison is remembered today as the quintessential American inventor and businessman, he seemed destined to a life of failure in his youth. His schoolteachers had given up on him as unteachable. His father suspected that he was mentally retarded. The family physician feared that he suffered brain damage at birth. The only person in his life who seemed to have an unwavering faith in his abilities was his mother, Nancy Elliott Edison.

Although we do not know what specific learning disability caused Thomas Edison's troubles in school, *Al*, as his family called him, had a number of health problems as a child. His general ill health and weakness often caused his mother to fear that he would not survive his youth. His hearing gradually decreased until he was completely deaf in one ear and 80 percent deaf in the other ear by age 12. He did not begin speaking until 4 years of age, furthering his father's belief that Al suffered from mild mental retardation.

Edison described himself as "a careless child," and this recklessness nearly resulted in his own death several times. He once fell into a commercial grain elevator while *exploring* and almost suffocated in the mountain of wheat. He was also notoriously impulsive and often acted on his ideas with little forethought, even losing the tip of a finger after holding a skate strap down and instructing a friend to shorten the strap with an axe. He started two major fires as a boy, one at age 6 (which promptly burnt the family barn to the ground) and another at age 12 in a railroad baggage car where he had stored some hazardous chemicals.

In 1854, at the age of 7, Edison began his brief period of classroom schooling at the Family School for Boys and Girls in Port Huron, Michigan. The school founder, Reverend George Engel, ran a firm and disciplined classroom where the children were expected to pay attention and sit quietly at their desks while the teachers lectured. Lessons were taught primarily by repetition and rote memorization.

Edison's inquisitive nature and creativity were unwelcome in this chilly academic setting. Al would often burst spontaneously into a series of questions when a subject intrigued him, disrupting the class and preventing the teachers from following their rigid lesson plans. On the other hand, Al quickly lost interest whenever the class seemed to move too slowly or the subject was boring. The teacher's monotonous drone would gradually fade away from Al's consciousness, and he would find himself doodling in his notepad or staring out of the window at the ferry crossing the St. Claire River.

Al's teachers would frequently ridicule him in front of the class or make him sit in the corner as punishment for not paying attention. "I was always," he recalled, "at the foot of the class, and had come almost to regard myself as a dunce. Even my father entertained vague anxieties as to my stupidity."[1]

Today, we understand that some children, such as young Thomas Edison, do not respond well to traditional teaching methods and require special attention to succeed in a classroom environment. Unfortunately, most educators in the mid-1800s believed that poor performance in school was due to either a lack of discipline or a fundamental inability to learn. Academic failure was nearly always presumed to be the fault of the child.

Predictably, Al's teachers took no responsibility when a visiting school inspector asked why the young lad was performing so poorly. Mr. Crawford, Al's teacher, explained that the boy's brain was *addled*, a term used to describe an egg that had gone rotten, implying that Al was too weak-minded to ever do well in school.

Al was devastated by Mr. Crawford's cruel remarks. He ran home crying and told his mother about the incident, which immediately stirred Nancy's anger. She reassured Al that he was a bright child with his own unique abilities and strengths, and urged him to not take the teacher's unkind words to heart.

Nancy marched Al back to the school and confronted the school staff. Although they explained their belief that Al was unable to learn, she countered with her knowledge that Al was smarter than any teacher in the school. Henceforth, she declared, she would teach Al at home.

Thus, after just 3 months of classroom instruction, Thomas Edison's formal education ended. For most of the next 5 years, he would spend his days being homeschooled by his mother.

EDISON'S LEARNING DIFFICULTIES

Modern parents of intelligent children who underperform at school can easily relate to this story. The problems Al experienced, such as a difficulty focusing for long periods of time on one topic, are common in many intelligent children. Their problems in school may be due to a number of different causes, ranging from sheer boredom to dyslexia or some other learning disorder.

Many sources attribute Thomas Edison's troubles in school to attention deficit hyperactivity disorder (ADHD). Edison did seem to share many common characteristics of children with ADHD, such as

- fidgeting or squirming frequently;
- drifting off into daydreams more than other children;
- having difficulty following instructions or finishing activities, such as homework;
- interrupting a speaker, such as the teacher;
- being easily distracted; and
- being impulsive.

Although ADHD is considered to be a health impairment that can adversely affect a child's learning, a number of persons in the field of child behavior now feel that this is a misnomer. Rather than thinking of ADHD as an impairment, this school of thought prefers to believe that *normal* children and ADHD children are primarily different only in *how* they learn, not in their *ability* to learn. An ADHD child, for example, might learn well in a visually oriented activity or a hands-on experiment, whereas a *normal* child might learn well by listening to a teacher give a lecture or completing a worksheet. One analogy is to think of ADHD children as being similar to left-handed children; they are certainly *different* than most other kids, but that is not to say that they are *wrong*.

Traditional educational systems in America often teach children as if they are all *linear thinkers*, who think in clear lines that focus on one subject at a time. Linear thinkers learn well in a normal classroom environment through lectures and repetition. Thomas Edison, in contrast, was a *tangential thinker*. His mind would grasp one thought and use it as a springboard to form associations with other ideas. He had trouble focusing on one idea because tangential thoughts were always popping up and vying for his attention.

Although many children with ADHD may be tangential thinkers, not all tangential thinkers necessarily have ADHD. Only an estimated 5–7 percent of the schoolchildren in America have clinical ADHD, meaning that the child is significantly impaired in social or academic functions by their ADHD symptoms. An untold number of tangential thinkers may display some ADHD behavior without having significant enough symptoms to warrant a diagnosis of ADHD. (Chapter 2 will go into more detail on this subject.)

THE POSSIBLE ADVANTAGES OF TANGENTIAL THINKING

A number of theories have been proposed in the last 20 years to explain the presence of ADHD children in our midst, ranging from excess television watching to modern food additives. The proponents of these theories suggest that something in our modern world is making these children go *wrong*. Otherwise, they ask, why is it that no one ever heard of an ADHD child 30 years ago, whereas now they seem to be abundant in every school system?

However, it is likely that ADHD is not exclusively *caused* by any one thing in our modern world that did not exist 100 years ago or even 1,000 years ago. For example, Thomas Edison did not have red food dye #5, monosodium glutamate, or potassium sorbate in his food. Neither was he subjected as a child to endless cartoons and reruns of "Gilligan's Island" on television, yet he appears to have exhibited the classic symptoms of a person with ADHD.

This is not to say that environmental or social factors, such as food additives, television, and computer games, and the fast pace of modern society do not have some effect of the incidence of ADHD in children. However, the reason that ADHD seems so prevalent today, compared to 30 years ago, may be simply that ADHD is now a recognized condition that doctors and educators are familiar with and are comfortable diagnosing.

Recent research suggests that our ancestors may have found some advantage to having a certain number of tangential thinkers in every group, possibly increasing the population's overall survival rate.[2]

The apparent evolutionary advantage afforded by having a certain amount of diversity in thinking styles arises from the common traits associated with ADHD: hyperactivity, frequent daydreaming and inattention, the ability to hyperfocus, and impulsivity (unpredictability and novelty seeking). While these traits may cause problems for modern children in a traditional classroom environment, an ancient hunter-gatherer society may have realized an overall advantage by having a small subpopulation of persons with these traits.

The basis for this argument stems from an apparent association between ADHD and a dopamine receptor gene labeled *DRD4*. Several studies show that a particular variation of this gene increases the tendency toward *novelty seeking* and occurs in a high number of children with ADHD. This does not mean that the *DRD4* variation *causes* ADHD, but it does indicate that this variation of this gene, when combined with other genetic variations (and possibly, other social or environmental conditions), can result in a child having a higher probability for ADHD.

This genetic variation may have spontaneously occurred more than 10,000 years ago, but remained in the gene pool instead of dying out as most mutations do. The fact that the mutation survived and replicated into future generations indicates that it had some positive effect, since mutated genes that have negative effects cannot usually compete with robust *normal* genes and therefore eventually die out of the population.

Having a genetic variation linked to ADHD helps to explain why ADHD seems to run in families. Thomas Edison's father, Samuel, was famously impulsive and grew bored easily. The National Institute of Mental Health reports that children who have ADHD usually have at least one close relative who also has ADHD. At least one-third of all fathers who had ADHD in their youth have children with ADHD, and when one twin of an identical twin pair has the disorder, the other is likely to have it too.

THE ADVANTAGE OF NOVELTY SEEKING

If ADHD is perceived as such a *problem* today, why was it an apparent advantage for our prehistoric ancestors to have a number of ADHD persons in their groups? This question seems particularly difficult to answer when you consider two of the complicating factors commonly associated with ADHD:

- ADHD individuals (especially, children) are generally more careless and prone to injury than are *ordinary* individuals.
- ADHD often co-occurs with other problems, such as depressive and anxiety disorders, conduct disorder, drug abuse, or antisocial behavior.

However, consider that ADHD is a name that we have given to a specific set of symptoms only recently. By definition, we designate the top 5 percent to 7 percent of the most hyperactive, inattentive, and impulsive persons as having ADHD. That does not mean that in a group of 100 persons, we will find 5 hyperactive or impulsive individuals and 95 *normal* persons. Hyperactivity, inattentiveness, impulsivity, and novelty seeking are traits that we all exhibit to some degree. These characteristics are spread over the population in the same manner as intelligence, height, weight, and shades of hair color. Persons we designate as having ADHD are merely those who exhibit their particular traits most profoundly. Tangential thinkers, however, may represent the top 10–20 percent of these persons, not just the 5–7 percent that we identify as having ADHD.

Tangential thinkers would have presented a number of advantages to a tribal hunter-gatherer group. For instance, their search for novelty may have made them more prone to explore or migrate, helping the group spread out and discover new environmental niches and sources of food. Tangential thinkers would also be less afraid to explore their own creativity, thus opening up new areas of art, social expression, and invention that the rest of the group could then exploit. They could also prove useful in testing and exposing false beliefs.

THE WONDER OF NANCY EDISON'S ACCOMPLISHMENT

While many successful methods for teaching tangential thinkers are known today, Nancy Edison could only follow her instincts when it came to deciding how to educate her son. It would have seemed a daunting task to even the most determined tutor of the mid-1800s, yet Nancy approached it with obvious optimism. She believed in Al's abilities as well as her own. Her unwavering faith and self-esteem were reflected later in her son as he persevered through thousands of dead ends in his experiments with the light bulb and other inventions.

Edison's astounding achievements speak highly of the education he received from his mother. He executed the first of his 1,093 successful U.S. patent applications in October of 1868, at the age of 21. In 1882, perhaps his most productive year, he completed 106 successful patent applications.

Who Was Nancy Edison?

Throughout the rest of this book, we will be exploring how Nancy Edison successfully taught Al at home. First, let's take a look at who this remarkable woman was.

Nancy Elliott was born on January 4, 1810, in Chenango County, New York, to a family of Scottish descent. Her father was Reverend John Elliott, a Baptist minister and the son of Ebenezer Matthews Elliott, a former captain in Washington's army.

Nancy moved to Vienna, Ontario, in her late teens to teach in the public high school. She met Samuel Edison there and married him on September 12, 1828. Nancy was just 18 years old, a bit stout and of medium height, with soft brown hair, large hazel eyes, and an easygoing, mild attitude toward life. Samuel was a 24-year-old tavern keeper who had moved with his family to Vienna 17 years earlier to establish a homestead. He was a restless and impulsive jack-of-all-trades, who had already tried his hand at being a tailor and carpenter before deciding to open a tavern. Contrary to Nancy's patriot heritage, Samuel's American grandfather had been loyal to the British Crown and had fled to Nova Scotia during the Revolutionary War.

Nancy and Samuel had four children together (Marion, William Pitt, Harriett Tannie Ann, and Carlile), and they appeared to live a quiet life over the course of their first 8 years together. Everything changed, however, in 1837, when Samuel became involved in a political struggle led by William Lyon McKenzie, the mayor of Toronto.

McKenzie was outraged by the British government's imposition of "taxation without representation" on Canadians. He hoped to enact a second American Revolution and establish a democracy in Canada. It is known that Samuel was said to have felt some guilt for his grandfather's refusal to take part in the American Revolution, although it is impossible to say whether or not this guilt helped to motivate him toward supporting McKenzie.

Despite the danger in which it placed his family, Samuel began secretly training volunteers in the woods outside of Vienna in anticipation of the rebellion's outbreak. In December of 1837, his group of rebels was called to action. They quietly began making their way toward a tavern north of Toronto to rendezvous with other rebels and receive further orders. Fortunately, word reached them before they had arrived at their destination that British troops knew of their plan. Many of their comrades had already been killed, and soldiers were reportedly heading toward Venice to track down Samuel's band of men.

The rebels split up, each man trying to get to a safe destination before they could be apprehended. Nine members of Sam's brigade were caught and hanged in London, Ontario, but Samuel eluded capture and made a desperate run for the United States border 80 miles away.

Samuel made the frigid journey on foot, hiding during the day and moving on deserted country roads at night. He eventually made it safely to the frozen St. Claire river and crossed over into Michigan. Cold, alone, homeless, and virtually penniless, Samuel realized that he would not be able to return to Nancy and his children in Canada. He therefore began wandering the American countryside, searching for a suitable place to settle and send for his family.

British soldiers spent an entire day searching for Samuel in Venice, ransacking Nancy's house and outbuildings in the course of their quest. Although the troops eventually departed, Nancy and her four young children were left alone to eke out a living as best they could while Samuel searched for a new home in America.

Samuel finally sent word for Nancy to join him in Milan, Ohio, after nearly a year and a half. She dutifully loaded a wagon and took her children on the arduous trek to reunite with her husband in June of 1839.

One of Samuel's new friends, a Great Lake's steamboat captain named Alva Bradley, helped Samuel set up a shingle mill and feed store in town to support the Edison family. A new canal that ran between Lake Huron and Lake Erie soon brought prosperity to Milan and success to Samuel's businesses. Farmers from 100 miles around Milan would bring grain to ship on the canal, making it for a time the busiest grain port in America. Al would sometimes spend hours watching from his bedroom window as the wagons full of golden grain wound down the road to the boat docks.

Nancy was content for a while to raise the children in a small leased home, but she soon became pregnant with their fifth child and insisted on a larger house. Although Samuel balked at the idea of building a new home, Nancy took it upon herself to purchase a lot in her own name. Samuel eventually complied with her wishes and built a splendid three-story Greek Revival home of sandstone and brick, topped with cedar shingles from his mill.

Sadly, their new home would be the scene of a series of tragedies. Samuel Ogden Edison III, Nancy's fifth child, was born on March 5, 1840, but would only survive to age 3 before succumbing to an unidentified illness. Six-year-old Carlile would die in February of 1842, barely a year before little Samuel passed away. Another daughter, Eliza, was born the following year but became ill and died a week before her third Christmas.

Nancy was emotionally devastated over the loss of three children within 5 years. She sought solace in the midst of all this tragedy by becoming pregnant one final time. It was a difficult pregnancy, complicated by her emotional duress and prenatal diabetes. To calm her nerves, she would knit baby clothing for 3 hours every day.

Thomas Alva Edison, Nancy's seventh and last child, was born on February 11, 1847. He was named for Samuel's uncle Thomas and their friend Captain Alva Bradley. Doctor Leman Galpin, the family physician, lived nearby and was able to arrive in time to deliver Al himself. He hesitantly observed that the child's head was *sorely misshapen* and feared that *brain fever* of some kind had caused damage to the newborn, setting the stage for Samuel's doubts as to his son's intelligence. Although the doctor's fears were unfounded, Al did prove to be a sickly child and was always small for his age.

Nancy now had only her newborn baby and three teenagers remaining at home. Of the teenagers, only 14-year-old Tannie was destined to stay with her for more than a few months. William Pitt was 16 years old and already looking for a job in town, while 17-year-old Marion would soon marry a local farmer and move away.

Nancy felt a great sense of loss from the five mournful years leading up to Al's birth and feared that she would lose him just as she had lost Carlile, Samuel, and Eliza. Nancy devoted herself to her youngest child, often praying for his health for long periods at a time. She managed to nurse him through his various illnesses until, at age 7, he was deemed well enough for the family to move to Port Huron, Michigan. Samuel felt the move was necessary, anticipating that the railroads in Port Huron would soon supplant the steamboat traffic on Milan's canal.

It was in Port Huron that Al had his brief exposure to classroom education at the Family School for Boys and Girls. After three short months, Nancy pulled Al out of school and once again devoted her life to her youngest child by pledging to teach him at home. Despite anyone else's opinion of Al and his abilities, she believed he was capable of learning.

Nancy's experience as a teacher was certainly a great help, although a greater gift may have been her intuition as a mother. She knew Al intimately and understood how to grab and retain his attention. Al's natural curiosity and her guidance would be more than enough to show the world that he was capable of great things.

2

WHY THOMAS EDISON WAS SUCH A POOR STUDENT IN SCHOOL

The question of why Thomas Edison did so poorly in school is a topic of great debate. Undoubtedly, Edison had learning differences compared to his classmates; he clearly did not learn in the same manner as most other boys and girls of his age. The real question is whether Edison had a specific health impairment, such as attention deficit hyperactivity disorder (ADHD). Unfortunately, a definite posthumous diagnosis is impossible, despite the many Web sites and articles that proudly list Edison and other famous persons as having had ADHD.

Perhaps it is best, however, if we do not insist on a positive diagnosis of ADHD or some other learning disorder for Thomas Edison. The fact that he obviously had difficulties learning in a conventional classroom despite his innate intelligence allows him to be an inspiration to every parent of a tangential thinker.

The classic classroom setting and teaching methods used by most schools may not be conducive to educating tangential thinkers. Sitting still and listening to verbal instructions are not strong points for children like Thomas Edison, yet these are the two skills needed for success in a conventional classroom.

ADHD OVERVIEW

Let us take a minute to consider how ADHD is diagnosed, and explore why many people suspect that Edison had the condition.

Diagnosing a child with ADHD can be a rigorous process. A qualified professional must conduct personal interviews with the child and his or her parents. The professional may also need to interview the child's teachers or review school records. Sometimes the professional must actually witness real-time interactions between the child and his or her teachers and classmates to see how the child responds to the classroom environment. In addition, standardized testing may provide an objective measurement of the child's ADHD tendencies.

ADHD is inherently difficult to diagnose. There is no definite laboratory test or blood work that will give a chemical signature for the condition, although laboratory tests may be performed in the course of the diagnosis to detect other conditions that could cause or exacerbate the observed symptoms. The particular ADHD traits displayed may vary greatly from one child to the next, and even a single child's symptoms can vary according to the environment in which he or she is observed. Sometimes the child may exhibit an almost complete inability to focus on a subject, while at other times he or she may hyperfocus on something for hours at a time.

All children occasionally act distracted or hyperactive, so the professional diagnosing ADHD must look at such things as the frequency and severity of these occurrences. Most importantly, the child's symptoms must significantly impair his or her social or academic life to warrant a diagnosis of ADHD.

Another factor that must be considered when diagnosing ADHD is the tendency of other conditions to masquerade as ADHD. For example, caffeine or drug use, chronic anxiety, hyperthyroidism, or dyslexia might manifest symptoms similar to those produced by ADHD. Several conditions sometimes coexist with ADHD, such as Tourette's syndrome, complicating the actual diagnosis of either condition.

A perplexing range of symptoms is classified as belonging to ADHD, causing the National Institute for Mental Health to recognize three subgroups of symptoms.

Predominately Hyperactive/Impulsive

These children display hyperactivity by being constantly *on the go*. They have a good deal of trouble sitting still for any length of time. They might dash around the room, and touch or play with whatever they can reach. Their feet may remain restless and constantly wiggle or tap the floor, even while they are sitting down. They might continually tap their knuckles or a pencil on the table. They are usually searching for some stimulation and feel a need to stay busy, even if it means doing two or three things at the same time.

Their impulsive nature makes them seemingly unable to think before they act. Their immediate urge is to act on a thought without considering the consequences of that action. These children often blurt out inappropriate comments or questions, and are subject to displays of unrestrained emotion. They are sometimes prone to sudden aggressive actions, such as taking toys away from other children. Waiting their turn in line can be a major struggle for these children.

Predominately Inattentive

Inattentiveness means that the child has difficulty maintaining his or her focus on one thing. These children may act confused or lethargic, and are sometimes described as *dreamers* or *spacey*. They can become bored easily, although they can also concentrate for long periods of time on things they enjoy. Distractions are a common problem among these children; practically any noise or movement is enough to attract their attention. They might also have trouble paying attention to details or following instructions. A widespread symptom is the tendency to move from one uncompleted activity to another.

Homework is a common problem for these children. They often misplace books or *forget* to bring books home. They tend to misunderstand or inaccurately copy their homework assignments. Even completed assignments may be full of obvious errors and inattention to detail.

These children are rarely impulsive or hyperactive. Still, they may have just as much trouble paying attention as a hyperactive child. Oral instructions are often the hardest for them to follow, but even written instructions can sometimes be difficult for them to comprehend.

These children do not *fit the mold* of the public's concept of a child with ADHD. They are not normally disruptive or loud in class, and can usually get along well with other children. Although they might need help just as much as a hyperactive/impulsive child, their condition is not as easily identified and can therefore be overlooked by parents and teachers.

Combined Type

Children with combined type ADHD can exhibit any mixture of traits from both the hyperactive/impulsive and the inattentive group. Their diagnosis can be particularly complex, since any number of combinations of symptoms are possible.

The final word: ADHD and other learning disorders can only be diagnosed by a qualified professional, such as a psychiatrist, psychologist, pediatrician, family physician, or neurologist. Treatment may involve a combination of medication and counseling for the child and parents. ADHD is listed as a health impairment under the Americans with Disabilities Act, and ADHD children may be eligible for special accommodations. Parents should consult with their school district about the availability of such programs or seek qualified legal help.

Although we cannot tell for certain if Thomas Edison had ADHD, it is fair to say that he displayed the following traits commonly accepted by the medical community to be ADHD symptoms:

Beginning One Project before Another Is Completed

Edison was famous for carrying on a number of simultaneous projects. Edison and his staff worked on as many as forty projects at one time at the Menlo Park laboratory.

True to his nature as a tangential thinker, Edison frequently allowed himself to be *carried away* when a new idea arose during the course of a project. The original project would sometimes even be forgotten as he pursued tangents created by the new idea.

An excellent example of this tendency occurred while Edison was attempting to develop an effective transatlantic cable. He used powdered carbon as a conductor in his experiments to simulate the electrical impedance of thousands of miles of electrical cable. His experiments were ruined when vibrations caused by everyday activities, such as footsteps in the laboratory, affected the electrical resistance and conductivity of the carbon. Although Edison was annoyed that his experiment was ruined, his tangential thinking caused him to become fascinated by this newly discovered property of powdered carbon. Edison followed this idea until it lead him to invent a "pressure relay" to control electric currents.

Although Edison abandoned the transatlantic cable project, his new pressure relay turned out to be a perfect tool for amplifying the voice signal in Alexander Graham Bell's newly invented telephone. His invention made the telephone so efficient and practical that it turned from being a mere laboratory novelty into a ubiquitous appliance in every house and business. Thus, Edison set the stage for the modern telecommunications industry.

Restlessness and the Need for Constant Stimulation

"I owe my success to the fact that I never had a clock in my workroom," Edison wrote in his diary. "Seventy-five of us worked twenty hours every day and slept only four hours—and thrived on it."

A Pattern of Disorganization

The collection of Edison's writings at the Edison National Historic Site is voluminous, spanning approximately 5 million papers in all. While the sheer vastness of the collection makes it difficult to locate any specific piece of information, the lack of systematic organization within the papers makes the task almost impossible.

Until 1871 Edison had no consistent organization methods at all. Driven by his need to provide documentation for patent and contractual litigation, Thomas Edison then vowed: "all new inventions I will hereafter keep a full record." Despite his best intentions, however, many important papers were lost or misplaced over the course of his career. He would often allow loose notes to pile up around his laboratory for days or weeks, and then order his assistants to gather them up and paste them into scrapbooks. Unfortunately, Edison usually had several projects going on at once, and the resulting piles of papers were usually a tangled mess of various dates and subjects.

Edison, in desperation, finally banned loose papers from his laboratory altogether in 1877, and used only 9" × 11" softcover tablets throughout the rest of his career. The following year he also hired his longtime friend Stockton L. Griffin to be his secretary, who organized his papers for him on a full-time basis.

Attention Span Ranging from "Easily Distracted" to "Hyperfocused"

Every parent or teacher of a child with ADHD knows that *attention deficit* can be an extremely inaccurate term when the child is interested in something. ADHD children can often focus for long periods of time on something they find interesting, but be unable to focus at all on something they find boring.

Edison himself acknowledged that he could be easily distracted by extraneous sights and sounds. For this reason, he counted his near deafness as a gift. The relative silence in which he lived allowed him to concentrate without many of the distractions of everyday life.

A classic example about the ease with which Edison could be distracted from one concern and subsequently hyperfocus on another concern involves his wedding night. One of his uncompleted projects had remained on his mind throughout the wedding ceremony, and he felt that all he might need was an hour or so to complete some work and then he would be free to concentrate on his new bride. Upon arriving at their home, Thomas announced that he had to go to work for a short session. He promised to only be gone a short time, and left for his laboratory.

Hours later, an assistant discovered Edison hard at work. The assistant was naturally surprised to see him there, and asked, "Why are you here after midnight on your wedding day?"

"Oh, dear," said Edison, "I've lost track of time. I had best get home and celebrate my wedding."

Troubles with Authority

Thomas Edison was never anyone's employee for very long. He seemed to become bored at every job he took, and often tried to alleviate his boredom by conducting unauthorized experiments while he was supposed to be working. He once accidentally spilled sulfuric acid he had secretly stored in an upstairs closet at his workplace while performing clandestine experiments on batteries. The acid ate through the floor and dripped all over his supervisor's desk, resulting in Edison's hasty termination.

One job as a telegraph operator ended in near tragedy when Edison disregarded company policy and fell asleep at his desk. Thomas had set up a system with another employee where they would alternately take naps through the night, each rousing the other as the need arose. The other employee was not in the room, however, when an urgent message came through that warned of an unscheduled train on the railway that night. Edison slept through the message and did not pass it on. Fortunately, an alert railway operator heard the unscheduled train approaching in time and diverted an oncoming train onto another track before disaster struck. Once again, Edison found himself unemployed due to his disregard for company rules.

Creativity and High Intelligence

Edison is best known as the inventor of the lightbulb, the phonograph, and the motion picture camera. However, he should also be remembered for developing entirely new industries. He is largely responsible for the beginning of electric power distribution in the United States, as well as the telecommunications, motion picture, recording, and concrete industries.

Edison showed perhaps his greatest creativity in developing the first full-time research and development laboratory, now a fundamental part of almost every major corporation. In so doing, Edison effectively invented the *inventing* industry.

A Pattern of Underachievement

ADHD interferes with a child's concentration and makes it difficult for a child to focus or process instructions correctly. The child consequently struggles in the classroom and with his or her homework. The child might score poorly on tests even if he or she has high intelligence and spends a good deal of time studying.

This lack of success can spawn a dangerous spiral of failure in the child, who may become convinced that he or she scores poorly on tests because he or she is *stupid* or *can't learn.* This belief leads the child to think that studying is useless, since he or she will *probably fail the test anyway.* The resulting lack of study brings another round of bad grades, fulfilling the child's self-prophecy and reinforcing his or her feeling of hopelessness. The child could quickly become entrenched in a pattern of underachievement unless someone intervenes to help him or her.

Even though Thomas Edison was a man of incredible achievements, he was feeling like an underachiever when he attended school in Port Huron. "I . . . had come," he recalled, "almost to regard myself as a dunce." Only his mother's timely action saved him from becoming trapped in a lifelong pattern of underachievement.

Impulsive Behavior

There are many indications that Edison had an impulsive nature, such as his tendency toward practical jokes at school that failed to amuse his teachers or many of his classmates. As an adult, he was known to shock his assistants with an electrical *corpse waker* if he thought that their naptime had exceeded a reasonable period.

Two childhood experiments on flight also show that he was prone to act on his ideas without considering the consequences of his actions:

First, Al guessed that a stomach full of carbon dioxide should provide enough lift to float a young boy up into the air. Al went to his friend Michael Oates, and convinced him that he would be able to fly high above the town of Port Huron after swallowing a huge glass of Seidlitz powders (a bicarbonate solution). Michael hesitantly agreed, only to find himself quickly in bed for the remainder of the day with stomach pains.

Next, Al noticed that birds ate worms. Perhaps eating worms gave birds the ability to fly. There was, of course, only one way to find out. Al mixed a potent mash of crushed worms together and promised a neighbor girl that she would soon be flying over the town if she drank it. Once again, one of Al's trusting friends ended up spending the rest of the day in bed nursing her sour stomach.

Family History of ADHD or Other Disorders

Samuel Ogden Edison, Thomas' father, was strangely impulsive throughout his life, such as when he decided to rebel against British rule of Canada at great risk to himself and his family.

Samuel rarely remained at any occupation for long. He was, at various times, a carpenter, a tailor, a tavern keeper, hotel operator, lumberyard proprietor, feed store manager, realtor, tourist attraction owner, and land speculator. He suddenly shut down his shingle mill without obtaining an alternate source of income after Thomas left home, placing himself and Nancy in severe financial distress.

Nancy, despite the warmth and tenderness that she displayed to Thomas in his youth, experienced some sort of mental disorder after Thomas left home. She became increasingly neurotic as she aged, but the social stigmas and scant psychological knowledge of the time prevented any detailed record of her symptoms or condition from being kept.

High Propensity for Accidents

Edison was careless to the point of recklessness, especially as a child. He burned down his family barn, had the tip of his finger accidentally chopped off with an axe, and started a chemical fire onboard a train. Several times in his life he suffered battery acid burns.

The Centers for Disease Control and Prevention reports that children with ADHD are significantly more likely to be injured as pedestrians or while riding a bicycle, to receive head injuries, injure more than one part of the body, and be hospitalized for accidental poisoning. Children with ADHD also tend to be admitted to intensive care units or have an injury result in disability more frequently than other children.

Children with ADHD also appear to have significantly higher medical costs than children without ADHD. Health care costs for each child with ADHD may be more than twice as high as medical costs for children without ADHD.

The main traits of ADHD—inattention and impulsivity/hyperactivity—may place a person with ADHD at greater risk for certain types of accidents and injuries.

Further research is needed to understand what role ADHD symptoms play in the risk of injuries and other disorders that may occur with ADHD. For example, a young child with ADHD may not look for oncoming traffic while riding a bicycle or crossing the street, or may engage in high-risk physical activity without thinking of the possible consequences. Teenagers with ADHD, who drive, may have more traffic violations and accidents, and twice as likely to have their driver's licenses suspended than drivers without ADHD.

Much of what is already known about injury prevention may be particularly useful for people with ADHD, such as

- Ensure bicycle helmet use. Remind children as often as necessary to watch for cars and to avoid unsafe activities.
- Supervise children when they are involved in high-risk activities or are in risky settings, such as when climbing or when in or around a swimming pool.
- Keep potentially harmful household products, tools, equipment, and objects out of the reach of young children.
- Teens with ADHD may need to limit the amount of music listened to in the car while driving, drive without passengers and/or keep the number of passengers to a chosen few, plan trips well ahead of time, and avoid alcohol and drug use and cellular phone usage.
- Parents may want to enroll their teens in driving safety courses before they get their driver's license.

We may safely say that Edison displayed a number of ADHD tendencies without insisting on a positive diagnosis of ADHD. These ADHD tendencies and his behavior at school clearly mark him as a tangential thinker, who experienced trouble learning in a conventional classroom. There may be as many as 10 million children in the school systems today that fit this same description to some degree but may not be affected seriously enough to obtain a diagnosis of ADHD or some other learning disorder. They may still benefit, however, from counseling or special attention with their schoolwork just as Edison benefited from the attention he received from Nancy.

In the next chapter, we will begin exploring specific examples of how Nancy taught her young son and began his extraordinary academic turnaround.

3

Nancy Edison: Advocate
for Her Son

Nancy Edison was a strong and capable advocate for her son at a time when there were no support groups, educational services, or government programs available to help her.

The family physician thought that some sort of brain damage caused Al's academic problems, and therefore nothing could be done to help him. The doctor's opinion was understandable, since diagnosis and treatment for conditions such as attention deficit hyperactivity disorder (ADHD) or dyslexia were unknown at the time.

Samuel Edison, while tolerant of his wife's desire to educate Al, was not convinced at first that the boy was even teachable.

The local schools had no interest in helping Nancy educate Al and probably assumed that she was doomed to failure. They may have even had reason to hope that she would become frustrated in her effort and validate their contention that Al was addled.

Nancy continued to believe in her son's ability to learn despite the opinions of others. Nancy did not consider Al to have a learning disability or a learning disorder; on the contrary, she understood that Al merely learned differently than other children. She was confident that he would thrive in an environment that emphasized his strengths rather than his weaknesses.

The Importance of a Parent-Advocate

Having the support of a parent is crucial to the success of any child, especially to a tangential thinker. According to a 15-year study of hyperactive children conducted by Gabrielle Weiss, Ph.D., and Lily Hechtman, Ph.D., the most important key to their success was having an accepting and supportive adult who believed in them.[1]

Nancy Edison's example to parents today is crucial; believing in and acting as an advocate for your child is a vital element to your child's success in school and life.

KNOW THY CHILD

Nancy Edison took the time to know her son Al intimately before he began attending school. She saw Al in a strictly positive light, through the glow of a mother's love. She knew that he was more than intelligent enough to succeed academically, and so she was able to reject his teacher's claims that Al was unteachable. While others pointed out Al's weaknesses, Nancy recognized Al's strengths. Some thought Al to be stubborn; Nancy recognized that he had a strong will. His teacher complained that Al did not follow instructions; Nancy knew that Al could follow instructions if they were properly explained. The teacher described Al as easily distracted; Nancy understood that Al was highly sensitive to—and easily stimulated by—his surroundings. His teacher claimed that Al was unable to learn; Nancy knew that Al learned *differently* than the other children.

Learning differences that remain unidentified or unaddressed can create a vicious cycle of failure. At first, the child may just feel frustrated at his or her inability to understand the lessons at school. His or her frustration then gradually turns into demoralization and finally to surrender. The child ultimately abandons all hope of ever doing well at school and sets his or her expectations accordingly.

The importance of a parent-advocate is vital even when the child is not dysfunctional enough to be diagnosed with a specific learning disorder or disability. The dysfunctional or significantly impaired child will have a number of special programs available to help him or her, whereas a functional child who struggles with a mild-to-moderate learning difference may not even be recognized as needing assistance unless the parent is actively monitoring the child's education.

Tangential thinkers may struggle with their grades, but they may also be the most creative thinkers in their class. They may thrive in an open environment that rewards self-initiative and spontaneity, but feel confined and repressed in a classroom. They may be highly visual and able to grasp complex concepts easily, yet have difficulty following the logic of a lecture or understanding verbal homework instructions.

These tangential thinkers could possibly be the premier business owners, inventors, scientists, researchers, artists, authors, educators, and engineers of tomorrow. On the other hand, they could be lost in the quagmire of a school system that has difficulty identifying and responding to their needs. Whether or not they realize success or become mired in mediocrity may be determined by one thing: a parent who recognizes their needs and becomes their advocate.

PARENT-ADVOCATES MUST WORK WITH THE TEACHER

To acknowledge that a parent must become a strong advocate for his or her child's education is not to imply that today's teachers are apathetic or intentionally unresponsive to the needs of tangential thinkers. Most teachers are dedicated professionals, who have only the best interests of each student at heart. However, every teacher is limited as to the time and resources they can spend on each student.

The "No Child Left Behind" (NCLB) Act of 2001 places severe penalties on schools that score below the required level on standardized tests. The schools, in turn, place pressure on each teacher to raise their student's scores. In my conversations with teachers, I have heard them lament that the pressure on schools and teachers is unbelievable. "We forget everything else other than scoring numbers on a test," many teachers complain.

Even while each teacher's workload has increased due to the NCLB Act, the resources available to each of them since 2001 have decreased in many states due to budget cuts. Thus, "Now we are being asked to do much more with less," has become another common complaint.

This rising pressure to do *more with less* is further complicated by the myriad discipline and social issues that teachers must face each day. Teachers must often confront family conflict, parental neglect, substance abuse, crime, violence, and other issues before any real education can begin.

Children with family or social problems frequently act out their frustration and anxiety by misbehaving at school. Their behavior can disrupt the entire class and effectively monopolize the teacher's time until the child's problem is recognized and addressed. All the while, the teacher feels the seconds ticking away toward the next series of mandated tests. "I had one student who witnessed a drug bust at his parent's house the night before a test. How was that student going to perform? These are life issues and parent issues that we have no control over," lamented one schoolteacher to me.

The pressures placed on teachers today make it even more paramount that the parents of a tangential thinker develop a cooperative relationship with their child's teachers. The best way modern parents can act as an advocate for their child is to become as involved as possible in the child's education.

The best research to date on the importance of parental involvement in education finds that neither income, race, ethnicity, the level of parental education nor social status were accurate predictors of a student's achievement in school.[2] The level of parental involvement is the only consistent ingredient in a child's academic success.

How does a parent best become involved in his or her child's education? I have included forty-two different ways in the list below, provided by The National Parent–Teacher Association (PTA), with comments and suggestions from various teachers:[3]

1. Give positive feedback and show appreciation for teachers and the principal. (Like many other professions, teachers are often contacted only when problems occur. It's always nice to hear from a parent when things are going *well.*)
2. Approach interactions with a positive attitude and an open mind. (Keep in mind that teachers and other school staff may have observed behaviors at school that you have never witnessed in your child at home. This

is understandable, as the environment at school is very different than the surroundings of home.)

3. Share your child's strengths, talents, and interests with your child's teachers. (Teachers are only human, and it is all too easy to identify a child's weaknesses without seeing his or her corresponding strengths. Your input may allow the teacher to see your child in a new light.)

4. Share expectations and set goals together for your child. (Developing a mutual understanding of goals and expectations can prevent misunderstandings between the parent and the teacher and keep the child away from being held to two different standards.)

5. Attend parent–teacher conferences with specific questions you want to ask. (Keep a notepad in a specific place at home to write down questions that arise during homework or discussions with your child.)

6. Indicate the best way for the teacher to give you information, such as phone, e-mail, notes, etc.

7. Understand and reinforce school rules and expectations at home.

8. Address concerns or questions honestly, openly, and early on. (Parents are sometimes surprised to find that the child's version of events differs greatly from the teacher's version. The only way to get the full story is to contact the teacher and discuss the situation as soon as possible.)

9. Attend PTA or parent meetings regularly.

10. Read classroom and/or school newsletters.

11. Visit your school's Web page.

12. Read and know your school's handbook. (Many schools now post their handbooks online, so be sure to look for one on the school Web site if your child *forgets* to bring one home.)

13. Share your perceptions with educators and school staff about how parents are treated. (Remember that teachers need to hear positive as well as negative feedback.)

14. Meet your child's friends and get to know their parents. (Other parents need to be aware of any ADHD behavior or similar differences that your child might have. Explain to the other parents what to expect from your child, and how they can help to avoid conflicts and other problems as your children play together.)

15. Contact your school for information on family programs and resources.

16. Assist in developing parent support programs/groups and attend them. (Many PTAs and other organizations now have support groups, where you can meet other parents and learn how to deal with the unique issues that come with raising tangential thinkers. If such a support group does not exist, perhaps you should look at starting one or finding an active group at another school nearby.)

17. Attend workshops or seminars on various parenting topics.

18. Attend parent fairs and other events, especially for parents and families.

19. Assist in creating and/or offer your services to before-school and after-school programs. (Recall that the highest success is achieved when parents become involved in coordinated efforts with the school staff.)

20. Ask teachers or counselors about how to talk with your children about tough topics. (Many school districts have behavioral specialists and other professionals available to help teachers with discipline problems and other issues.

They will probably be delighted to talk to you and help you resolve whatever concerns you might have with your child.)

21. Discuss your child's school day and homework daily. (A daily discussion of school and homework lets your child voice the issues that are important to him or her, both good and bad. Let the child brag about something he or she accomplished, or give him or her a chance to tell you about a problem he or she is experiencing.)

22. Learn your child's strengths and weaknesses in different areas of school. (You might be surprised when you discover exactly where your child excels in school and where he or she struggles.)

23. Provide a quiet, well-lighted place with basic school supplies for studying/homework. (All children need to have distractions kept to a minimum to do their homework, but this is essential for tangential thinkers. If possible, have an area that is dedicated to just homework.)

24. Help your children break down projects into smaller, more manageable steps. (The U.S. Navy learned decades ago that sailors learned and retained their knowledge better when training was conducted in short sessions. They break each job down into a series of small steps that can be taught individually.)

25. Develop a consistent daily routine and time for studying and homework. (Thomas Edison recalled many afternoons when his play was interrupted by his mother calling him inside to attend to his studies. Nancy set definite times each day for his schoolwork and chores to be done.)

26. Provide encouragement and approval for effort and schoolwork. (Look for little successes. Encouragement based upon their efforts will help motivate them to continue working on a big goal until it is achieved.)

27. Provide children with books and magazines, and develop a nighttime reading routine.

28. Attend meetings on learning expectations, assessments, and grading procedures.

29. Participate in fairs and fests for math, science, history, and so forth. (Science and history fairs are great opportunities to let your child's creativity run free. There may be no better place for your child to demonstrate his or her unique abilities.)

30. Let school staff know your availability to volunteer days, times, and how often.

31. Assist your child's teacher in the classroom or on field trips whenever you are able to. (You might be amazed at how much you can learn about both the teacher and your child while helping in the classroom or on a field trip.)

32. Help provide child care and/or transportation for volunteering parents.

33. Learn and uphold school discipline, confidentiality, and other policies as a volunteer. (Learning how the school enforces discipline can also help you enforce your own discipline at home. Having the same methods of discipline at home and at school gives your child a consistent set of rules by which to live.)

34. Voice your support or concerns on any issue that will affect your family.

35. Participate in meetings to determine special educational needs and services.

36. Serve on school advisory councils or committees on curriculum, discipline, and so forth.

37. Attend PTA, school board, and/or town meetings, and speak about the issues of concern.
38. Write, call, or travel to state capitals to support or oppose proposed legislation.
39. Participate in petition drives or letter-writing campaigns to Congress on legislation.
40. Give testimony at public hearings in support of or opposition to education legislation.
41. Vote in local, state, and federal elections for public officials who support education.
42. Be a role model, and be active in community service yourself or together with your child.

Nancy Edison had very little support or help as she educated her son. Fortunately, parents today have a host of resources available to help them participate in their child's education. Ask your child's teacher or consult your school's PTA to help locate local support groups. There are also a number of online support groups that can be found through the Internet.

PEER RELATIONSHIPS AND ADHD

ADHD can have many effects on a child's development. It can make childhood friendships, or peer relationships, very difficult. These relationships contribute to children's immediate happiness and may be very important to their long-term development. In some cases, children with peer problems may also be at higher risk for anxiety, behavioral and mood disorders, substance abuse, and delinquency as teenagers.

The Centers for Disease Control report that children with ADHD may be less likely to play with groups of friends or be involved in after-school activities. An ADHD child may also find that his or her circle of close friends is relatively small. Compared to other children, a child with ADHD may be more than twice as likely to be *picked on* at school or have trouble getting along with other children.

Not all children are tangential thinkers, and because of this your child may have difficulty relating to and communicating with his or her peers. As your child's parent and main advocate, you may have to be keenly aware of any problems your child may experience as he or she meets and forms relationships with other children.

Exactly how conditions such as ADHD contribute to social problems is not fully understood, but several studies have found that children with predominantly inattentive ADHD may be perceived as shy or withdrawn by their peers. Other research strongly indicates that aggressive behavior in children with symptoms of impulsivity/hyperactivity may play a significant role in peer rejection. In addition, other behavioral disorders often occur along with ADHD and may further impair your child's ability to form relationships with peers.

Of course, having ADHD does not mean a person has to have poor peer relationships, and not everyone with ADHD has difficulty getting along with others. For those who do, many things can be done to improve the person's relationships. The earlier a child's difficulties with peers are noticed, the more successful intervention may be. Although researchers have not provided definitive answers, some things parents might consider as they help their child build and strengthen peer relationships are as follows:

- Recognize the importance of healthy peer relationships for children. These relationships can be just as important as grades to school success.
- Maintain ongoing communication with people who play important roles in your child's life (such as teachers, school counselors, after-school activity leaders, health care providers, etc.). Keep updated on your child's social development in community and school settings.
- Involve your child in activities with his or her peers. Communicate with other parents, sports coaches, and other involved adults about any progress or problems that may develop with your child.

Peer programs can be helpful, particularly for older children and teenagers. Schools and communities often have such programs available. You may want to discuss the possibility of your child's participation with program directors and your child's care providers.

4

CURRENT RIGHTS OF CHILDREN WHO LEARN DIFFERENTLY

Nancy Edison essentially had no choice but to teach her son Al at home; after all, she had removed him from the only elementary school in Port Huron, Michigan. Fortunately, Nancy had an educational background and was able to commit her expertise, time, and energy to Al's schooling.

Al was fortunate to have a mother who was capable and willing to teach him at home; certainly, not every child in such a circumstance was as fortunate as Al Edison. No one knows how many children in the history of our nation were expelled or withdrawn from school as a *trouble child*, because they could not concentrate or sit still in class due to a learning difference or disability. It is likely that a large number of these children received no alternative education at all.

This sad situation began to change with passage of the Education for All Handicapped Children Act in 1975. This law, which later came to be known as the Individuals with Disabilities Education Act (IDEA), gave all children the right to a free and appropriate public education, including due process protections.

The "due process" protections were inserted in IDEA to prevent schools from ignoring children who were found to be *difficult* or expensive to educate. Discipline in the classroom has always been an excuse to exclude children who do not fit in traditional classroom environments, and the National Council on Disability reports that disciplinary actions are disproportionately applied to students with disabilities, particularly if they are a member of a minority group. "Historically, the need for 'discipline' and 'order' has been a pretext for the full-scale exclusion from education of hundreds of thousands of children," the Council reports.[1]

IDEA also introduced individualized education programs (IEPs) that include special education and related services the child might need. In theory, a dyslexic, attention deficit hyperactivity disorder, or otherwise diagnosed child with a properly designed and implemented IEP would be able to learn even in a crowded public school classroom. The IEP would, if necessary, include "behavioral intervention strategies" that would help the child to control his or her behavior and minimize any discipline problems he or she might otherwise have.[2]

The U.S. Department of Education describes the IEP as "the cornerstone of special education." Each child who receives special education and related services must have an IEP developed exclusively to meet his or her unique educational needs.

An effective IEP can only be created as a cooperative effort between the child's parents, teachers, school staff, and possibly the child him- or herself. The collective knowledge, experience, and commitment of all involved will ideally come together to form an educational program that will help the student actively progress in the general curriculum.

IDENTIFICATION

A child must first be identified as having a disability or qualifying health impairment and needing special education and related services before he or she falls under the special protections offered by IDEA. A school professional may ask that your child be evaluated to see if he or she has a disability, since each state is tasked with identifying, locating, and evaluating all children with disabilities in the state who need special education and related services. However, you may proactively request that your child be evaluated by contacting your child's teacher or other school professional to request the evaluation. The request can be written or verbal, but a written request may be helpful later in case a dispute arises.

Your child cannot be evaluated against your will, as the school system needs parental consent prior to evaluating any child. The evaluation needs to be completed within a *reasonable time* once you have given your consent.

EVALUATION

The evaluation must assess the child in all areas related to the child's suspected disability to determine if your child is eligible for special education and related services. The results will also be used to decide what might be the most appropriate educational program for the child. You have the right to take your child for an independent educational evaluation (IEE) if you disagree with the school's evaluation. (You can even ask the school system to pay for this IEE.)

ELIGIBILITY

You and a group of qualified professionals should look at the child's evaluation results together to decide if your child is a "child with a disability," as defined by IDEA.

If your child is listed as ineligible for benefits under IDEA, you may challenge the decision and ask for a hearing.

Once your child is determined to be eligible for benefits under IDEA, the IEP team has 30 calendar days to meet and write an IEP for your child. The school system schedules and conducts the IEP meeting. School staff must

- contact the participants, including the parents;
- notify parents early enough to make sure they have an opportunity to attend;
- schedule the meeting at a time and place agreeable to parents and the school;
- tell the parents the purpose, time, and location of the meeting;
- tell the parents who will be attending; and
- tell the parents that they may invite people to the meeting who have knowledge or special expertise about the child.

PREPARING FOR THE IEP

The IEP can be an empowering event that lays out the blueprint for your child's academic success. The meeting should be a collaborative effort between you, your child's teachers, school administrators, related services personnel, and your child (when appropriate). However, some parents have voiced frustration after attending an IEP meeting, saying that they felt "outnumbered, intimidated, or confused." Another common complaint from parents is that the "school staff already had the IEP made out before the meeting," leaving the parents to feel that their input was neither welcome nor desired. Both of these problems can largely be overcome with adequate preparation by the parents.

Prior to the IEP, take the time to prepare yourself. For example, review your child's school records ahead of time, or let the school staff know that you wish for your child's records to be made available for review at the IEP. Write down any information you have on the following topics:

- your child's abilities, interests, performance, and school history;
- recent progress (or regression);
- things that you have taught your child at home;
- the types of situations where you have observed your child learning best;
- how your child interacts best with other people;
- any professional advice given to you by counselors, therapists, or physicians;
- pertinent medical information or prescriptions for your child; and
- specific areas in which you feel your child requires attention, such as behavioral issues or academic subjects.

The IEP Team Members

By law, certain individuals must be involved in writing a child's IEP. These are

- you, the parent(s);
- at least one of the child's special education teachers or providers;
- at least one of the child's regular education teachers (if your child is, or may be, participating in the regular education environment);

- a representative of the school system;
- an individual who can interpret the evaluation results;
- representatives of any other agencies that may be responsible for paying for or providing transition services (if your child is 16 years or, if appropriate, younger);
- your child, as appropriate; and
- other individuals who have knowledge or special expertise about the child. (This may include individuals that *you* have invited to the IEP, such as a professional advocate or special education attorney.)

Any IEP team member may fill more than one of the team positions, as long as they are properly qualified and designated. For example, the school system representative may also be the person who can interpret your child's evaluation results.

Participation and Attendance of Team Members

Some team members, such as the regular education teacher, may not be required to participate in every decision or even be present throughout the entire meeting. Depending upon the circumstances, certain members may not even be required to attend every meeting. For example, your child's speech therapist may leave the meeting after the discussion of speech therapy is complete. At subsequent meetings, the speech therapist may not even need to be present unless there are modifications needed in that area of service.

Ask for an open discussion to take place at the IEP meeting if you have concerns about which team members are absent or present at various stages of the meeting. Ultimately, your consent should be given before any team member is excused from an IEP meeting.

Your Role as a Team Member

You, as your child's parent, are a key member of the IEP team, since you probably know his or her strengths and needs better than anyone else. You should be able to give the rest of the team valuable insight into how he or she learns, what his or her interests are, and other aspects that only a parent can know. You can also report on whether the skills he or she is learning at school are being used at home.

The Teacher's Role

Teachers are vital participants in the IEP meeting as well. At least one of your child's regular education teachers must be on the IEP team if your child is (or may be) participating in the regular education environment. The regular education teacher should be able to give input on the school's curriculum, helpful changes or additions to the educational program, and strategies to deal with behavioral issues.

The regular education teacher may also point out various support services that the school staff needs to help your child reach his or her academic, social, and extracurricular goals. For example, the school staff may require professional development or training in areas that pertain to your child's needs.

Special Education Teacher's Role

The special education teacher contributes specific information and experience about educating children with disabilities. This teacher can suggest such things as modifications to the general curriculum that might help your child learn, or how to modify testing so that the student can show what he or she has learned.

The special educator will also be involved in the IEP implementation, working with your child in a resource room or special class devoted to students receiving special education services. The special education teacher may also instruct other school staff about how to address your child's unique needs.

The Role of Interpreting Evaluation Results

The team member who interprets your child's evaluation results is responsible for explaining the results and guiding the team as they design appropriate instruction. The evaluation results will help to determine how your child is currently doing in school, and what his or her *areas of need* might be.

Again, this role might fall to a separate team member or it could be the responsibility of an existing team member, such as the special education teacher.

The School System Representative

The individual representing the school system should know a great deal about special education services and educating children with disabilities. More importantly, he or she should have the authority to commit resources, and be able to ensure that whatever services are set out in the IEP will actually be provided. It would be an exercise in futility to write an IEP calling for resources that either do not exist or might be unavailable for your child. The school system representative should know the system's resources well enough to know what services are or are not available for your child's benefit.

The Role of Other Individuals

Both you and the school system can invite individuals to participate on the team if they have knowledge or special expertise about your child. You could, for example, invite a tutor who has had success teaching a subject to your child, or a therapist or other professional with special expertise about your child and his or her disability or health impairment. The school system may also invite one or more individuals who can offer special expertise or knowledge about your child, such as a paraprofessional or related services professional.

A child may require any of the following related services in order to benefit from special education. Related services, as listed under IDEA, include (but are not limited to)

- audiology services;
- counseling services;
- identification and assessment of disabilities;
- interpretation services, such as a sign-language interpreter if your child is deaf or hard of hearing;
- medical services;
- occupational therapy;
- orientation and mobility services;
- parent counseling and training;
- physical therapy;
- professional advocacy;
- psychological services;
- recreation;
- rehabilitation counseling services;
- school health services;
- social work services in schools;
- speech-language pathology services; and
- transportation.

The appropriate service professional, such as an occupational or physical therapist, adaptive physical education provider, psychologist, or speech–language pathologist, should be involved in developing the IEP if your child needs their particular service to benefit from special education.

Role of Transition Service Agencies

Transition refers to activities meant to prepare your child for adult life. This can include developing postsecondary education and career goals, getting work experience while still in school, and setting up linkages with adult service providers such as the vocational rehabilitation agency—whatever is appropriate for your child, given his or her interests, preferences, skills, and needs.

The school must invite a representative of any other agency that is likely to be responsible for providing or paying for transition services whenever transition services will be discussed during a meeting. This individual can help the team plan any transition services the student needs, and can ideally commit the resources of the agency to pay for or provide needed transition services. The school must take alternative steps to obtain the agency's participation in the planning of the student's transition services if he or she does not attend the meeting.

Role of the Student

The student may or may not be involved as a member of the IEP team, although he or she must be invited to attend if transition service needs or transition services are going to be discussed at the meeting. More and more students are participating in and even leading their own IEP meetings. This allows them to have a strong voice in their own education, and can teach them a great deal about self-advocacy and self-determination.

Interpretive Services

If you, the parent, are deaf or have a limited proficiency in English, you may need an interpreter in order to understand and be understood. In this case, the school must make reasonable efforts to arrange for an interpreter during meetings pertaining to the child's educational placement. For meetings regarding the development or review of the IEP, the school must take whatever steps are necessary to ensure that you understand the meetings, including arranging for an interpreter.

Let the school know ahead of time so that they can make arrangements for an interpreter, and check with the school before the meeting to ensure that an interpreter will be there.

THE IEP MEETING

The initial IEP meeting will probably be a face-to-face meeting at the school. Subsequent follow-up meetings can continue to be face-to-face meetings or via videoconferencing or teleconferencing, as long as you and the school administrators are in agreement.

It is important for you to go into each IEP meeting with an open mind. Assume that every member on the team is a capable and caring professional, who desires your child to succeed in school. Entering the meeting with an adversarial attitude could cause ill will that might never be overcome. The success of the IEP depends in large part on the cooperation of all parties involved. Treat each team member with the respect that they deserve, and they will probably respond to you with the respect that you deserve.

By law, the IEP must include certain information about the child and the educational program designed to meet his or her unique needs. At a minimum, this information is

1. *Current performance.* The IEP must state how the child is currently doing in school, and may include evaluation results such as classroom tests and assignments, individual tests given to decide eligibility for services or during reevaluation, and observations made by you, teachers, related service providers, and other school staff. The statement about *current performance* includes how your child's disability affects his or her involvement and progress in the general curriculum.

2. *Annual goals.*   These are goals that your child should reasonably be able to accomplish in a year. The goals may be broken down into short-term *objectives* or *benchmarks*, but this is no longer required as of 2004. Goals may be academic, address social or behavioral needs, relate to physical needs, or address other educational needs. The goals must be concrete and unambiguous enough that your child's progress can be accurately measured.

3. *Special education and related services.*   The IEP must list the special education and related services to be provided to your child, including supplementary aids and services that he or she needs. It also includes modifications (changes) to the program or supports for school personnel, such as training or professional development, which should be provided to assist the child.

4. *Participation with nondisabled children.*   The IEP must explain the extent (if any) to which the child will *not* participate with nondisabled children in the regular class and other school activities.

5. *Participation in state- and districtwide tests.*   The IEP must state any modifications your child will need when standardized tests are administered. The IEP must state why the test is not appropriate, and how the child will be tested instead if a test is deemed as inappropriate for your child.

6. *Dates and places.*   The IEP must state when services will begin, how often they will be provided, where they will be provided, and how long they will last.

7. *Postschool goals.*   Beginning when your child is of age 14 (or younger, if appropriate), the IEP must address the courses he or she needs to take to reach his or her postschool goals, such as attending college.

8. *Needed transition services.*   Beginning when your child is of age 16 (or younger, if appropriate), the IEP must state what transition services are needed to help him or her prepare for leaving school.

9. *Age of majority.*   The IEP must include a statement that your child has been told of any rights that will transfer to him or her at the age of majority, beginning at least 1 year before he or she reaches that age. (*This statement is needed only in those states that transfer rights at the age of majority.*)

10. *Measuring progress.*   The IEP must state how your child's progress will be measured, and how you will be informed of that progress.

Some states are authorized to develop multiyear IEPs for up to 3 years that coincide with natural transition points for your child, such as the move from elementary school to middle school. This multiyear IEP is optional, and can be used only with your consent.

Special Factors

The IEP team will need to consider what the law calls *special factors*. These include the following:

- Strategies and supports to address your child's behavior if it interferes with his or her learning or the learning of others.
- Your child's language needs as they relate to his or her IEP if he or she has limited proficiency in English.

- The need for instruction in braille or the use of braille if your child is blind or visually impaired.
- If your child is deaf or hard of hearing, the IEP team will consider his or her language and communication needs, including how he or she will have opportunities to communicate directly with classmates and school staff in his or her usual method of communication, such as sign language.
- Any other communication needs that your child might have.
- The need for assistive technology devices or services.

Any particular device or service that is needed for your child's education must be written in the IEP.

Deciding Placement

Placement is a term that specifies where your child's IEP will be carried out. The placement decision is made by a group of people, including yourself and others who know about your child. In some states, the IEP team serves as the group making the placement decision. In other states, this decision may be made by another group of people. *You have the right to be a member of the group that decides the educational placement of your child.*

IDEA states that your child should be placed in what is called the *least restrictive environment*. This means that your child must be educated with children who do not have disabilities, to the maximum extent appropriate.

Your child may be placed in special classes or in a separate school only if the nature or severity of his or her disability makes education in a regular class impossible or impractical.

Depending on your child's needs, his or her IEP may be carried out in a variety of different settings. The child may be placed in a regular class and given appropriate supplementary aids and services, or go into a special class where every student in the class is receiving special education services for some or all of the day. He or she could also be placed in a special school or in alternative setting, such as your home. (See Chapter 6 about homeschooling.)

In some cases, the IEP may have to be carried out wherever the child resides at the time, such as a hospital or institution. The school system can provide its own services or contract with another agency to provide services, as long as the IDEA requirement is met to provide an appropriate education program to every child.

Reaching Consensus on the IEP

Ultimately, you must give your consent before the school system may enact the completed IEP. *The IEP cannot be implemented until you are reasonably satisfied with it.* Do not allow yourself to be rushed through the meeting; ask that it be resumed at a later date if the allotted time is insufficient to address all your concerns.

You have the right to challenge any decisions made about your child's eligibility, evaluation, placement, or the services that the school provides. In the event of a dispute over any of these matters, first try to reach a reasonable agreement with the rest of the IEP team, even if it is just for a temporary concession. For example, the IEP team might agree to try a plan of instruction or a placement for a certain period of time, and see how your child does.

If you cannot reach an agreement with the IEP team, you may request mediation. During mediation, you and school officials sit down with someone who is not involved in the disagreement and try to reach an agreement. Mediation is designed to be a simple, fast, and amiable method for resolving disputes.

You can ask for a due process hearing if mediation fails or is unavailable. Due process involves both you and school personnel appearing before an impartial hearing officer, who listens to both sides of the story and decides how to solve the problem.

You can file a complaint with the State Education Agency (SEA) if you feel that your child's school has violated some part of IDEA. Write directly to the SEA and explain the alleged violation in as much detail as possible. The agency must resolve the complaint within 60 calendar days, unless exceptional circumstances exist. You should consider obtaining legal counsel or professional advocacy services with an expert familiar with state and federal education law at any time during the dispute resolution process.

Your child should begin to receive services as soon as possible once your written consent has been given to the IEP.

AFTER THE IEP

You should be given a copy of the IEP, and the school should ensure that your child's IEP is being carried out as it was written. Each of your child's teachers and service providers has access to the IEP and knows his or her specific responsibilities for carrying out the IEP. This includes the accommodations, modifications, and supports that must be provided to your child, as specified in the IEP.

IEP Measurements and Reports

Your child's progress toward the annual goals will be measured in accordance with the instructions in the IEP. You should be regularly informed of his or her progress, and whether or not he or she is on track to achieve his or her goals by the end of the year. Although the frequency of these progress reports may vary, they must occur at least as often as regular progress reports or report cards are issued.

IEP Reviews

Your child's IEP must be reviewed by the IEP team at least once a year, but you or a school staff member may request more frequent reviews if needed. You are a part of the IEP team and must be invited to attend these meetings. The review meetings are an opportunity for you to make suggestions for changes and voice your concerns with the IEP goals or your child's placement.

You may also amend or modify your child's IEP without having to convene a new meeting. Simply contact the responsible teacher or service provider and work out the issue with them.

As always, try to work out an agreement at the meeting if you do not agree with the IEP and placement. You can suggest several options if you feel they are needed, including additional testing, an independent evaluation, or asking for mediation or a due process hearing. As a last resort, you may file a complaint with the SEA. When appropriate, seek the services of a legal advisor who is familiar with your state and local education laws.

Periodic Reevaluations

Your child must undergo a reevaluation at least every 3 years. (Sometimes called a *triennial*.) Its purpose is to find out if he or she is still a "child with a disability," as defined by IDEA, and what his or her educational needs are. However, you or a school staff member can request a reevaluation before the scheduled triennial if it is needed.

Differences in IEPs

Although the minimum content of the IEP is laid out in federal law, many states and school systems include additional information to document their compliance with state and federal requirements. You may see documents showing when each meeting or review was scheduled and held, for example, or verification that you have received all copies of all necessary documents. The sheer volume of information in the IEP may seem overwhelming, but the school staff should be eager to explain it to you and answer any questions you might have.

While the law tells us what information must be included in the IEP, there is no *standard* IEP form nationwide, and the actual forms used might vary from one state to the next. In some states, individual school systems design their own IEP forms, so it may be a good idea for you to obtain a copy of your local school system's form and become familiar with it prior to the IEP meeting.

5

USING A PROFESSIONAL ADVOCATE

Nancy Edison was an advocate for her son Al at a time where there were no laws demanding equality for all children in the educational system. Today, there are a number of state and federal laws that require states to provide each child with access to a free and appropriate education in the least restrictive environment. Like most sets of rules and regulations, these laws can be very complex and difficult to understand. This often makes it hard for parents to adequately represent their child at an individualized education plan (IEP) meeting. What most parents need is an expert in special education law and someone who knows the in and outs of IEP meetings. And special education advocates do just that.

A well-trained and experienced advocate can be a godsend to a parent who feels overwhelmed by the entire IEP process. The advocate can

- provide a premeeting consultation to prepare the parent for the meeting (this consultation can be face-to-face, over the telephone, or in person);
- perform a postmeeting review of the IEP to suggest changes; or
- actually lead the IEP meeting for the parent, acting in the role the parent normally plays.

In the event in which mediation or a due process hearing is required, most advocates will step aside and bring in the services of a special education attorney. The advocate may be used in the hearing as an expert witness. Also, some special education attorneys will become involved early in the process and act as an advocate at the IEP meeting.

In late 2006, I discussed the advantages of using a professional advocate with Mr. Louis H. Geigerman, the founder of National ARD/IEP Advocates in Sugar Land, Texas. (*Note:* ARD stands for "Admission, Review, and Dismissal," the terms used in the state of Texas to describe the IEP process.) He has been a professional advocate since 1995, and is a charter member of the Council of Parent Attorneys and Advocates (COPAA).

Scott: Louis, could you explain what your role is as a professional advocate?

Louis: Essentially, I act as a sort of a *guide dog* to lead parents through the special education maze. Through years of being in ARD/IEP meetings, I have found it to be a unique process full of special procedures. Parents who don't know the procedures will find plenty of potholes they can fall through. So, helping a parent understand the process they must go through is important.

Most parents try to deal with their child's difficulties, but the whole concept of special education, with laws such as Section 504 (of the Rehabilitation Act of 1973) involved, can really be intimidating. Not having a background in the special education process can prove to be quite a barrier to the child's progress.

Scott: How did you become involved in this process? What caused you to become a special education advocate?

Louis: Most people who work in special education advocacy became involved because of a connection with a loved one. That is how I got my start. My son was diagnosed with a pervasive developmental disorder, which later manifested itself as Asperger's syndrome in the autism spectrum. He was diagnosed at about the age of 3, and my wife and I felt as if the world was caving in on us. "Oh my gosh," we thought, "what do we do?" We were absolutely stunned. The clinics didn't really give us much information after his evaluation, other than telling us that the school district would give us help. So, we went through the initial intake process with the school, and we acquired some services. I remember distinctly one thing. A Ph.D. level psychologist came over to our house and talked to my wife and myself. This was the first time this person had ever seen our son. While she hadn't observed him previously, she felt comfortable sharing her knowledge of the many years of experience she had had with children in the autism spectrum. She sat us down and told us that we needed to be prepared for the *reality* that our child *might have to be institutionalized for the rest of his life.*

Scott: That must have been quite a blow to hear those words.

Louis: Oh, it was! My wife was in tears, but I took a different tact. Frankly, I became angry, and I just wanted to show her up. "Oh, yeah," I said, "we'll see about that!" From that point on, we did everything we could to prove her wrong. In reality, we certainly succeeded. That was the *lightbulb* that went off in my brain to start me to engage the special education system.

Scott: That's very interesting, because I know of other advocates with the same sort of background, where the beginning of their process was finding that their own child had a learning disability or some other special need. Once they discovered how difficult the process was and how cumbersome everything was, they made it their mission to help others go through, as you say, the special education maze.

Louis: In my case, I really started getting into advocacy when my son was around 6 and starting school. We tried public schools first, and then turned to private schools. When the private schools began turning him away due to his special needs, we felt as if we had no recourse. They were telling us that "he can't do this" or "he can't do that." The word *can't* kept coming up. But I knew from working with him that he could learn. You just had to spend some one-on-one time with him to get there. I got tired of the word *can't,* and wanted to change the discussion. So, we put him back into a public school, and at that time I decided that I needed to impress upon the school just where my son needed to be (academically). That's when I began reading everything I could about the Individuals with Disabilities Education Act (IDEA), court decisions, hearings, and everything else I could get my hands on. I was a sponge for information. I took part in every training program that was out there. One day, a school district person that I had known for a long time took me aside and told me that I needed to find a way to offer my services to other parents.

Scott: You mentioned all of the training you have had, and that should be an issue on a parent's mind when he or she looks for an advocate. How would a parent know, for example, if an advocate has the expertise needed to properly guide him or her through the process?

Louis: Unfortunately, there aren't any real standards yet. There is a group called COPAA that provides some standardized training. Unfortunately, most of the training has been offered on the East or West Coast, so there hasn't been much going on in the central part of the country. What I think important is to look for an advocate who has gone to every bit of training they can find, someone who has taken every opportunity to learn.

There are lots of training classes available across the country; for instance, by a well-known group called Wrightslaw. Peter and Pam (Wright) know me as the "rebel rouser," which is my moniker to them. We're part of a mutual admiration society (Louis chuckles). They conduct training meetings across the country. Usually once a year or so, they'll be in Texas, for example, then later they'll be in another part of the country.

The ARC (Association for Retarded Citizens, a national organization for people with mental retardation and related developmental disabilities) also runs training programs. Most states also have an Advocacy and Protection office that offers training. Your state education agency may conduct trainings as well.

So, whenever and wherever the trainings are done, it's a good thing (for an advocate) to be there. Finally, COPAA does its own training at its annual conference. Now, not everyone has the money or time to travel to a conference, but the bottom line is there are multiple ways for an advocate to obtain training.

Personally, from a professional perspective, I feel that both parents and advocates should be affiliated with an organization like COPAA, an organization of parents, attorneys, and advocates. Parents especially should be involved in the process. COPAA provides training, and it provides a terrific listserv. It's worth every penny you pay to that organization. It's something that is essential. It gives us strength in numbers, and it has wonderful information to share.

Parents should look for an advocate who has received a good deal of training, but they should also look at how many ARD/IEP meetings they have been to. In truth, it's like anything else. The more you write, the better writer you become. The more meetings they have gone to, the better advocate they are. I think it's just simply having the hours under their belt that is crucial.

Scott: Louis, you mention COPAA and how it is trying to standardize training for advocates. Does it have any sort of designation that would tell a parent that an advocate has been through a particular training program?

Louis: No, not yet. COPAA does have what's called special education advocate training, and graduates obtain a certificate of completion. Unfortunately, it has only obtained grants at this time to hold trainings in a few areas of the country.

Scott: You are a charter member of COPAA. How did you become involved with them?

Louis: S. James Rosenfield was the founder of COPAA back in the late 1990s. He had established an organization known as the Ed Law Center. When I started doing advocacy in 1995, I began searching for an association of advocates. I thought that there should be a way for us to ban together and share information, discuss case law, and discuss where the various states are going in their special education programs. So, I had made contact with James, and he discussed wanting to get such an organization going. Well, I automatically knew that I wanted to help, and I've been a member since their inaugural meeting.

My original thinking was that I wanted some sort of certification process to be there. I believe that advocacy is a true profession, there's no getting away from that, and it should have a certification process. So, I believe that COPAA will ultimately be a conduit toward that goal, to establish the necessary standards.

Scott: Louis, you mentioned earlier that COPAA is an organization of parents, advocates, and attorneys. How does your role as an advocate differ from the role of a special education attorney?

Louis: This might be a convoluted answer, because the roles might differ from one state to the next, and the roles are still evolving in many states. In Texas, for example, up until recently it was acceptable for an advocate to bring a case to an administrative hearing. Now, it seems as though Texas is leaning toward that not being acceptable. In some states the lines are fairly clear, and in other states the lines are not so clear.

Personally, I do not execute legal documents nor dispense legal advice, which is the business of an attorney. I am considered a person with specialized knowledge. What I do is help people navigate through the system and advocate for appropriate services for their child. Now, parents are their children's best advocate, but unless you are acquainted with the rules and regulations regarding special education, you are going to get eaten alive by the schools. The reason is that there are two very different agendas going on; the school's goal is to save money, and the parent's goal is to save their child.

Even if parents are well informed and understand the system, they still have the problem of emotions. Often, their emotions get in the way of their clear thinking. An advocate can help them rechannel their emotions and think objectively. So, I help them organize their thoughts. Now, if they end up having to go to a due process hearing to obtain the services their child needs, my job is to set things up for the attorney to enhance the chances of winning their case. Once the lawyers come in to litigate, they need to see good documentation. They need to see that we are on good solid ground, and that we have established a firm position on which they can build their case and win.

Scott: Of course, one of your main goals is to avoid litigation, right?

Louis: Absolutely, that's the first goal, to avoid litigation and still meet the child's needs. Bringing in a professional advocate can do just that. When you bring in an advocate, the school district realizes that you mean business. They know they are now dealing with someone who understands the system and knows what's going on. They know that we can't be pushed or bullied through the system.

Unfortunately, as we go on without Congress adequately funding IDEA (the Individuals with Disabilities Education Act of 1997, reauthorized in 2004), the problem is that conflicts will arise between parents and the school districts because of the money issue.

Scott: So, you're saying that the school districts are being forced to save money however they can, because they simply have not been given the money they need to meet the needs of special education children.

Louis: Right, so conflicts are inevitable. But, it's like anything in life; the best way to avoid war is to prepare for war. That's what I use for my mantra.

Scott: Louis, I hear you discuss the need for parents to prepare for the ARD/IEP meetings, and yet I know from talking to persons in the education system that some parents don't even bother to show up at the meetings. How do you feel that we can get the word out? What can be done to make parents understand the need to fight for their child and to understand that the school may not automatically do everything in the best interests of the child?

Louis: That's dreadful to hear about situations where parents don't go to the ARD/IEP meetings. I have heard of that happening especially with teenage students, in high school, and I can't for the life of me understand that. Part of the problem is that parents might go to one meeting and experience how the special education process is run, and frankly it can be intimidating. Sometimes games are being played against them, and the bottom line is that many parents end up being disenchanted. They feel that they were stonewalled, their concerns were not listened to, and it gets to a certain point where the parents just throw up their hands and say, "The school's going to do what they want to do anyway! Why should I even go? They're just going to tell me what they plan to do, regardless of what I think." Sadly, that's where the story ends for many parents.

Scott: All too true. I have had parents telling me that they felt the IEP was written before they even stepped into the room, and the purpose of the ARD/IEP meeting was just to inform them about what the school planned to do with their child.

Louis: You also have those parents that are themselves uneducated or disadvantaged. You know, people discriminate against people with disabilities, but disabilities don't discriminate against people. For instance, take a poor family with a language barrier. Even though they may have an interpreter at the meeting, it's that much easier for them to get *buffaloed*. They're probably not going to know what to do, and they may not have the money to fight the school even if they wanted to. These people feel like they're being hit with a sledgehammer in an ARD/IEP meeting, and they don't know what to do about it. As for the school district, their motivation is very limited to give that child all of the resources available. I mean, this child is a liability to the school district!

Scott: Right, because there are such limited resources available to the school.

Louis: That's right. I know of one principal who once told a parent that his school did not want to be known as the *special education school.* This was in a fairly affluent school district, and it was obviously maddening to hear. The school would like to be known for its advanced placement program, or drill team or football team, but not special education. It's a financial drain to the school. The only way that some schools will provide special education services is if they know they will lose in a (due process) hearing or otherwise avoid a public relations black eye to the district.

Scott: It sounds as though you frequently find there to be an adversarial relationship between the parents and the school staff. Is that how it really is, that you and the parents are on one side of the table and the school is on the other side? Isn't this supposed to be a cooperative relationship, not an "us against them" scenario?

Louis: Yes, that is the way it is "supposed to be"; however, the reality is something else entirely. The root cause of most of the problems is the school attorneys. Most school districts outsource their special education legal services to law firms that specialize in school law. It is my opinion that because they are paid with public tax funds, they have little incentive to settle and tend to string the process out with the parents. The school attorneys have set up systems of games, like using various methods against the parents. Things like the Delphi method where the parent's ideas are isolated and ridiculed in hopes that the parent gives up. The entire meeting is set up to intimidate the parents into giving up their ideas and goals. These types of strategies are widely used in Texas, as well as in other states.

So, is it adversarial? Yes, it's adversarial, because the schools were developed under the pretense of *in loco parentis*, or "in place of the parent." The school is seen as the expert, and therefore the school makes decisions for the parents about how the child should be educated. The reality is that the parents are the real experts. They are the ones living with the child, interacting with the child 16–18 hours a day, whereas the school just has the kid 6–8 hours a day. The school is taking the attitude that it knows what is good for the kid better than the parent knows, and therein lies the problem.

Scott: Of course, no one knows and understands the child's needs, strengths, and weaknesses like the parent.

Louis: Absolutely, and I'm sure that was the case with Thomas Edison.

Scott: Definitely! Not only was his mother the only one who believed in him, she was also the only one who truly understood him, who knew his capabilities and limitations. And the school took the easy way out and labeled him as unteachable.

Louis: Sadly, that's kind of where we are today. Believe me, I don't go into a meeting with a belligerent attitude. I'm courteous and professional. I present my ideas and suggestions in a calm, professional manner, and I'm sure that I have my facts down before the meeting. But, there comes a time when you have to stand up for the kid, even though the school sees the kid as a liability. It's like any other problem. You just have to follow the money. People will say, "No, this isn't about money," but it's simply not true. It's always about the money. The schools just don't have it, so they try to save it however they can. Unfortunately, minimizing services to a special education child is one way to do that.

Basically, some school districts see it as their job to wear down the parents. It's a battle of attrition. The school districts know that most parents will lose at a due process hearing unless they have professional help, so it's easier and cheaper to go that route than it is to provide services to the kid. Think of it—the school district has staff attorneys to fight on their behalf, but most parents don't have the resources to fight a large organization like that. A lot of parents just pull their child out of public school in frustration, which is fine with the school district; it's one less special education kid that they have to deal with. So, the parents either accept the school's program or they homeschool or send the child to a private school. Some parents, in effect, end up paying an equivalent of college tuition to give their children a chance in life, when the public school that has gladly taken their tax dollars should have provided a free and appropriate education for the kid in the first place. For many though, the option of self-paying for private school is not possible.

Scott: Louis, let's go to a positive note. What are some personal experiences you have had as an advocate, where you felt that you made a real difference in a child's education?

Louis: The cases that I have made the most impact are related to behavioral issues. Sometimes a child's disability results in behavioral problems, and the school personnel don't always have the training or the desire to help the child work through the behavioral problems. I've had cases where disability-related behavior issues were referred to juvenile court, where they were treated as a delinquency issue rather than as a disability. It was once again a matter of the school not wanting to deal with the real cause, and it was easier for them to off-load the matter to juvenile court. Getting kids like that back into school and set up with an appropriate education plan has been extremely rewarding.

Scott: Excellent! Any last thoughts you'd like to leave on us?

Louis: Two things: Special education needs to be thought of as a war. The parents and the school districts are the soldiers, but the children are the true casualties. You've got to fight for your kids. Also, when advocating for your child, never ever say that you want the "best for your child." The public schools are only required to provide an *appropriate* education and not the *best* education. If you say that you want the best, it could potentially compromise your chances of success in due process.

Note: You can find out more about Mr. Geigerman's services by visiting his Web site at www.narda.org or by calling (281) 265–1506.

6

THE HOMESCHOOLING OPTION

Individualized education plans (IEPs) and the other specialized protections offered by the Individuals with Disabilities Education Act have helped to transform the public school system into a much friendlier and effective environment for children with diagnosed learning difficulties. However, some parents still feel that a classroom does not provide the ideal learning environment for their child. Their choice is to remove the child from a classroom completely and place him or her in an environment with much more controlled conditions—the home.

Thomas Alva Edison is only one of many famous Americans who received a significant amount of their education at home. The list includes a number of past presidents, such as George Washington, James Madison, John Quincy Adams, Woodrow Wilson, William Henry Harrison, Abraham Lincoln, and Franklin D. Roosevelt, as well as Edison's fellow inventors Benjamin Franklin, Alexander Graham Bell, George Washington Carver, and the Wright Brothers.

The most obvious commonality between these famous homeschooled Americans is that they were all raised during the eighteenth and nineteenth centuries before the rise of universal truancy laws, mandating that all children enter into an accredited public or private school. In the late 1800s and early 1900s, homeschooling eventually became illegal in a majority of the states, and the long tradition of children being taught at home practically disappeared from American society.

The swing back toward homeschooling began in the 1970s, led by the late John Holt's "unschooling" movement that emphasized giving freedom to the student to explore and discover.[1] Holt championed the idea that teaching the child *how to learn* was more important than forcing the child to follow a predetermined curriculum. This was a very radical idea in its time that challenged many of the contemporary ideas about educating children.

Holt believed that each child was born with a natural inclination to learn, but that traditional schooling methods went contrary to natural learning. Modern education's attempt to control or regulate learning was, in effect, smothering the child's innate ability and desire to learn.

Holt promoted homeschooling as an intimate environment, where the parent and the child could enjoy a flexible schedule and respond directly to the needs and interests of the child. The natural mood and energy swings of the child could be taken into account. For example, the parent-child team could take it easy when the child felt tired or sick, or move ahead at a quick pace on days when the child was full of energy.

Holt encouraged the parents to let the child share in the daily life of the family rather than follow a prescribed curriculum. The child would be certain to ask questions to better understand the day's activities, opening up teaching situations throughout the day for the parent to exploit in lieu of a curriculum. The parent's role as an educator was, therefore, to expose the child to as much of the world as possible, and then satisfy the child's curiosity by answering his or questions or showing him or her how to find answers by going to a library or finding someone who had the knowledge they sought.

Holt emphasized that this sort of education placed everything in the context of real life, rather than the artificial environment of the classroom. For instance, the child could learn arithmetic and finances by balancing the family checkbook, giving him or her perspective on the family's financial situation and teaching him or her the value of money.

Many of Holt's followers faced formal opposition from school districts and teachers unions who were quick to point out that homeschooling violated truancy laws in many states. The *unschoolers* had no consolidated lobbying group to champion their cause in the various state legislatures, and therefore experienced difficulty getting their views accepted as a valid and legal method of educating a child.

The homeschooling environment nationwide experienced a major change in the 1980s when Holt's group was joined by a growing number of conservative Christians seeking a nonsecular school environment for their children. Soon, the Christians became the most powerful force in the homeschooling movement. In contrast to the unschooling crowd, the Christian homeschoolers were highly organized with well-established communication networks and significant political clout. Before the end of the decade, every state in the United States of America had passed legislation to make homeschooling legal.

The homeschooling segment of the population today is a diverse and growing group. The National Center for Education Statistics reported that in 2003, there were 1.1 million children schooled primarily at home in the United States, an increase of approximately 250,000 over 1999 figures. About 80 percent of these students are taught exclusively at home, while the rest of the students are enrolled at least part-time in a public or private school.[2] (Many states allow homeschooled children to take part in extracurricular activities or have an IEP developed for special education programs, such as speech therapy. Contact your local school board for your state's policy on support for homeschooling.)[2]

WHO DOES HOMESCHOOL THEIR CHILDREN?

Roughly three out of four homeschooled students are white children, with one or more siblings who live in urban areas with both parents.[3] More than two-thirds of such households have only one parent in the workforce, leaving the other parent free to manage the household and teach the children.

Homeschoolers are more likely to live in the South and least likely to live in the Northeast. The Midwest and Western states share about an equal number of the remaining homeschool population.

Slightly less than one-half of homeschool parents have a bachelor's or graduate degree, and about the same number have household incomes of $50,000 or more.

All ages of children are represented in the homeschool population, with about two out of five children being of elementary school age and the rest about equally split up between middle school and high school ages.

CREATING A BETTER LEARNING ENVIRONMENT

Homeschoolers give a number of reasons for why they homeschool, but the most common reply is that they have concerns about the environment in other schools. Parents of children with attention deficit hyperactivity disorder (ADHD) or other learning differences are particularly sensitive to the stress that their child can face in a school environment, including cruel abuse and teasing from other children.

"I home school my son, who's 14 and has ADHD, obsessive-compulsive disorder and Tourette's syndrome," one mother told me. "We home school because he had so many problems at school. He was really tormented in public school by other children who teased him about the stuff he did."

"My son talked 'all the time' without really saying much," another parent shared with me, "getting him in trouble with teachers, who developed an attitude toward him that transferred to the other kids. By junior high, he was willing to do almost anything to have friends. (This was a) very dangerous situation."

Moving the learning environment to home relieves the daily social frustrations for these children and allows them to focus on academics. The parent can also modify the school day to fit the child's natural schedule, catching the child when he or she is active and receptive to learning.

"My 5th grader has increased his abilities in all subjects since coming home, testing almost 100% in some subjects," a mother proudly reports. "Yes, I am bragging. I always knew he was smart; he just needs to be approached at his teachable moments. I know I can adjust the day around his super activity and I know when he needs a break. It's not always by the clock on the wall."

"Learning should happen all the time, not just during supposed school hours," another mother explains. "Think of all the learning opportunities you have every day, such as changing measurements in a recipe or determining the amount of time required to get from your home to the doctor's office."

Of course, working with an ADHD child is not always easy. It can be a terrible strain on a parent to spend all day, every day with a child who has so much energy. "A day with my son is like trying to keep a tornado contained in a crystal shop," confessed one mother.

Homeschooling a child with a learning difference takes patience, understanding, and creativity. One mother laments that "what works one day may never work again or it could go smoothly for two weeks and flame out the next month." The flexibility afforded by the home environment allows the parent to adapt to the child's needs, as opposed to a classroom where it is difficult or impossible for a teacher to adjust to the varying needs of each child on a daily basis.

Many parents choose to homeschool for religious or moral reasons, while others reply that they were dissatisfied with the academic results of other schools. Parents of gifted children, in particular, may choose to homeschool their child in a self-paced program, where he or she may learn as fast as possible rather than be restrained to the speed of his or her less gifted classmates.

One mother stressed to me that the flexibility she found in homeschooling was very important to her. "When my son understands something, we move forward," she explains. "When he doesn't understand then we remain at that point in the lesson until he does. I don't feel that he has to remain on the same rigid timetable as the public school."

About one in seven homeschooling parents say that they homeschool specifically because their child has one or more special needs, such as a learning disability, or a physical or mental health problem. These parents feel that the home environment is far more effective in meeting the specific needs of their child. "I think there are so many distractions at school that kids with ADHD miss out on a lot," explains one father.

RESULTS OF HOMESCHOOLING

Homeschooled students tend to do extremely well as a group on standardized testing, regardless of their parent's income level, ethnicity, or education level. A 1997 study by Dr. Brian Ray of the Home Education Research Institute found that homeschooled children outperformed their public school peers by an average of 30–37 percentile points across all subjects.[4]

Surprisingly, the homeschooled children whose parents had a teaching degree performed at about the same level on standardized tests as other homeschoolers. A parent's certification as a teacher seemed to make little difference in his or her child's test scores.

Another unexpected result from Dr. Ray's study was that the amount of state regulation had little-to-no impact on the standardized test scores. States that mandate testing and evaluation of homeschooled students saw their students score about the same as states that had very little regulation of homeschooling.

While just over 2 percent of students across the country were homeschooled in 2005, it is interesting to note that 31 of the 271 contestants in that year's Scripps National Spelling Bee were homeschooled (more than 11 percent).[5]

SHOULD YOU HOMESCHOOL YOUR CHILD?

Homeschooling is definitely not for everyone. I asked a number of experienced homeschooling parents for questions that a parent should ask himself before choosing to homeschool his or her child, and received the following responses:

- Ask yourself why you want to homeschool. You should be able to answer that question rather specifically.
- Are you willing to go through a trial and error period? (More than once, if needed?)
- Are you sure that you want to spend time, i.e., all day every day, with your kid(s)?
- If you are married, can you count on your spouse's support?
- Do you have access to a support group of experienced home schoolers, either in real life or online?
- Are you getting resistance from anyone to do this? If so, is the resistance perhaps indicative of a valid reason for you not to home school?
- Is your child in need of special services due to a medical condition, learning disorder, developmental disorder, disability, behavioral disorder, or delinquency? If so, are you in a position to see to it that those services are accessible, available, and provided? Or, are you otherwise prepared to deal with your child's particular issues? Do you have a plan (and a backup plan)?
- Are you ready and willing to spend some time and money investigating the various home schooling options available?
- Don't make the mistake of believing that you are above the law. Are you ready and willing to investigate and abide by the local laws concerning home schooling? If not, are you willing to work to change the laws?
- Everyone has to make their own decisions and be comfortable with that decision. Are you truly committed to home schooling? If you have any serious doubts about it then it may not be the right time for you and your child.
- Are you willing and financially able to let go and find a tutor if you encounter problems teaching a subject?
- How will you hold yourself accountable? How will you know that your child is getting it?
- Are you willing to challenge your child academically? Do you have the time and energy needed to keep up his education and not fall behind?
- How does your child feel about home schooling? Be sure to include him or her in the decision.

BUILDING SOCIAL SKILLS

Perhaps the most frequent criticism aimed at homeschooling is that homeschooled children are deprived of socialization. The conventional assumption is that the daily interactions among children that occur at school are a beneficial and necessary part of *growing up*.

In contrast to this traditional view, one homeschooling mother told me that she viewed school as "the absolute worse place" for children to socialize. "Learning social skills from other children is *not* a good thing," she insisted. "Watching what adults model, specifically parents but also grandparents, extended family and even older siblings is a much better scenario."

Dr. Brian Ray's 1997 study showed that the average homeschooler does participate in a fair amount of outside activities that allow for socialization. It was most common for homeschoolers to participate in more than five outside activities, including scouts, ballet or dance classes, 4-H clubs, volunteer work, outside classes, music classes, group sports, church activities, and field trips.

"Most home schoolers understand the need to get their child out of the house and out into the real world," a father told me, "and it is easy to find good activities, particularly if you are part of a home school support group."

Choosing a Homeschool Curriculum

There are myriad ways and methods to teach your child at home, ranging from the unstructured *no curriculum* philosophy of pure *unschooling* to highly structured turnkey systems that provide an academic road map for both the parent and the child to follow. Both secular and religious curricula are now available in abundance for homeschoolers.

Educational programs can be delivered via DVD or VHS video, interactive CD-ROMs, online Web-based training, or old-fashioned textbooks. (Thomas Edison, a highly visual learner, expected textbooks to become obsolete and be replaced by motion pictures.) Many homeschoolers find that combining different types of media is useful to provide variety and expose the child to different styles of teaching.

Parents can explore the many different programs available by conducting a Web search for "homeschool curriculum" on any good search engine. Most communities now also have homeschool support groups, where parents can share their experiences and gain advice from other homeschooling families about different educational programs. Ask other homeschooling parents to show you their curriculum and discuss how it might work for your unique child.

Homeschooling Tangential Thinkers

In reality, every parent homeschools their child to some extent, even if it just involves helping the child do his or her homework. Here are some general tips from the Department of Education on teaching children like Thomas Edison, who are tangential thinkers.[6]

Introducing Lessons

Children with ADHD and other learning differences learn best with a carefully structured academic lesson, so it is a good idea to explain what you want the child to learn and place the lesson in the context of previous lessons. So, review past lessons first, and then preview the coming lesson. For example, explain that a language arts lesson will involve reading a story about Paul Bunyan and identifying new vocabulary words in the story.

Provide an advance organizer that summarizes the order of various activities planned. That way he or she will know exactly what is expected of him or her each day.

Simplify instructions, choices, and scheduling. The simpler the expectations communicated to an ADHD student, the more likely it is that he or or she will comprehend and complete them in a timely and productive manner.

Conducting Lessons

Periodically question your child's understanding of the material throughout the lesson. Probe for correct answers and identify if you need to go back over material before moving forward in the lesson.

Transitions from one lesson or class to another are particularly difficult for students with ADHD. Help prepare him or her for transitions by

- *Being predictable.* Structure and consistency are very important for children with ADHD; many do not deal well with change. Minimal rules and minimal choices are best for these children. They need to understand clearly what is expected of them, as well as the consequences for not adhering to expectations.
- *Perform ongoing evaluation.* Watch for signs of lack of comprehension, such as daydreaming, or visual or verbal indications of frustration.
- *Help him or her correct his or her own mistakes.* For example, remind the child that he or she should check his or her calculations in math problems, or remind him or her of particularly difficult spelling rules, and how he or she can watch out for easy-to-make errors.
- *Help him or her focus.* Periodically remind him or her to keep working and to focus on his or her assigned task.
- *Provide follow-up directions.* These follow-up directions should be provided in writing.
- *Divide work into smaller units.* Break down assignments into smaller, less complex tasks. For example, allow him or her to complete five math problems before presenting the remaining five problems.
- *Highlight key points.* Highlight key words in the instructions on worksheets to help him or her focus on the directions. Prepare the worksheet before the lesson begins, or underline keywords as you read the directions together. In math, for example, show him or her how to underline the important facts and operations; in "Mary has two apples, and John has three," underline *two*, *and*, and *three*.

- *Eliminate or reduce frequency of timed tests.*　Tests that are timed may not allow the child to demonstrate what he or she truly knows due to his or her potential preoccupation with elapsed time. Allow him or her more time to complete quizzes and tests in order to eliminate *test anxiety*, and provide him or her with other opportunities, methods, or test formats to demonstrate his or her knowledge.
- *Try interactive computer programs.*　Try these computer programs to make instruction more visual, and allow him or her to participate actively.

Language Arts and Reading Comprehension

To help children, who are poor readers, improve their reading comprehension skills, try the following instructional practices:

- *Silent reading time.*　Establish a fixed time each day for silent reading.
- *Follow-along reading.*　Ask your child to read a story silently while you read the story aloud.
- *Storyboards.*　Ask your child to make storyboards that illustrate the sequence of main events in a story.
- *Storytelling.*　Schedule storytelling sessions where your child can retell a story that he or she has read recently.
- *Playacting.*　Schedule playacting sessions where your child can role-play different characters in a favorite story.
- *Word bank.*　Keep a word bank or dictionary of new or *hard-to-read* sight-vocabulary words.
- *Board games for reading comprehension.*　Play board games that provide practice with target reading comprehension skills or sight-vocabulary words. (Educational stores near you should have a number of board games from which to choose. Ask members of your local or online homeschooling support group for suggestions.)
- *Computer games for reading comprehension or phonics.*　Schedule computer time for him or her to have drill and practice with sight-vocabulary words.
- *Recorded books.*　These materials, available from many libraries, can stimulate interest in traditional reading and can be used to reinforce and complement reading lessons.

Writing

Children with ADHD have been found to benefit from the following practices:

- *Standards for writing assignments.*　Set a consistent standard for acceptable written work, such as format and style.
- *Recognizing parts of a story.*　Teach him or her how to describe the major parts of a story (e.g., plot, main characters, setting, conflict, and resolution). Use a storyboard with parts listed for this purpose (or have him or her create the storyboard as a project).
- *Visualize compositions.*　Ask him or her to close his or her eyes and visualize a paragraph that you read aloud.

- *Proofread compositions.*   Require that he or she proofreads his or her work before turning in written assignments. Provide him or her with a checklist of items to check when proofreading his or her own work.
- *Tape recorders.*   Ask the student to dictate writing assignments into a tape recorder, as an alternative to writing them.
- *Dictate writing assignments.*   Write down a story told by your child to spur his or her creativity.

Spelling

To help children who are poor spellers, the following techniques have been found to be helpful:

- *Everyday examples of hard-to-spell words.*   Take advantage of everyday events to teach difficult spelling words in context. For example, ask him or her to spell *sandwich* during lunch.
- *Frequently used words.*   Assign spelling words that he or she routinely uses in his or her speech each day.
- *Dictionary of misspelled words.*   Have him or her keep a personal dictionary of frequently misspelled words.
- *Manipulatives.*   Use cutout letters or other manipulatives to spell out hard-to-learn words. (This is an especially helpful tool for tactile-kinesthetic learners.)
- *Color-coded letters.*   Color code different letters in hard-to-spell words (e.g., receipt).
- *Movement activities.*   Combine movement activities with spelling lessons (e.g., jump rope while spelling words out loud).
- *Word banks.*   Use 3" × 5" index cards of frequently misspelled words sorted alphabetically.

Handwriting

Students who have difficulty with manuscript or cursive writing may well benefit the following:

- *Individual chalkboards.*   Have him or her practice copying and erasing the target words on a small chalkboard.
- *Spacing words on a page.*   Teach him or her to use his or her finger to measure how much space to leave between each word in a written assignment.
- *Special writing paper.*   Have him or her use special paper with vertical lines to learn to space letters and words on a page.
- *Structured programs for handwriting.*   Teach handwriting skills through a structured program, such as Jan Olsen's "Handwriting without Tears" program (available at http://www.hwtears.com).

Math Computation

Numerous practices can help children improve their basic computation skills. The following are just a few:

- *Patterns in math.* Teach him or her to recognize patterns when adding, subtracting, multiplying, or dividing whole numbers. (e.g., the digits of numbers which are multiples of 9 [18, 27, 36, ...] add up to 9).
- *Mastery of math symbols.* If children do not understand the symbols used in math, they will not be able to do the work. For instance, do they understand that the *plus* in 1 + 3 means to add and that the *minus* in 5 − 3 means to take away?
- *Mnemonics for basic computation.* Teach mnemonics that describe basic steps in computing whole numbers. For example, "Don't Miss Susie's Boat" can be used to help the student recall the basic steps in long division (i.e., divide, multiply, subtract, and bring down).
- *Real-life examples of money skills.* Provide real-life opportunities to practice target money skills. For example, ask him or her to calculate the change when you buy something at a store, or set up a *pretend* store at home where he or she can practice calculating change.
- *Color coding arithmetic symbols.* Color code basic arithmetic symbols, such as +, −, and =, to provide visual cues for him or her when he or she solves arithmetic problems.
- *Board games for basic computation.* Play board games that use adding, subtracting, multiplying, and dividing whole numbers.
- *Computer games for basic computation.* Schedule computer time for him or her to drill and practice basic computations, using appropriate games.
- *"Magic minute" drills.* Have him or her perform a quick (60-second) drill every day to practice basic computation of math facts, and have him or her track his or her own performance.

Solving Math Word Problems

To help children improve their skill in solving word problems in mathematics, try the following:

- *Reread the problem.* Teach him or her to read a word problem *two times* before beginning to compute the answer.
- *Clue words.* Teach him or her clue words that identify which operation to use when solving word problems. For example, words such as *sum, total,* or *all together* may indicate an addition operation.
- *Guiding questions for word problems.* Teach him or her to ask guiding questions in solving word problems. For example, what is the question asked in the problem? What information do you need to figure out the answer? What operation should you use to compute the answer?
- *Real-life examples of word problems.* Have him or her create and solve word problems that provide practice with specific target operations, such as addition, subtraction, multiplication, or division. These problems can be based on recent, real-life events in his or her life.
- *Calculators to check word problems.* Let him or her use a calculator to check computations made in answering assigned word problems.

Use of Special Materials in Math

Some children benefit from using special materials to help them complete their math assignments, including:

- *Number lines.* Provide number lines for him or her to use when computing whole numbers.
- *Manipulatives.* Use manipulatives to help him or her gain basic computation skills, such as counting poker chips when adding single-digit numbers.
- *Graph paper.* Ask him or her to use graph paper to help organize columns when adding, subtracting, multiplying, or dividing whole numbers.

Organizational and Study Skills

Many tangential thinkers are easily distracted and have difficulty focusing their attention on assigned tasks. However, the following practices can help them improve their organization of homework and other daily assignments:

- *Color-coded folders.* Provide the child with color-coded folders to help organize assignments for different academic subjects (e.g., reading, mathematics, social science, and science).
- *Clean out desks and book bags.* Ask the child to periodically sort through and clean out his or her desk, book bag, and other special places where written assignments are stored.
- *Visual aids as reminders of subject material.* Use banners, charts, lists, pie graphs, and diagrams situated throughout the classroom to remind students of the subject material being learned.

Time Management

Children with ADHD often have difficulty finishing their assignments on time and can thus benefit better time management skills, including the following:

- *Use a clock or wristwatch.* Teach the child how to read and use a clock or wristwatch to manage time when completing assigned work.
- *Use a calendar.* Teach the child how to read and use a calendar to schedule assignments.
- *Practice sequencing activities.* Provide the child with supervised opportunities to break down a long assignment into a sequence of short, interrelated activities.
- *Create a daily activity schedule.* Tape a schedule of planned daily activities to the child's desk.

Helpful Study Skills

Children often have difficulty studying effectively on their own, but these tips may help them improve their self-study skills:

- *Adapt worksheets.*   Teach a child how to adapt instructional worksheets by folding his or her reading worksheet to reveal only one question at a time. The child can also use a blank piece of paper to cover the other questions on the page, helping him or her focus on the question at hand.
- *Venn diagrams (two or more overlapping circles).*   A Venn diagram is a highly visual way to show relationships between objects or ideas. Venn diagrams are often used in mathematics to show relationships between sets, and in language arts they can be used to examine similarities and differences in characters, stories, poems, etc. You can also use them as a prewriting activity to help organize thoughts. Try a Web search for "Venn diagram," and you should find dozens of creative ideas to help you implement them into your instruction.
- *Note-taking skills.*   Show your child how to outline a lesson or story to pick out the most important concepts and pieces of information. Do an outline together first, and then let him or her try it again on his or her own.
- *Checklist of frequent mistakes.*   Provide your child with a checklist of mistakes that he or she frequently makes in written assignments (e.g., punctuation or capitalization errors), mathematics (e.g., addition or subtraction errors), or other academic subjects. Teach the child how to use this list when proof-reading his or her work at home and school.
- *Uncluttered workspace.*   Having an uncluttered workspace can help reduce distractions during schoolwork.
- *Tangible rewards.*   Use tangible rewards to reinforce appropriate behavior. These rewards can include stickers, such as *happy faces* or sports team emblems, or privileges, such as extra time on the computer or lunch with the teacher. Ask your child to help select the reward to ensure that he or she will be motivated by it.
- *Intangible rewards.*   Praise and encouragement should be frequent, sincere, and appropriate for the child's work. Don't fall into the trap of finding fault first—look for the goods things he or she does and reinforce that behavior before you begin correcting mistakes.
- *Token economy systems.*   Use token economy systems to motivate your child to achieve a goal identified in a behavioral contract. For example, he or she can earn points for each assignment completed on time. In some cases, he or she might lose points for each homework assignment not completed on time. Give him or her a tangible reward for earning a specified number of points, such as extra time on a computer or a *free* period on Friday afternoon.

7

THE IMPORTANCE OF SELF-CONFIDENCE AND SELF-ESTEEM

Young Al Edison's short but unsuccessful stint at the Family School for Boys and Girls in Port Huron, Michigan, caused him to lose great confidence in his own abilities. "I...had come almost to regard myself as a dunce," he later remembered. Nancy Edison knew that her son's self-confidence needed to be restored, and wasted no time in setting the matter straight. As Edison told the story, his mother "brought me back to the school and angrily told my teacher that he didn't know what he was talking about, that I had more brains than he himself."

Nancy instinctively understood that Al needed self-confidence to balance his learning differences. A popular story in the Edison family demonstrates Nancy's emphasis on self-confidence and refusal to identify with failure. Al, as a preschooler, had watched in wonder as little goslings hatched from the family goose's eggs. After the goose had laid her next clutch of eggs, Al waited until she got up from her nest and carefully set himself in her place. He was discovered still sitting on the eggs several hours later by the rest of the family who had come in search of him. Although his siblings all laughed at him for being so silly, Nancy comforted him and said, "Al, you did a smart thing, even if you didn't get any of the eggs to hatch. If no one ever tried anything, even what some folks say is impossible, no one would ever learn anything."

SELF-CONFIDENCE FACTS AND MYTHS

Self-confidence and self-esteem are thought by some to be an answer to many of life's problems. Everything from drug abuse, criminal activity, teen pregnancy, and poor academic achievement are sometimes blamed on a fundamental lack of self-confidence, self-respect, and self-esteem. One late 1980s report funded by the State of California concluded that most of the state's problems could be traced back to the low self-esteem of many Californians.[1] The implication was that raising those individuals' self-esteem would subsequently correct most of the state's ills, including balancing the state budget. While this report's conclusions may have been a bit extreme, the overall premise that a high feeling of self-worth can greatly benefit an individual sounds intuitively correct. How can we tell if this is true?

Designing an experiment to prove the value of high self-confidence and self-esteem in children is an extremely complicated task. For example, how do you measure the self-esteem and confidence of a child? Most researchers, for lack of a better idea, resort to merely asking the children to rate their own levels of confidence and self-esteem.

As you can imagine, it is difficult to draw a scientific conclusion based solely on someone's opinion of him- or herself, especially a child. Complicating the situation is the tendency of most people to report that they are better than they actually might be. (One recent college survey found that 70 percent of students considered themselves as above average, while just 2 percent admitted that they were below average.[2])

The correlation between self-confidence and good grades can also suffer from a chicken-or-the-egg problem. For example, a group of self-confident students might have good grades, but that does not prove that their self-confidence caused the good grades. On the contrary, their good grades may actually be the basis for their self-confidence, meaning that they had to score good grades *before* their self-confidence developed. Researchers must be careful to not jump to conclusions about cause and effect when two events are shown to correlate with one another.

Fortunately, there have been a small number of studies that studied causation closely and used various objective ways of measuring self-confidence and self-esteem rather than merely relying on people's personal opinions of themselves. The American Psychological Society sponsored a comparison of these studies and published the results in 2003.[3] The following conclusions help to confirm the common beliefs about the importance of high self-esteem and personal confidence:

- Persons with high levels of self-confidence tend to excel at meeting new people and forming friendships, while people with lower levels of self-confidence fear rejection and thus avoid meeting new people.
- Persons with high levels of self-esteem are happier and less prone to depression than persons with lower levels of self-esteem.
- Persons with high self-esteem usually find it easier to work in groups than their colleagues with lower self-esteem.
- Persons with high self-esteem and confidence do not give up as easily as someone with lower self-esteem (probably because the confident individual has a deeper belief in his or her own ability to solve the problem at hand).

However, the study also showed the following surprises that challenge our traditional beliefs:

- Children with high self-esteem are just as likely as other children to be bullies or exhibit other aggressive behavior. There is even some evidence to suggest that bullies actually have higher self-confidence levels than have other children.

- High self-esteem did not seem to reduce the tendency for adolescents to use alcohol, tobacco, drugs, or have premarital sex. In fact, teens with high self-esteem may be overconfident and less adverse to the risks associated with sex.
- High self-esteem does not seem to significantly improve scholastic or vocational performance in the general population. We will discuss more on this later, because many experts feel that high self-esteem is essential for success in a child with learning differences.
- False (or *feel-good*) self-esteem may actually backfire and produce negative results. For example, in 1999 one group of students was encouraged and praised in an effort to raise its self-esteem, even though its students were all getting a D or an F in a particular course. The result was their average test scores dropped below 50 percent. On the other hand, a group of similar students that were consistently encouraged to accept responsibility for their grades managed to raise their average score up to a passing grade.

SUMMARY

We cannot deny the importance of children having high self-esteem and confidence. They will develop better social skills, live a happier life, and learn to not give up as easily as their lower self-esteem classmates. These benefits are certainly worth the time spent each day to cultivate self-esteem, as long as you recognize that it is not an end-all cure for the various woes of childhood.

EDISON'S SELF-CONFIDENCE

The benefits of high self-esteem and confidence were undeniable in Thomas Edison's life. His belief in his own abilities helped him succeed in projects long after other inventors would have given up. The most famous example is the story of the lightbulb, where Edison unsuccessfully tested thousands of materials before he found a suitable carbon filament. Time after time for several years he tried new materials, only to have each test end in failure. Each time, he merely recorded the results and confidently moved on to test the next material. "The trouble with other inventors is that they try a few things and quit," he explained. "I never quit until I get what I want!"

SELF-CONFIDENCE AND LEARNING DIFFERENCES

Children with learning differences commonly suffer from a lack of confidence from their failures at school. According to a recent Presidential Commission Report on Excellence in Special Education, "the current system uses an antiquated model that waits for a child to fail, instead of a model based on prevention and intervention."[4] Children who learn differently are therefore *required* to fail before they can obtain help. Unfortunately, this often sets a pattern of chronic and severe underachievement that can be very hard to break out of once it is in place. Maintaining a confident self-image would be difficult for anyone who was placed in such an overwhelming situation.

Although confidence and self-esteem can be quickly lost by one or two failures, gaining that self-esteem and confidence back is a slow process that must be gradually earned with small *wins*. Undeserved praise or artificial success in an easy environment builds false confidence that can be quickly lost again as soon as the child is placed in a challenging situation.

ACCEPTING RESPONSIBILITY–BOTH GOOD AND BAD

Before you begin building your child's confidence, it is important to understand how your child views his or her successes and failures. Children with a history of academic failure frequently develop a defensive thought pattern that denies any personal responsibility for their education. For example, a child may believe that there is no use in studying for a test, since his or her inability to learn will cause him or her to fail anyway. This becomes a self-fulfilling (and self-reinforcing) prophecy, since the child's lack of study causes him or her to fail the test. Thus, the child perceives the failing grade as confirmation that he or she cannot learn. Failure, the child surmises, is inevitable. The child's life is hopelessly out of his or her control.

Paradoxically, the same type of thought pattern might cause a child to not accept responsibility for his or her success. For example, a child may dismiss a good score on a test as *pure luck*. He or she may not believe that the success was a result of hard work or good study habits on his or her part, and may therefore benefit little from the accomplishment. Once again, events (good and bad) are perceived to be out of his or her control.

Why would a child want to deny him- or herself credit for achieving success? There are a number of possible reasons, such as the following:

- Admitting that good study habits lead to good grades would place pressure on the child to continue studying and getting good grades. It is much easier to take the path of least resistance and believe that nothing could help him or her in school.
- If your child does not study for a test and consequently fails the test, he or she can always claim that he or she could have passed it if he or she had really tried. However, it may make the child appear to be stupid or unteachable if he or she studies hard but fails anyway. Therefore, it is psychologically safer for the child to not study and leave him- or herself an excuse.
- Your child may be afraid of the fear and humiliation that is part of the learning process. We all make mistakes when we learn new things; it is normal to not understand a new idea or skill the first time we are exposed to it. However, the frequent frustrations and failures that your child may have experienced in school might cause him or her to seek refuge in the idea that he or she is not responsible for his or her mistakes—or his or her successes.

Children who feel that they are not in control of their life usually develop strategies to avoid stressful situations, such as quitting an activity as soon as it becomes frustrating or refusing to take part in the activity at all. Unfortunately, these coping strategies just exacerbate the problem and make it harder for the child to regain control.

This "my life is out of my control" mentality will sabotage any efforts you make to improve your child's self-esteem. Therefore, the first step in building your child's sense of self-worth must be to instill the belief in him or her that he or she is responsible in large part for what happens to him or her.

Changing your child's thinking to accept responsibility for his or her own success and failure can be a slow process, but it is absolutely critical to any long-term improvement in his or her education. Your child's feeling of hopelessness will only grow as long as failure is perceived as inevitable and success is discounted as luck.

You may have to repeatedly find small successes and point out to your children how their actions caused those successes to come about. Conversely, you will need to point out how failures or disappointments in their life were caused by the choices they made and the actions they undertook.

Ultimately, you must look for opportunities on a daily basis to lovingly and patiently demonstrate that their actions, both good and bad, caused consequences. Your child must feel that he or she is in control of his or her life before self-confidence and self-esteem can take root and develop.

THE RESILIENT CHILD

Resiliency is a term applied to children exposed to severe risk factors, such as poverty, sickness, or learning difficulties, who nevertheless thrive and excel. It is the ability to spring back from and successfully adapt to adversity.

Helping your child overcome the "my life is out of my control" mentality is a key step toward developing his or her resiliency. The child must be firmly rooted in reality before he or she can begin to develop a healthy and confident self-image.

Emmy Werner is called "The Mother of Resiliency" from her work on the island of Kauai, studying disadvantaged children. She noted that the most important factor in developing a child's self-esteem was a relationship with at least one adult who showed him or her unconditional love.[5]

Of course, Nancy and Al Edison could be the archetype of this sort of relationship. Al experienced great adversities with his partial deafness, frequent illnesses as a child, and difficulties learning in school, but his mother's unfailing love and devotion gave him the support he needed to bounce back and thrive. Just as Nancy Edison ensured that Thomas Edison was unconditionally loved as a child, your child needs to know that you are going to accept him or her for who he or she is and unconditionally help him or her discover and develop his or her own unique strengths.

WHAT IS SELF-CONFIDENCE?

The U.S. Department of Health and Human Services defines self-confidence as "having a positive and realistic opinion of yourself and being able to accurately measure your abilities."[6]

Perhaps the most interesting part of this definition is its description of self-confidence as a *realistic* opinion. Healthy self-confidence must be based on reality. That is why it is so crucial that your children understand that they are in control of their lives. They can learn to identify their weaknesses and work with parents, counselors, and educators to solve problems that previously may have seemed insurmountable. They can learn to identify their strengths and use them as a foundation for positive self-esteem. But it all has to be based on reality.

A faulty self-image can be skewed either too high or too low.

Low self-confidence can lead your children to underestimate their talents and abilities. They may fear failure and never risk trying to achieve their true potential.

Overconfidence can be just as bad, getting your child in over their head in situations that they cannot handle. They may unknowingly set themselves up for failure, disillusionment, and despair. Overconfidence is not ability based. It is imagination based, and often children with Edison-like characteristics have *tremendous* imaginations. That's why it can be so dangerous to build up their self-esteem with false *feel-good* affirmations. Their vivid imaginations can literally take flight into a fantasyland of self-confidence.

The second part of the definition of self-confidence is important as well: "being able to accurately measure your abilities." Imagine that you have an old balance scale like Lady Justice holds in her hand, with a left and a right weighing pan on either side of a central balance point. You measure something on a balance scale by placing the object you are weighing on one side, and then adding various weights to the other side until the scale reaches equilibrium or balance. You usually don't guess the correct weight perfectly on the first try. You add a weight, and then add or subtract more or less weight, depending on whether you guessed high or low on the previous attempt. Eventually, through trial and error, you come up with a very accurate idea of how much the object weighs.

The process of measuring is not the important part. What matters most is that we end up with an accurate weight for the object we wished to measure. Whether it took us ten tries or twenty tries to get the scale balanced is really unimportant. When we still don't have the scale balanced after the first four or five tries, we don't throw up our hands in despair. We simply make an adjustment and try again.

That's exactly how measuring our abilities should be. We should accept our mistakes as merely part of the process. Make an adjustment and move on, and try again. Success will come to he who does not give up.

When your children measure their abilities, they might start off a little lighter than they really should, just testing themselves on something easy to ensure that they can do it. That's fine. Eventually, they will probably overstep their abilities and go for more than they can handle. That's fine as well. They will never know how far they can go unless they overextend their reach a bit. Just be sure to be there when they fall, help them up off the ground, dust them off, and encourage them for giving their all.

Of course, your children will not ever truly complete the testing of their abilities. Throughout most of their lives, they will continue to grow, continue to learn, and continue to develop. They will always have to be testing their true abilities, just as you and I should. Otherwise, how would we really ever know how much we might be able to accomplish? The important point is to let your children know that failing to reach a goal does not make them a failure; it merely gives them an accurate measure of their abilities at the time. Failure is a reality check, and one should never be afraid or ashamed of reality.

ACHIEVABLE, INCREMENTAL GOALS

Once your children have measured their abilities, you can begin setting realistic goals together. Let them choose goals of their own from two or three choices that you give them. Develop an action plan for how they will achieve each goal, be it memorizing a multiplication table, cleaning their room, or studying 2 minutes longer than normal. Talk to them about their progress on a regular basis. Allow praise to be appropriate and timely, but not artificial or undeserved.

Goals should be a bit of a stretch without being overwhelming. Set a long-term goal first and then break it down into bite-size pieces that are attainable, but still will allow the achievement of the long-term goal in a reasonable amount of time.

Make a visual aid such as a daily calendar or list that will remind your children of their goal and what they need to do each day to achieve it. Discuss appropriate rewards and punishments for staying on track or falling behind.

EMPHASIZE STRENGTHS AND IDENTIFY WEAKNESSES

Your child's strengths are the basic building blocks on which his or her self-esteem and identity will be built. You must work hard to identify these strengths and learn to nurture them as he or she develops a positive self-image.

Your child's teachers may be able to help you identify his or her strengths and weaknesses. Their insight is based on how your child responds to various subjects and activities at school, which may be very different from how he or she acts at home. The child's teachers are also probably a bit more objective than you might be when they evaluate your child, since they do not have complex emotional family ties to cloud their vision.

You may wish to have your child tested professionally to further identify his or her strengths and weaknesses. This may identify some specific areas for you and your child's teachers to work on. Ask your school's staff for help in finding qualified testing facilities in your area.

Remember that strengths and weaknesses extend beyond school subjects, such as reading and arithmetic. For example, arts, social skills, kindness, empathy, the ability to play well, etc. are all important skills that should be considered.

Besides identifying your child's strengths and weaknesses, each parent should give thought to his or her own skill sets. What subjects do you really excel in that you can best help your child with? What subjects are you fairly weak in and could probably use some help? Both Nancy and Samuel Edison gave up and hired a tutor when Al asked them to explain Isaac Newton's *Principia Mathematica.*

It is no crime to ask for help. Thomas Edison knew that he was weak in mathematics and had no qualms about hiring mathematicians to help him when needed. "I can always hire them, but they can't hire me," he confidently explained. Ask your child's teachers or inquire at Parent–Teacher Association meetings about other parents who might help your child with particular subjects. You might even be able to arrange an exchange of help if you are willing to tutor other children in subjects that you enjoy.

Physical Activity and Self-esteem

"Physical activity appears to relieve symptoms of depression and anxiety and improve the mood," according to a 1996 Surgeon Generals report.[7] Specifically, positive results appear after 10–15 weeks of regular exercise, and the exercise is most effective when it is an aerobic activity, such as running, swimming, soccer, basketball, or cycling.

Some nonaerobic activities, such as strength training or baseball, may also increase a person's self-confidence as he or she practices and gets better at the sport, but anxiety levels may not be reduced as with an aerobic sport.

The President's Council on Physical Fitness reports that "female athletes do better academically and have lower school dropout rates than their nonathletic counterparts." In addition, 69 percent of the studies reviewed by the President's Council showed a positive relationship between physical activity and self-esteem in school children.[8]

Should you encourage your children to enter into competitive sports so they can reap all of the benefits cited above? Well, probably yes. Just don't overdo it. As the President's Council reports, "Left unchecked, highly competitive sports contests can lead to stress and anxiety. For example, in a significant number of children and youth . . . stress, anxiety and burnout are of major concern."

The problems seem to come when sports are overemphasized in some way. Interviews with fifteen *burned-out* adolescent athletes showed that they "saw themselves and were viewed by others only in terms of their specialized athletic roles." They also reported that they felt as control over their own lives had been lost to other *power relationships* (coaches, parents, athletic peers, etc.).

Female athletes, in particular, noted the potential for physical and emotional damage from an excessive need to please others and strive for perfectionism. Females in top athletic condition would see themselves as *fat cows*, sometimes stemming from verbal abuse given by overzealous coaches who wished for their teams to win at any cost.

The bottom line on sports is *balance*. Sports can provide both mental and physical health benefits, instill self-confidence, teach team-building skills, and reduce anxiety levels for youths. The possibility of a sports scholarship could be a tremendous benefit as your child approaches college. However, sports can also be a source of extreme anxiety and stress to your child. Let the child have fun and encourage him or her to become as proficient at his or her sport as he or she can, but stop short of driving your child to stress, anxiety, and burnout.

BULLYING AND SELF-CONFIDENCE

Children with learning differences are also more likely than other children to encounter problems with bullying at school. Being bullied can be a terrorizing experience to a child and can seriously damage his or her self-image and confidence. The U.S. Department of Health and Human Services reports that children with learning disabilities or health impairments such as attention deficit hyperactivity disorder are at increased risk of being teased and physically bullied, as well as being somewhat more likely than others to bully their classmates.[9]

Bullying can take many forms, but it is always an aggressive behavior that is intentional, and involves an imbalance of power or strength. Although bullying may be isolated to a single instance, it is often a repeated offense. Bullying can be either physical or emotional, including hitting, kicking, shoving, teasing, name-calling, making intimidating gestures, excluding a child from a social circle, or sending threatening or insulting messages through notes, text messages, or e-mail.

Bullying or being bullied was once thought to be a normal childhood rite of passage, but it can have serious consequences. Children who are bullied are more likely to show signs of depression and anxiety. Their self-esteem suffers, and they may experience somatic symptoms, such as headaches, stomachaches, fatigue, or poor appetite. Absences from school are likely to increase as the classroom environment becomes more and more hostile. Some children have even reported thoughts of suicide as a result of being bullied.

If you feel that your child is being bullied, it is important that you encourage him or her to tell you who was involved and how it happened. Write down exactly what he or she tells you as soon as you can; it is best to not trust your memory on as emotionally charged subject as this, and you want to be as accurate as possible when you talk to school officials. Let your child know that it is not his or her fault, and that you are proud of him or her for being brave enough to tell you about it. Let him or her know that fighting back might just make the problem worse, especially since it could lead to your child being suspended or expelled. Talk to your child's teacher or principal immediately; they may be able to resolve the problem quickly, with no further actions needed on your part.

Parental instinct might cause your temper to flare up when you discover that your child has been intimidated or harassed by another child, but you should not let your anger cause you to do or say anything that you will later regret. Keep your emotions in check when you report bullying to school officials. In all likelihood, they want to stop the bullying as much as you do. Just give them the facts and let them know that you want to work with them to find a solution. Listen carefully to any suggestions they have for you, such as encouraging your child to make friends with specific children. Write down exactly what they intend to do and ensure that you understand the steps to be taken, as well as the expected time frame of the actions. Although they will probably work to resolve the problem quickly, it will be good for you to have notes in case you need to escalate the problem to school administrators or the superintendent later.

Give the school reasonable time to investigate and hear both sides of the story. This entire process should not take longer than a week.

Keep in touch with the school staff politely but persistently until you are sure that the bullying has stopped.

Although your first impulse might be to contact the parents of the bully, this could actually escalate the problem. If necessary, school officials should be the ones who initiate contact with the bully's parents.

If your child is being bullied based on a disability, the bullying may in fact be *disability harassment.* The Department of Education defines this as "intimidation or abusive behavior toward a student based on disability that creates a hostile environment by interfering with or denying a students participation in or receipt of benefits, services, or opportunities in the institutions program."[10] Immediately contact staff at your child's school if you feel that disability harassment has occurred. They should investigate promptly and respond appropriately. More information is available at www.ed.gov.

What if it is *your* child who turns out to be a bully? At first, you may be shocked to hear or even suspect that your child may be bullying another child. Unfortunately, adults are often unaware of bullying problems because the bullying usually takes place in unsupervised areas. Even if bullying happens near you, it might sound like mere teasing or roughhousing unless you listen closely. Adults are also unaware of bullying, because many children don't report it for fear of retaliation by the bully.

Your first impulse might be to panic when you discover that your child is acting like a bully, but bullying is more common than many adults realize. It is estimated that between 15 and 25 percent of American students are bullied at some time. It is most likely that your child does not understand how fearful the other children may be of him or her, or how dire the consequences of bullying might be.

One clue as to whether or not your child has bullying tendencies is to watch them with their siblings or friends at home. Children who bully other students at school are more likely than other children to also bully their siblings at home. Similarly, children who are bullied at school are somewhat more likely than other children to be bullied by siblings at home.

The Federal Health and Resources Service Administration lists the following steps that parents should take if they suspect that their child is acting like a bully[11]:

- Make it clear to your child that you take bullying seriously and that you will not tolerate this behavior.
- Develop clear and consistent rules within your family for your children's behavior.
- Praise and reinforce your children for following rules and use nonphysical, nonhostile consequences for rule violations.
- Spend as much time as possible with your child and carefully supervise and monitor his or her activities.
- Find out who your child's friends are, and how and where they spend free time.
- Build on your child's talents by encouraging him or her to get involved in social activities, such as clubs, music lessons, nonviolent sports, etc.
- Share your concerns with your child's teacher, counselor, or principal. Work together to send clear messages to your child that his or her bullying must stop.
- If you or your child needs additional help, talk with a school counselor or mental health professional.

You can find more resources to help you deal with your child, such as a quiz he or she can take to help determine if he or she is acting like a bully, at www.stopbullyingnow.hrsa.gov.

8

INDEPENDENT LEARNING AS
A CORE STRENGTH

Although Nancy devoted much of her time to one-on-one schoolwork with Al, perhaps her biggest contribution to his education was teaching him how to teach himself. Edison was very much an autodidact from roughly the age of 12 through the rest of his life. He read everything he could get his hands on, both technical and literary works. "If ever there was a man who tore the heart out of books it is Edison," wrote one of his staff members, "and what has once been read by him is never forgotten if useful or worthy of submission to the test of experiment."[1]

Also, Al never stopped his childhood habit of posing an inexhaustible amount of questions to anyone who might be able to teach him something, once describing himself as "more of a sponge than an inventor." He experimented endlessly, and kept copious and meticulous (but poorly organized) notes of his observations, hoping to illuminate the elusive properties of the world around him.

THE JOY OF READING

Edison's love of books was legendary. As a newsboy working on the Grand Trunk Railroad, he would spend his 5-hour layovers in Detroit at the newly opened Free Library. (His card number was 33.) Edison is rumored to have read the entire library, starting at the bottom shelf of each aisle and working his way through every row, one book at a time.

At age 20, he worked as an itinerant telegraph operator in order to afford used books. One associate at the time claimed that Edison spent so much money on books that he had no money left over to buy a coat, preferring to be cold rather than run short of reading material.

In his later years, he often received weekly deliveries of books to feed his voracious desire to read. His West Orange laboratory, built in 1887, contained a great library with 30-foot ceilings and two galleries with some 10,000 books.

Edison even chose the main library hall as the place he wished to lie in state and have mourners come pay their last respects.

Edison loved all literature, not just technical books on science. He discovered Victor Hugo's *Les Miserables* at the library in Detroit and talked so much about it that his friends temporarily nicknamed him "Victor." He enjoyed reading Shakespeare and even briefly entertained a desire to become a Shakespearean actor.

Edison particularly loved poetry, and enjoyed quoting stanza nine from Thomas Gray's *Elegy to a Country-Churchyard*:

> The boast of heraldry,
> the pomp of power,
> And all that beauty,
> all that wealth e'er gave,
> Awaits alike the inevitable hour:
> The paths of glory
> lead but to the grave.

HELPING YOUR CHILD TO LOVE READING

Nancy began instilling a love of reading in her son by first reading literary classics to him aloud, and then gradually having Al join in the reading until he could read the books himself aloud to her. In this manner, they finished Gibbon's *Rise and Fall of the Roman Empire*, Burton's *Anatomy of Melancholy*, and Sears' *History of the World* by the time Al was 12 years old. Samuel Edison helped to encourage this practice by giving Al a small coin as a reward for finishing each book.

The parental involvement that both Nancy and Samuel showed was a key ingredient in building Edison's lifelong enthusiasm for reading. As the Department of Education states in its booklet, *Helping Your Child Become a Reader*,[2]

> Years of research show clearly that children are more likely to succeed in learning when their families actively support them.
> Other than helping your children to grow up healthy and happy, the most important thing that you can do for them is to help them develop their reading skills. It is no exaggeration to say that how well children learn to read affects directly not only how successful they are in school now, but how well they do throughout their lives.
> *When children learn to read, they have the key that opens the door to all the knowledge of the world (emphasis mine)*. Without this key, many children are left behind.

Perhaps the best thing you can do to encourage your child to read is to take him or her to the library as often as possible. Get the child a library card of his or her own and show him or her how to use it responsibly. Introduce the child to encyclopedias and other resource materials available at the library. Show him or her how to look up a subject in the library computer database, and then locate the associated books on the shelf. Most importantly, let him or her see you using and enjoying the library yourself.

If your child finds books to be *boring*, try directing him or her to exciting subjects, such as pirate stories about Blackbeard or Robert Louis Stevenson's *Treasure Island*. Books on space or sports' figures might also pique his or her interest. Do not despair if he or she does not show interest at first in the subjects you pick; if you keep trying and give him or her a wide assortment of books from which to choose, you will eventually find the one or two key areas that will grab his or her attention and get him or her on the road to reading.

START AS YOUNG AS POSSIBLE

The ability to read is rooted in a child's understanding of language, and this begins when your child is a baby. Every time you speak, sing, or otherwise communicate with him or her, you are helping to build his or her language skills and lay the foundation for reading.

Even toddlers can learn to love books as you read to them and discuss the book's story and pictures. Taking time such as this to show your child that you enjoy books is often the first step toward getting him or her interested in reading.

The U.S. Department of Education's suggestions to involve young children with reading include the following[3]:

- *Making a special time each day that is devoted to reading.* Ensure that this time is fun by choosing periods when your child is in a playful mood.
- *Pointing word by word as you read to young children.* This will help the child learn that reading goes from left to right and understand that the word he or she says is the word he or she sees.
- *Reading a child's favorite book over and over again.* Look for something new occasionally to keep it interesting.
- *Reading many stories with rhyming words and lines that repeat.* Invite the child to join in on these parts. Point, word by word, as he or she reads along with you.
- *Discussing new words.* For example, "This big house is called a castle. Who do you think lives in a castle?"
- *Stopping and asking.* Stop and ask about the pictures and about what is happening in the story.
- *Helping your child learn the basic relationships between written letters and spoken sounds, or phonics.* Children need to be taught the sounds individual printed letters and groups of letters make. Knowing the relationships between letters and sounds helps children to recognize familiar words and *decode* new words.
- *Reading from a variety of children's books.* It includes fairy tales, song books, poems, and information books.

Control the Television Set and Video Games

Kids love to watch television and play video games, and not all television shows and video games are bad. However, unbridled use of the television set and video games can be a serious obstacle to reading. Every minute that your child spends watching television or playing video games is a minute that he or she is not reading, doing homework, being physically active, or learning social skills by playing with other children. Time limits and rules must be established and monitored to ensure that your child is watching only approved television or playing video games at designated times.

Not all television or video games are bad, of course. Nature documentaries, adaptations of classic books and stories, music, and so forth can make television a very rewarding experience for your child. However, a lot of sex, violence, commercials, and plain, old numbskull entertainment can also be delivered into your living room through television shows and video games. Selection and control are the issues at hand:

- *Selecting* the right programs or games for your child; and
- *Controlling* the amount of time and the specific times of day your child is allowed to watch television or play video games.

Here are some helpful tips for controlling the amount and quality of *video time* your child experiences:

- Predetermine what shows your child should see and prerecord them. The child can then watch them during his or her designated viewing times, preventing him or her from randomly channel surfing or watching shows on impulse.
- Control your own viewing to demonstrate proper use of the television, especially when you are supposed to be interacting with other family members or helping your child with homework.
- Be with your child when he or she is allowed to watch television or play games. You can open discussions about the show or game, such as "Was that real or make-believe?" or "Do people really act like that?"
- Limit the number and location of television sets in your house. Keeping a set *out* of your child's bedroom is a great idea.

Experimentation

Experimentation is an integral part of independent learning, and Thomas Edison's natural skepticism caused him to rely on experimentation to determine whether the things he read were true or not. As one of Edison's biographers pointed out, Edison never accepted "any statement of fact or experiment therein, but worked out every one of them himself to ascertain whether or not they were true."[4]

Edison's need to prove things to himself was so strong that he sometimes performed careless experiments just to test what he was reading, such as sniffing a small vial of phosphoric anhydride to see if it really could suffocate a person. After recovering from a "blood-spitting convulsion," he admitted that "the book was right that time." While your child will hopefully not go to such an extreme, this story does demonstrate the overwhelming compulsion that tangential thinkers have to learn by experimentation.

Nancy sparked Al's lifelong love of experimentation by giving him a copy of R.G. Parker's *School of Natural Philosophy*, describing a series of experiments he could perform at home. Young Al loved the book and performed every experiment from cover to cover. Nancy then provided him with the *World Dictionary of Science* and other similar books to further feed his interest in experiments. He quickly became consumed with interest in chemistry, obtaining as many chemicals as he could and setting up a small laboratory in the cellar of the family's house in Port Huron.

Nancy learned what interested Al, and ignited his desire to learn by encouraging and enabling him to follow his interests.

Develop your child's desire to experiment and explore by exposing him or her to a variety of different objects and experiences. Observe the child's reactions and talk to him or her after each new experience to see which ones catch his or her interest. Some suggestions are as follows:

- Get a book from the library on chemistry experiments the child can do at home. If he or she likes that, consider getting him or her a small chemistry set at home. (One great book you might try is *Science Experiments You Can Eat: Revised Edition* by Vicki Cobb, HarperTrophy, November 14, 1984.)
- Buy or borrow a telescope and explore the heavens on a clear night. Many telescopes now come with a computerized map of the sky that makes it easy to locate constellations, planets, and stars. Ask your librarian or search the Internet or local newspaper for an astronomy club near you. These clubs of amateur stargazers often invite novices to attend their meetings and use their telescopes.
- Get a microscope and explore the world of really small things. Let him or her discover what he or she might find in a drop of water from a ditch, or how a bee stinger is shaped. Teach him or her how to make salt or sugar crystals and look at their shapes.
- Get a magnifying glass and go on an outdoor bug hunt together. Encourage your child to look at the bugs carefully and tell you what he or she sees. Look up the names of unknown bugs when you get home and find out how they survive.
- Go hiking in a local nature center or park.
- Get a bird feeder for your home and help your child keep track of the different birds that arrive. If that piques his or her interest, think about getting several different feeders with various types of bird seeds to see which birds like different types of food.
- Give your child an inexpensive digital or film camera and let him or her explore photography.
- Go bird watching. All you need is a book on local wild birds from your library or bookstore and a pair of binoculars. Head to a park, river, or shore, and

begin cataloging how many different types of birds the two of you can spot. (*Note*: Local Audubon Clubs usually have lists of birds that are commonly found in your area.)

- Have your child start and maintain an aquarium, be it an inexpensive goldfish bowl or a lavish saltwater tank.
- Get a candle-making kit from a local hobby store and let your child experiment with different types of wax and techniques of candle making.
- Collect coins. The U.S. Mint has a great Web site for kids to help your child get started (http://www.usmint.gov).
- Start a stamp collection. Stamp clubs can be a great source for new stamps and for stamp-collecting advice. These clubs often meet at schools, YMCAs, and community centers. Ask your local postmaster or librarian for the locations of stamp clubs in your area.
- Cloud watching. This can be as simple as lying on the grass with your child looking up at the clouds and trying to see animals or other objects in them. You can then teach him or her the different names of cloud types, such as cirrus, usually the highest cloud of all, medium-height alto clouds, fluffy cumulus clouds (the easiest to spot), towering nimbus rain clouds, or low-level stratus clouds that look like a gray blanket.
- Make soap together. There are lots of different types of soap you can easily make at home, from basics soaps to milled soaps, glycerin soaps, and scented soaps.
- Learn magic. Start at your local library to find books on card tricks and other types of illusions your child can learn to perform. Many children are interested in magic, and the practice it takes to become proficient teaches perseverance.
- Join a pottery course or bring a do-it-yourself pottery kit home from a hobby shop. For minimum expense and mess, you could start with polymer clay that will fire easily in your oven at home.
- Go fly a kite. You can start with an inexpensive kite from the local discount store, and later move up to a more advanced kites that can perform aerodynamic aerobatics. Your child can also obtain instructions from the Internet or a library book on how to make his or her own kite.
- Buy a metal detector and go treasure hunting.
- Visit an old cemetery and try to find the oldest tombstone or the oldest person buried there. Read the epitaphs (older tombstones often contained epitaphs, some touching and poignant, some surprisingly humorous). Many people even make and collect tombstone rubbings. Your child might surprise you with his or her questions after visiting an old cemetery. One good topic of conversation is to imagine what the lives were like of the people who were buried there long ago.
- Head to a seashore and comb the beach for shells, flotsam, and other collectible paraphernalia. A small pail, garden trowel, putty knife, and magnifying glass, while not necessary, can be useful. The types and numbers of organisms will vary with the weather, seasons, tides, and numbers of passersby. Go slowly, be patient, and look carefully. Dig into the sand and mud to investigate the water's edge.
- Go rock collecting. You do not need any special equipment to get started other than good sturdy footwear and a book to help identify the rocks you see.

Dry creek beds are a great place to start exploring. (Keep your eye out for fossils along the way.)

A pencil and notebook are a good idea so that your child can record directions to the site, sketch the surroundings, or describe and label the rocks he or she is collecting. If he or she wants to become more involved later, you can get him or her a chisel-edged hammer, a short pry bar, cloth or leather gloves, newspapers for wrapping the best pieces, and safety glasses or goggles. An inexpensive rock tumbler kit from a hobby shop can even enable him or her to turn certain rocks into pieces for jewelry.

- Make jewelry beads out of polymer clay. Your local library or hobby store should have books with instructions showing how to do it.
- Start an indoor or outdoor garden or purchase some indoor plants, and place your child in charge of their care. The child could look after flowers, a small herb garden, or even a bonsai plant.
- Sewing, weaving, and knotting are three fun activities that also teach your child a wide variety of things. He or she will learn about different fabrics; he or she will have to use some arithmetic skills to find the right measurements from a pattern; and he or she can also make useful things and clothing items. This can be a good outlet for creativity, as well as developing a number of skills.
- Does your family have a collection of old photos tucked away in a drawer, shoebox, or storage bin? Set your child to organizing those photos into scrapbooks. Materials are easily obtained at hobby stores, and instructions and inspiration can be found for free on Web sites or at the library. Give guidance, but let him or her figure out the best ways to arrange, organize, and decorate the scrapbooks.
- Flower arranging with either live or silk flowers can also be a fine way to encourage creativity and teach your child about different types of flowers and design. He or she can also explore the differences between western and eastern (Asian) styles.
- Develop writing skills through an overseas pen pal. Your librarian or school staff should be able to help you find an international pen pal for your child. Today, a number of pen pal communications are done online through e-mail or on *blog* pages. This will expose him or her to another culture and give him or her daily writing practice.
- Find a machine or appliance of some sort and take it apart with your child to see how it works. Then let him or her put it back together and make it work again. (Buy a cheap used toaster or some other item if you do not want to place your real appliances at risk.)

IMPORTANCE OF THE ARTS

The arts may open the world of learning to students who have trouble with traditional learning methods. The arts are intellectual disciplines requiring complex thinking and problem-solving skills, such as learning how to maneuver correctly across the spatial differences of a keyboard.

Visual arts offer a student the opportunity to construct his or her own understanding of the world. Drawing and painting reinforce motor skills, and can also be a way of learning shapes, contrasts, boundaries, spatial relationships, size, and other math concepts.

Edison himself was known to be constantly making sketches and drawings as he worked his way through an idea. "It has been noted by intimate observers of Thomas A. Edison," wrote Dyer and Martin, "that in discussing any project or new idea his first impulse is to take up any piece of paper available and make drawings of it. His voluminous notebooks are a mass of sketches."[5] (*Note: Voluminous* might be an understatement, as the Edison archives contain literally millions of notebook pages full of ideas, observations, and sketches.)

This need by Edison to get his ideas down on paper where he could visualize and organize his thoughts is common among tactile–kinesthetic thinkers who learn best through a hands-on approach, actively exploring the physical world around them. Drawing his idea on paper gave it substance and brought it out of the abstract realm of pure thought.

If your child is a tactile-kinesthetic thinker like Edison, it is likely that he or she has encountered difficulties in a traditional classroom environment that have caused him or her to experience him- or herself as somewhat of a failure or misfit. However, music, arts, crafts, and dance can give such students a chance to express themselves through different media and gain confidence along the way. The arts may provide a *window of success*, wherein he or she can blossom and grow confident.

THE IMPORTANCE OF A ROLE MODEL

Helping your child find a role model can be an extremely important part of molding his or her character. It is interesting to note that Edison's idol, Michael Faraday, was largely self-taught and learned primarily through reading and experimentation. Edison obtained a complete set of Faraday's works when he was a young telegraph operator in Boston, and obviously identified with Faraday immediately. Faraday's success and acceptance in the scientific community despite his lack of formal education gave Edison the encouragement and inspiration he needed to embark on his own career in science.

Although Edison's initial field of interest was chemistry, he devoted himself to the study of electricity soon after reading Faraday's book *Experimental Researches in Electricity*. "I think I must have tried about everything in those books," Edison later recalled. "His explanations were simple . . . he was the Master Experimenter."[6]

Faraday was born in a poor area of London in 1791, the son of a blacksmith, and noted in his autobiography that he, like Edison, had very little formal education beyond the rudiments of reading, writing, and arithmetic.

Another trait Faraday shared with Edison was an aversion to complicated mathematics, causing both men to focus their attention on performing practical experiments and creating new inventions. Just as Edison hired mathematicians to work with him, Faraday left a mathematical analysis of his work to be done by a Scottish physicist named James Clerk Maxwell, who used Faraday's work to develop the modern field theory of electromagnetism.

Both Edison and Faraday found it helpful to sketch out their ideas before starting an experiment, and both men regularly carried sketchpads or notebooks around with them to capture ideas as they occurred.

Despite Faraday's lack of education, he was perhaps the only inventor in the industrial age that rivaled Edison's own abilities. Faraday was the first person to isolate benzene and liquefy chlorine. He developed the laws of electrolysis and our modern system of oxidation numbers, as well as the process of electroplating metals. Many of the electrochemical terms commonly used today, such as electrode, electrolyte, anode, cathode, and ion, were coined together by Faraday and William Whewell. Of perhaps most importance, he laid the groundwork for Edison's work by creating the first electric motor in 1821. Within ten more years, Faraday had also uncovered the secrets behind electrical induction theory and invented the first electric generator or dynamo.

A paramount trait that Edison and Faraday shared was the love of reading. Faraday left his family at age 14 to work as an apprentice bookbinder, and often read the books that he was binding. He soon became enamored with the new and growing field of electrical research after reading Jane Marcet's *Conversations on Chemistry* and the science portions of *Encyclopedia Britannica.*

Faraday began attending scientific lectures to learn even more than his books could teach him, and in doing so he managed to meet Sir Humphrey Davy. Faraday latched onto Sir Davy as a role model, and used his meeting with him as an opportunity to become a laboratory assistant at the Royal Institution in London. Eventually, Faraday managed to become Davy's personal assistant and followed him on tours, where Davy demonstrated his discoveries to the scientific community and the press.

The parallels between Davy, Faraday, and Edison are striking. Davy's father died when he was very young and left no money to his family, so Davy's mother could not afford to place him in school. With very little formal training, Davy had to teach himself from whatever books he could find. Fortunately, he loved to read as much as Faraday and Edison did, and managed to learn geography, languages, and philosophy as a boy. At age 19, he obtained a book on chemistry written by Antoine-Laurent Lavosier, and devoted his life thereafter to the pursuit of science.

Davy was the first person to isolate the elements sodium, potassium, magnesium, calcium, strontium, and barium. He gave chlorine gas its name, and introduced nitrous oxide (*laughing gas*) as an anesthetic. Davy also invented the carbon arc lamp and the miner's safety lamp. His use of *cathodic protection* to prevent corrosion is still in use today on ships and other metal objects.

Davy could also be as impulsive as Edison was in the laboratory, and sometimes even endangered his own life in pursuit of a discovery. He nearly suffocated twice from inhaling gasses, and discovered the anesthetic effects of nitrous oxide by accidentally breathing it in while working in his laboratory.[7]

Perhaps the best way to expose your child to role models is to have him or her read biographies of great men and women. Make a good portion of his or her reading time be spent on historical figures that exemplify your family's values and share interests that your child displays.

LEARNING ON THE WEB

The Internet is a vast source of learning materials for your child. Your child can explore Web sites online from all over the world, perform research on his or her family genealogy, find out about outer space, or go any subject that his or her heart desires.

There are many great Web sites for your child to explore, but a great place to start is www.kids.gov, a project of the Federal Citizen Information Center. It provides links to Federal educational sites for children along with some of the best children-oriented sites from other organizations, all grouped by subject. You can find agricultural ideas for science fair projects, games that teach your child about protecting the environment, the history of the electric guitar, reading comprehension games, and lessons on how to solve real-world problems, using the scientific method and problem-based learning. Links include sites in arts, computers, fighting crime, geography, government, global village, health, history, homework, money, music, plants and animals, recreation, safety, science and math, space, state Web sites, and transportation.

Another great site is run by the National Weather Service (http://www. nssl.noaa.gov/edu/). Your child can investigate weather phenomena, such as tornadoes, thunderstorms, lightning, and hurricanes. He or she can also download coloring books, with safety tips about tornadoes and other dangers.

Of course, the National Zoo (http://nationalzoo.si.edu) has a wonderful site for children. When I visited it in the course of writing this book, they even had a live webcam, displaying a busy nest of black-footed ferrets.

The U.S. Forest Service highlighting its NatureWatch program provides nature-viewing opportunities over the Internet in all fifty states. So, your child can catch the view from a slope of Mount Baker in Washington State from the comfort of his or her home in New Jersey or anywhere else in the nation (http://www.fs.fed.us/outdoors/naturewatch/).

The National Park Service runs a great site for children on Yellowstone National Park (http://www.nps.gov/yell/kidstuff). It even has an online album of over 9,000 print-quality photos you can download of park scenery and wildlife.

National Aeronautics and Space Administration (NASA) has sites specifically devoted to students and teachers from kindergarten through high school. You can get to them through the main NASA site, www.nasa.gov. One example of NASA's extensive number of Web sites is SpacePlace (Spaceplace.nasa. gov), with games, animations, projects, and fun facts about earth, space, and technology. Your child will find word puzzles, scrambled pictures, crazy quizzes, and even a board game in the game area. Games include "Let's go to Mars!," where he or she must choose ten items to take on the 9-month journey through space as he or she travels to Mars. Your child will also learn about concepts, such as zero gravity, which causes some things that work fine on earth to not work so well in space.

The projects area of SpacePlace contains a coloring book, a star finder, how to make a potato into an asteroid or a cardboard roll into a fizz-tablet rocket, and other fun activities.

9

THE IMPORTANCE OF DISCIPLINE

Tangential thinkers such as Thomas Edison are notoriously independent. They become bored and distracted easily. They act unpredictably and impulsively, sometimes little to no regard for the consequences of their actions. They want to do things and see things for themselves, and hate to be restricted by rules. They seem to have only three speeds, *hyperfocus, fidget,* and *daydream.* All of these tendencies make it very difficult for parents and teachers to teach them self-control.

Nancy Edison believed strongly in the need to discipline her children. As an adult, Thomas Edison would often recount how his mother kept a birch switch in the kitchen for the sole purpose of ensuring that he was a well-disciplined lad. Nancy, as did most parents living in America in the 1800s, felt that a good switching was the most practical and proper way to discipline a child.

Corporal punishment was also the accepted method of discipline in nineteenth-century schools across the nation. None less than John Witherspoon, the eminent sixth president of Princeton University (then College of New Jersey), one of the signers of the Declaration of Independence and an early advocate for education in America, recommended that schoolteachers freely use corporal punishment in his *Letter on Education.* "Since the rod is the evidence of love," Witherspoon wrote, "what is said of our Father in heaven, 'whom the Lord loveth he chasteneth, and scourgeth every son whom he receiveth.'"

The New England Primer even worked corporal punishment into its alphabet lesson, reminding the children that the letter "F" stood for *the idle fool* who is "whipt at school."

Mark Twain's fictionalized portrayal of his own childhood experiences, *Adventures of Tom Sawyer,* described a stern schoolmaster:

> Vacation was approaching. The schoolmaster, always severe, grew severer and more exacting than ever, for he wanted the school to make a good showing on "Examination" day. His rod and his ferule were seldom idle now...

Mr. Dobbins' lashings were very vigorous ones, too; for although he carried, under his wig, a perfectly bald and shiny head, he had only reached middle age, and there was no sign of feebleness in his muscle. As the great day approached, all the tyranny that was in him came to the surface; he seemed to take a vindictive pleasure in punishing the least shortcomings. The consequence was, that the smaller boys spent their days in terror and suffering and their nights in plotting revenge.

The use of such severe punishment would likely be considered as child abuse if it happened today, whether by a teacher in school or by a parent at home. Yet, such harsh discipline was widely accepted at the time as the proper method to teach obedience in children. By contrast, the great majority of public schools today choose to use no corporal punishment at all.

What brought about this great change, from the extensive and sometimes harsh use of corporal punishment in Nancy Edison's time to its very limited usage today? Sadly, the initial catalyst for this change came from the growing public awareness of child abuse.

CHILD ABUSE IN EARLY AMERICA

It is a distressing fact that child abuse was rarely recognized in the days of early America; few communities even had laws protecting children until the mid-1870s. Until that time, children were considered to be the property of their fathers (a carryover from English Common Law).

The public recognition of child abuse in America began in the early 1870s when the case of 9-year-old Mary Ellen Wilson was reported in several New York newspapers. Young Mary had been routinely abused both physically and mentally by her foster mother for more than 7 years. Her punishments consisted of being beaten, cut, and burned, and she had reportedly never been allowed outdoors. The child was locked inside a tiny, dark closet whenever her foster mother left the house.

A concerned social worker named Etta Wheeler learned of the child's horrible plight and unsuccessfully tried to obtain the help of police and the courts. Amazingly, Etta learned that the foster mother was not violating any known laws. Both the police and the court system turned a blind eye to the child's situation and refused to intervene in what they considered a purely parental matter.

Fortunately, Etta Wheeler was not easily deterred. Just a few years before, in 1866, a New Yorker named Henry Bergh had established the first American Society for the Prevention of Cruelty to Animals (ASPCA) and championed new anticruelty laws for animals. Etta approached Bergh for help, believing that the ASPCA attorneys could argue in court that a child had at least the same rights as an animal. Bergh agreed with Etta, and convinced a court to hear the case. The ASPCA successfully pleaded for Mary, and had the foster mother sentenced to 2 years in prison for assault and battery.

Public outcry over the much-publicized trial eventually led Mr. Bergh and other New Yorkers to establish the first society for the prevention of cruelty to children. Child protection laws were passed soon afterward in New York and other states, beginning the path of progress to child protection as we know it today.

In Nancy Edison's defense, Thomas Edison always spoke in reverent and loving tones about his mother, and there is no indication to suspect that she ever took corporal punishment to the point of child abuse. She was merely following the accepted child-rearing practices of her time.

Today, corporal punishment is a controversial and emotionally charged topic in the United States. Many modern American adults were spanked as children, and to suggest that there are better ways of disciplining a child is to imply that their parents did not raise them correctly. Many parents also belong to religious denominations that sincerely teach corporal punishment as scripturally based. Yet, experts such as the American Academy of Pediatrics officially discourage its use.[1]

Why is corporal punishment still a popular form of discipline among many parents when there is so much opposition to spanking or switching a child in the medical and educational communities? The answer may be that it simply *seems to work.* The child reaches for something that he or she should not have, and the mother instinctively swats his or her hand. It is a quick and convenient method of correcting the child. In addition, it allows the mother to vent a little frustration at the child's unacceptable behavior.

Opponents of corporal punishment would argue, however, that physically punishing a child seems to work only in the short term. Over time, a child who is physically punished might grow resentful of the punishment and vent his or her anger by showing hostility toward others. Also, spanking a child when you are angry teaches him or her that it is appropriate to strike another person in anger.

Several studies, such as the 1980s work of Malcolm Watson and Ying Peng at Brandeis University or the work of Murray Straus, Ph.D., at the University of New Hampshire in Durham, showed that children who were spanked at home were more likely to display aggressive behavior toward other children. In addition, spanking can lead to other antisocial behaviors, such as cheating.

ALTERNATIVE FORMS OF DISCIPLINE

The American Academy of Pediatrics recommends nonphysical methods of discipline, referred to as behavior management methods.[2] Disciplining negative behavior may include activities such as a *time-out* or removal of privileges. Rewarding good behavior and providing encouragement when the child does something correct is perhaps even more important than punishing the bad behavior.

These recommendations bring up an important distinction: the difference between discipline and punishment. The word discipline comes from

Latin *disciplina*, meaning teaching or learning. Merriam-Webster defines discipline as "training that corrects, molds, or perfects the mental faculties or moral character." This imagery of molding or perfecting the child tells us that discipline should be undertaken with a long-term goal in mind—that of developing a child with self-discipline and self-control—as well as accomplishing the short-term goal of immediately stopping inappropriate or unsafe behavior.

When you regard discipline as the act of teaching the child how to behave, it makes sense to consider praising him or her for good behavior as a form of discipline. Discipline does not have to be thought of as merely a set of rules and punishments. Discipline should be as much about positive and loving reinforcements as it is about negative punishments.

One rule that I have found to have practically universal endorsement is "Effective discipline should take place around the clock, whether your child is behaving or misbehaving."

This means that encouragement should be a large part of your child's discipline program. Making him or her feel encouraged and rewarded for displaying appropriate behavior makes it much more likely that he or she will want to repeat that behavior. Your attention will have a positive impact on him or her, as opposed to showing only negative attention to him or her when he or she acts inappropriately. Your child will feel better about him- or herself and about his or her relationship with you.

Punishment means something entirely different from discipline. The Latin root is *poena*, or penalty, from whence we also get the word *pain*. Merriam-Webster defines punishment as imposing "a penalty for a fault, offense, or violation." Punishment provides the consequences for violating a rule or acting inappropriately.

Sometimes, the act or violation provides its own natural consequence, such as when a child breaks a toy and can therefore no longer play with it. Your job as a parent would then be to explain the loss of the toy to your child and refuse to replace it. Another example is when your child refuses to eat supper, with the natural consequence being that he or she will go to bed hungry.

No additional punishment is needed when the natural consequence is sufficient and acceptable; in fact, any additional punishment might only cause your child to harbor anger and resentment toward you.

Of course, not all natural consequences are acceptable forms of punishment. The natural consequence of your son not doing homework, for example, is that his grades will fall. No parents want to see their son fail in school, so some other combination of support, rewards, and punishment must be used to induce him into doing his homework.

Sometimes you will find that there is no significant natural consequence to your child's misbehavior, such as when he or she does not make up his or her bed or pick up his or her toys. Although the bed is unmade, the child can still sleep in it. Although his or her toys are strewn all over the bedroom floor, he or she can still probably find the one he or she wants, with a little searching. Therefore, the parent must provide an appropriate reward for performing the desired behavior or an appropriate punishment for misbehavior, such as a removal of certain privileges.

Setting Boundaries

Clearly defining the boundaries of acceptable behavior allows the child to know what is appropriate and what is inappropriate.[3] This, in turn, gives the parent more control and consistency when it comes to administering discipline. Defining specific punishments for different misbehaviors ahead of time reduces stress on the parent, and prevents arbitrary and uneven discipline. The child gains security in knowing what his or her boundaries are and what the consequences might be for violating these boundaries. It sets the stage for the *avoidance* of misbehavior, and provides opportunities to positively reinforce good behavior.

Behavior boundaries must not only be clearly defined, but also periodically subjected to a reality check. Examples of questions you can ask yourself:

- Are the expectations too high or too low for your child's age and temperament? If in doubt, find a book on child development and ensure that your expectations are realistic.
- Are all of the boundaries important enough to keep? Can you simplify the rules without jeopardizing some aspect of your child's discipline? No child is perfect, and having too many rules may be setting him or her up for failure.
- Are you placing your child under undue stress by placing him or her in situations that are beyond his or her present capabilities (i.e., expecting a 5-year-old child to sit still during a long church service, etc.)?
- Does he or she remember all of his or her boundaries, or should you review them to refresh his or her memory?
- How does your child feel about his or her boundaries? You might be surprised to find that he or she feels ready to take on more responsibility.
- Are you praising him or her enough for his or her good behavior? Have you taken time each day to tell him or her all of the good things he or she did, or have you fixated on the one or two times that he or she misbehaved?
- What new goals and rewards could the two of you set together, such as seeing a new movie as a reward for a day or two with no misbehavior?
- Are you consistently applying the rules? Your child needs to feel secure that he or she will be treated fairly and predictably.
- Do the punishments fit the crimes? Are you allowing natural consequences to be the punishment when possible, and only creating your own punishments when no natural consequence exists?
- Are your rewards and punishments still effective, or have they become *stale* over time? Both rewards and punishments may need to be periodically changed and updated to remain useful.
- Are both rewards and punishments immediate? Delayed consequences are never as powerful as immediate feedback.

Managing Aggression and Frustration

Tangential thinkers often need to be taught how to manage their aggression and frustration. Sometimes these children just have too much energy and need to let off harmless steam. Parents need to provide healthy outlets for this energy to minimize the amount of frustration the child feels. Gymnastics, martial arts, or other physical activities can give your child an outlet for this energy while helping him or her gain self-confidence.

Focus on Important Behaviors

As a parent, you are only human and should learn to recognize your limits. Even though your child may sometimes seem to have an endless supply of energy, you have only a limited amount of energy available to manage him or her. You cannot possibly step in to correct every objectionable or undesirable behavior he or she displays.

One way to compensate for this is to write down the various types of aggressive or negative behavior he or she exhibits. Consider each item and prioritize the behaviors from most objectionable to least objectionable. Write them in descending order from top to bottom on a clean paper, with the least desirable behaviors at the top of the page. Determine which behaviors you can live with, and draw a line above that point. Set rules for everything above the line, and let everything go that falls below the line. These are probably mildly disruptive behaviors that your child may outgrow. Not harping on him or her about these behaviors will keep you from wasting time and energy that could be better spent on more positive activities.

Review your list also for behaviors that may merely reflect your child's tangential thinking, such as not sitting still. He or she may just be trying to pay attention, using frequent motions to keep his or her brain awake. Constant or frequent movement may be distracting to you, but to your child it may be an important coping skill. Consult with your child's pediatrician or school counselor if you have any doubts about how much you should limit his or her *fidgeting*.

You should always review your list periodically to see if some behaviors have gotten out of hand and need to be included on the *forbidden* list.

If there is a consistent problem with a specific misbehavior, such as a refusal to go to bed, talk to your child to determine the underlying cause. Children do not usually display continual defiance unless there is an underlying reason. Seek professional help from your pediatrician or a family counselor if you cannot find a definite cause and corresponding solution on your own. The solution may be simpler than you think.

Time-out

Time-outs are a good form of punishment when other responses have not worked, although a time-out may have limited value if your child has been diagnosed as hyperactive. As always, the behavior boundaries should have been clearly defined beforehand. Explain to your child what a time-out is and let him or her know the specific misbehaviors that will result in a time-out. Time-outs can be especially helpful as a *cooldown* period to calm a troubled or angry child. You can begin using short time-outs after your child is 1 year old.

Choose a consistent time-out spot, preferably a quiet place with no distractions. A chair in a corner can be good, but bathrooms and bedrooms might contain too many distractions.

You can give your child one warning when he or she violates one of the specific rules that result in a time-out. This gives him or her an opportunity to correct his or her actions. Send him or her to his or her time-out spot immediately if the misbehavior persists. No second warnings should be given.

Tell your child what he or she did wrong in a calm voice. If you show anger and hostility, you are inviting the same emotions from him or her as he or she mirrors your behavior. Think of a highway patrolman who has stopped you for speeding. They are taught to maintain control of the situation by being very calm and professional. They don't yell or scream at you, nor do they act overly friendly. If you have trouble displaying a calm outer composure, have some fun and practice your very best highway patrolman impersonation in front of a mirror before the next time-out session. Practice looking unruffled but stern as you go through your time-out speech.

A common rule of thumb is 1 minute of time-out for every year of your child's age. (For example, a 5-year-old child would get a 5-minute time-out.)

It is okay to pick up your child and carry him or her to the time-out spot if he or she resists going on his or her own volition. You may have to stand behind him or her and hold him or her gently but firmly by the shoulders or restrain him or her in your lap. Calmly explain that you have to hold him or her there because he or she has a time-out. Above all, do not get into an argument with the child. He or she misbehaved, was warned, and continued to misbehave. Now, he or she has a time-out. End of discussion.

Your child may have difficulty accepting the time-out at first. Do not despair. He or she should begin cooperating in a couple of weeks (perhaps a little longer for very strong-willed children).

After your child has accepted the time-out process, you can begin to introduce a timer so that he or she will know when the time-out is over. If the child starts to fuss or get up prematurely, reset the timer.

After the timer goes off, it is time to accept your child back with no reservations, frustrations, or anger. Give him or her a hug and immediately steer him or her into a positive activity. After a few minutes, you can bring up the previous misbehavior if you need to discuss it, but don't nag him or her about it.

Find out How Your School Disciplines

Many parents find that duplicating the discipline system at school helps to maintain a consistent set of rules for the child to follow. Many schools are going to a color-based system that is easy for the children to understand:

- Each child has a green, yellow, and red card with his or her name on it. At the start of each day, all cards will be of the color green. The goal is to remain on green for the entire day.
- A verbal warning is given to the child upon the first offense each day.
- The child's green card is moved to a yellow card upon the second offense, indicating a 5-minute time-out during recess and no sticker for the day on his or her behavior calendar.
- The child's yellow card is moved to a red card on the third offense. A red card indicates a 10-minute time-out at recess, no sticker for the day on the behavior chart and a note home.

It is very important that parents back up the school in this discipline program. Parents can have rewards or punishments based on the color of the child's card at the end of the school day. Parents can also have their own card system to use at home so that the child is on a consistent program both at home and at school.

Beware of Power Struggles

A young mother tells her son, "Almost time for bed, Tommy. Stop playing and put up your toys." Little Tommy ignores her and continues playing with his action figures. Mom repeats her command, only louder. This time Tommy stares her in the eye and says, "No, I don't wanna go to bed!" Mom raises her voice even more, saying, "Don't backtalk to me, young man. Pick up those toys now!" Little Tommy throws his toy down on the floor and begins yelling angrily at his mother, who in turn yells back at him. Soon, Tommy is standing in the middle of the room in tears watching his mother furiously throw his toys in the toy box. Tommy is spanked and sent to bed, where he screams for 30 minutes before going to sleep. The next night, the entire scene is repeated.

Your child's ability to engage you in a power struggle is one of his or her most powerful tools. Arguing with your child effectively negates your position as an authority figure, and elevates the child to an equal status. Although the situation caused by your child's defiance is unpleasant and stressful for both of you, it does manage to give your child a sense of control over his or her life. You requested him or her to do something, and he or she was able to create enough chaos that he or she avoided having to submit to your request. In the mind of a defiant youngster, that is a *win*.

The alternative to this power struggle is to ensure that you, the parent, remain in positive control. Remember, your ultimate goal is not to have Tommy pick up his toys tonight; it is to build self-control and self-discipline in Tommy so that he will eventually pick up his own toys, without having to be told to do so. How can you build self-control in your child when he or she can manipulate you into losing your self-control by simply arguing with you?

It takes two persons to engage in an argument; your child cannot argue with you if you do not participate. This takes self-discipline on your part, but is the only way to break out of the parent-child power struggle.

Stopping a power struggle requires you to commit to a few easy steps:

1. Sit down with your child at an opportune moment and discuss an activity that he or she finds most difficult, such as picking up toys, getting dressed in the morning, doing homework, etc. Discuss one activity at a time, rather than bombard him or her with numerous activities at the same time.
2. Develop a clear choice for each action. For example, if he or she does not stop and pick up his or her toys when you tell him or her to, let him or her know that you will pick up the toys and put them up high in his or her closet where he or she cannot reach them for the entire next day.
3. Maintain your self-control and do not lose your temper or raise your voice the next time he or she defies you and tries to draw you into an argument.
4. Give your child the clear choice that you discussed earlier, such as "Pick up your toys now or I will put them away and you won't be able to play with them tomorrow."
5. Be prepared to live with your commitment. Do not falter or appear wishy-washy. Your child needs you to be strong and consistent.
6. Be prepared to heap lavish praise on him or her when he or she complies without an argument. Celebrate his or her victory!

Do not be surprised if your child chooses his or her own battles. He or she might gladly comply with one request but dig in his or her heels and defy you at your next request. Take advantage of both occasions—hug him or her and congratulate him or her for being so good when he or she complies without a fight, and dig in your own heels when he or she defies you and tries to start an argument. It may not be easy to listen to him or her cry and scream as he or she tries to get you to give in. Remain calm and composed. He or she will eventually figure out that you mean what you say.

How long will you have to wait before you begin to see improvement in your child's behavior? It is impossible to say. Some children respond in just a few days, while more *difficult* children may test you for days or weeks to see if you will give in. It is up to you to be stronger than your child. In the long run, you and your child will have a happier and less chaotic life after your child learns to not engage in power struggles with you.

The Importance of Routines

Having a consistent daily routine can provide your child a great deal of security. He or she will know what is expected of him or her on a daily basis, and conflicts over poorly communicated expectations will be reduced or eliminated.

Routines, such as getting up in the morning and preparing for school, should be taught to him or her in short steps rather than broad sweeps. Many tangential children have problems with multistep tasks, so breaking down the routines into easily managed steps can make the learning process easier for him or her. Allow him or her to master each task before moving on to the new item on the list.

Set times for getting up in the morning, doing homework, playing and watching television, and doing daily chores. Spell out exactly what is expected of him or her at each time, so that "clean your room" has an agreed-upon meaning for both you and her.

Some children benefit from a visual aid, such as a daily chart or calendar where they can check off each routine activity as is it performed.

Everybody Sings out of the Same Songbook

It is common now for children to have multiple caregivers, such as ex-spouses, grandparents, or nannies. Ensure that every caregiver understands and consistently applies the rules of conduct and routines that you have at home. The child will feel more secure at each location and with each adult who cares for him or her.

You may find it helpful to provide written copies of rules and procedures that you have for your child. Ensure that everyone has *bought into* these rules by discussing them at length with each adult. They may need to be educated about why the rules are important and how they help your child.

It's Not Personal

Perhaps one of the most important things parents can do is to learn to speak and act in nonpersonal terms when they discipline their child. For example, imagine that your daughter Suzie carelessly runs through the house, hitting a coffee table and knocking over a framed photograph that falls to the floor. The glass in the frame shatters all over the floor. Do you

- explode in anger and yell "you're such a klutz!" at her, then send her to her room in tears; or
- show obvious disappointment at the picture being ruined and explain to her how much the picture meant to you. Ask her questions about why the picture broke until she acknowledges that she was careless and broke the rules by running in the house. You then supervise her as she carefully cleans up the glass off the floor (assuming she is old enough to perform this task safely) and places the photograph in a new frame.

The first scenario completely personalizes the situation and works to convince the child that she is an awkward klutz who cannot control herself. The second scenario blames the broken glass on her breaking a rule and focuses her energy on repairing the damage that she did. It is a much more constructive approach, and it avoids applying an ugly label to the child.

10

THE MEDICATION QUESTION

Nancy Edison never had to face the question of whether or not to place her son on medication to control his hyperactive behavior. However, any parent of a child with attention deficit hyperactivity disorder (ADHD) cannot avoid the issue today. During the 1990s, prescriptions for ADHD medications increased dramatically across the United States, with consumption in many states more than quadrupling. Today, the use of medications for ADHD children is widespread. According to the Centers for Disease Control, nearly one in twelve children between 4 and 17 years of age has been diagnosed with ADHD, and more than one-half of these children have had medication prescribed to them.[1]

WHY ARE SO MANY CHILDREN TAKING MEDICATION?

Although medication for ADHD children is still a hotly contested issue, the consensus within the medical community is that properly prescribed and administered medication can often be a safe and effective form of therapy.

Most of the medications taken for ADHD are classified as stimulants. These drugs, such as Ritalin, increase the amount of dopamine available for the brain to use. This increase in dopamine appears to help many children focus on activities and curb behavioral problems.

Medications are not always an answer for every child; some children react adversely to drugs and find that the side effects are worse than the ADHD itself. Other children might react well to the drugs but still not experience the same benefit from them as other children. One mother, for example, expressed her disappointment to me that her son improved somewhat from his medication, but not as dramatically as other mothers had told her to expect.

Even though a child may find that medication helps him or her focus and control his or her behavior, it is still not a *cure-all* for the challenges the child faces. Other types and methods of treatment must often complement drug therapy in order to achieve the best result. The most common method recommended today is a *multimodal* treatment that uses drugs in combination with behavioral therapy, based on research conducted in 1999 by the National Institute of Mental Health.[2]

This study included 579 elementary schoolboys and girls with ADHD, who were randomly assigned for up to 14 months to one of four groups. Both groups A and B received medication therapy, while Group C received just behavioral therapy and no medications. Group D received the benefit of both medication and behavioral therapy.

All of the children were reassessed regularly throughout the study period by both teachers and parents. The children were rated on hyperactivity, impulsivity, inattention, social skills, and symptoms of anxiety and depression.

The children in groups A (medication only) and D (medication plus therapy) met a physician monthly for one-half hour at each medication visit, during which the physician spoke with the parent, met with the child, and sought to determine any concerns that the family might have regarding the medication or the child's ADHD-related difficulties. The physicians also sought input from the teachers on a monthly basis.

Groups C (therapy only) and D (medication plus therapy) met up to thirty-five times with a behavior therapist, mostly in group sessions. These therapists also made repeated visits to schools to consult with children's teachers and to supervise a special aide assigned to each child in the group. In addition, children attended a special 8-week summer treatment program where they worked on academic, social, and sports skills, and where intensive behavioral therapy was delivered to assist children in improving their behavior.

Group B (community-based medication only) children saw the community-treatment doctor of their parents' choice, one to two times per year for short periods of time. There was no interaction between community-based physicians and teachers.

The results of the study indicated that a long-term combination of medication and behavioral therapy (Group D) produced better results than medication only (groups A and B) or therapy without medication (Group C). The combination treatments especially helped children who exhibited other conditions concurrent with their ADHD, such as anxiety, poor academic performance, underdeveloped social skills, parent–child relationship issues, or opposition to authority.

Another advantage of combined treatment was that children could be successfully treated with lower doses of medicine, compared with the medication-only group.

Not surprisingly, the children on medications in Group A who had regular visits to a physician had significantly better results than the Group B children who obtained their medications from a community-based service. This may be due to the fact that the doctors who saw their patients regularly had more opportunity to adjust the dosage or change the medication as needed to best fit each child.

Information on the long-term effects of all treatments is lacking, as is knowledge of the effects of long-term use of ADHD medications in children. Ongoing studies of ADHD, its comorbidities, and different methods of treatment will be needed before physicians understand these long-term issues.

WHICH TREATMENT SHOULD MY CHILD HAVE?

The choice of how to best treat and manage your child's hyperactivity is a very personal decision, and should be made only after consulting appropriate health care professionals. No single treatment is the answer for every child with ADHD. One child may exhibit undesirable side effects to a particular medication, while the child next door may be fine taking the same medication. One mother told me that her son's physician varied both the medication and the dosage until he found the best solution for her 12-year-old son.

If a child with ADHD also has anxiety or depression, a treatment combining medication and behavioral therapy might be best. Each child's needs and personal history must be carefully considered.

Stimulant Medications

Most of the drugs given to treat ADHD are classified as stimulants. The stimulant drugs come in long-term and short-term forms. The newer sustained-release stimulants can be taken before school, and are long-lasting so that the child does not need to go to the school nurse every day for a pill. The doctor can discuss with the parents the child's needs and decide which preparation to use, and whether the child needs to take the medicine during school hours only or in the evening and on weekends too.

If the child does not show symptom improvement after taking a medication for a week, the doctor may try adjusting the dosage. If there is still no improvement, the child may be switched to another medication. About one out of ten children is not helped by a stimulant medication.

Other types of medication may be used if stimulants don't work or if the ADHD occurs with another disorder. Antidepressants and other medications may help control accompanying depression or anxiety.

Some people get better results from one medication, some from another. It is important to work with the prescribing physician to find the right medication and the right dosage. For many people, the stimulants dramatically reduce their hyperactivity and impulsivity, and improve their ability to focus, work, and learn. The medications may also improve physical coordination, such as that needed in handwriting and in sports.

The stimulant drugs, when used with medical supervision, are usually considered quite safe. Stimulants do not make the child feel *high*, although some children say they feel different or funny. Such changes are usually very minor.

Although some parents worry that their child may become addicted to the medication, to date there is no convincing evidence that stimulant medications, when used for treatment of ADHD, cause drug abuse or dependence. A review of all long-term studies on stimulant medication and substance abuse, conducted by researchers at Massachusetts General Hospital and Harvard Medical School, found that teenagers with ADHD who remained on their medication during the teen years had a lower likelihood of substance use or abuse than did ADHD adolescents who were not taking medications.

One common stimulant medication is methylphenidate, known by such name brands as Ritalin, Metadate, and Concerta. A number of the name brands of this medication have been formulated to last longer than the original version, allowing the child to take the medication less frequently throughout the day. These drugs are usually given only to children 6 years old or older.

Other drugs for children of age 6 or older are dexmethylphenidate, known by the brand name of Focalin, and pemoline, known by the brand name of Cylert. Because of its potential for serious side effects affecting the liver, the U.S. Food and Drug Administration (FDA) has stated that Cylert should not ordinarily be considered as "first-line drug therapy for ADHD."[3]

Drugs approved for children of age 3 or older are dextroamphetamine, known by the brand names of Dextrostat and Dexedrine, and an amphetamine named Adderall.

The FDA is continuing to evaluate reports of serious adverse events in children, adolescents, and adults being treated with Adderall and related products. Although a number of sudden deaths among Adderall users were reported between 1999 and 2003, the FDA reports that this number is about what would be expected to occur naturally in a group of this size. (There were approximately 30 million prescriptions written in this period.) For this reason, the FDA had decided to not take any further regulatory action at the time of this writing. However, because it appeared that patients with underlying heart defects might be at increased risk for sudden death, the labeling for Adderall XR was changed in August 2004 to include a warning that these patients might be at particular risk, and that these patients should ordinarily not be treated with Adderall products.[4]

On April 6, 2006, the FDA approved Daytrana, the first transdermal (skin) patch, for treating ADHD in children 6–12 years of age. Daytrana is a once daily treatment, containing the drug methylphenidate, a central nervous system stimulant.[5]

Daytrana is applied each morning to the alternating hip, and worn for 9 hours. Parents and caregivers should keep a chart to track the application and removal of the patch.

The prescribing physician may change the amount of time the patch is worn to help manage how long the medication works each day and some of the side effects that may be caused by methylphenidate. Side effects such as insomnia may occur with greater frequency in some children if the patch is worn for longer than the recommended 9 hours. Other possible side effects include blurred vision, mild skin irritation or an allergic skin rash, and slower weight gain and height growth.

Daytrana should not be used if the child

- has significant anxiety, tension, or agitation, since methylphenidate may make these conditions worse;
- has allergies to methylphenidate or other ingredients in Daytrana;
- has glaucoma, an eye disease;
- has discontinued a monoamine oxidase inhibitor, a treatment for depression, in the last 14 days, or is currently taking it; and
- has motion or verbal tics or Tourette's syndrome, or a family history of Tourette's syndrome.

Potential Side Effects of the Medications

You should always discuss possible side effects with your child's physician before giving your child any medication. Most side effects of the stimulant medications are minor and are usually related to the dosage of the medication being taken. As one might expect, higher doses tend to produce more side effects than lower doses. The most common side effects are decreased appetite, insomnia, increased anxiety, and/or irritability. Some children report mild stomachaches or headaches.

Some medications may cause your child's appetite to fluctuate, usually being low during the middle of the day and more normal by suppertime. In these instances, you should ensure that your child receives good amounts of highly nutritious foods when he or she is hungry. Sometimes other drugs, such as Periactin, are prescribed to help increase your child's appetite.

If the child has difficulty falling asleep, several options may be tried: a lower dosage of the stimulant, giving the stimulant earlier in the day, discontinuing the afternoon or evening dosage, or giving an adjunct medication such as a low-dosage antidepressant. A few children develop tics during treatment. These can often be lessened by changing the medication dosage. A very few children cannot tolerate any stimulant, no matter how low the dosage is. In such cases, the child may be given an antidepressant instead of the stimulant.

You may see that your child's schoolwork and behavior improve soon after starting medication. Although this is a welcome event, do not think that the medication has cured your child. Medications do not cure ADHD; they only control the symptoms on the day they are taken. Although the medications may help him or her pay better attention and complete schoolwork, they can't increase knowledge or improve academic skills. The medications can only help him or her use the skills he or she already possesses.

On May 2, 2006, the National Institutes of Health (NIH) reported that ADHD drugs do suppress a child's growth to some degree.[6] While the effect found was statistically significant, the average growth suppression for a 10-year-old boy was estimated to be about three-quarters of an inch in height and a little more than 2 pounds in weight. For this reason, your physician will probably pay attention and monitor your child's growth, possibly changing the dosage or dosing schedule if necessary.

This drop in growth may be a side product of the appetite suppression that many medicated children experience. The NIH stresses that these changes may not be permanent, as the children might catch up when they go off the medications or as they grow older.

The risk of growth suppression must be weighed by the parents against the improvement to the child's life caused by the medications. If the child is able to function better at home and at school with the drugs, then many parents feel that the risk of growth suppression is acceptable.

More studies need to be performed to look at the long-term effects these drugs have on children's growth, and whether other factors may help to counteract the growth suppression. For example, giving the medication only after a meal might help to reduce appetite suppression and minimize the resulting suppression of growth.

Behavioral therapy, emotional counseling, and academic support are often needed to help children with ADHD cope with everyday problems, whether they are taking medication or not.

Nonstimulant Medication

The FDA has approved a medication for ADHD, which is not a stimulant. The medication, Strattera, or atomoxetine, works on the neurotransmitter norepinephrine, whereas the stimulants primarily work on dopamine.[7] More studies will need to be done to contrast Strattera with the medications already available, but some evidence suggests that over 70 percent of children with ADHD given Strattera manifest significant improvement in their symptoms.

THE FAMILY AND THE ADHD CHILD

Every family experiences conflicts between family members, and it is normal for families with ADHD children to experience more than their share of conflicts. Although medication might help your ADHD child control some of his or her behavior problems that created these conflicts, it may take time to undo the frustration, blame, and anger that may have developed within the family.

Interpersonal tensions may still exist long after your child's behavior has improved, and breaking out of patterns of behavior that were set in place long ago might prove to be extremely difficult for both parents and children. Professional counseling may still be necessary for one or more family members to develop new skills, attitudes, and ways of relating to one another. You may even consider having the entire family benefit from counseling; the problem does affect the family as a whole, and it may also help your ADHD child to not feel that he is the only person who needs to be *fixed*.

Several different types of counseling are available, and you may find that one or more types would be best for your needs. Your child's physician might also be able to refer you to counselors or recommend different types of counseling for your family.

Psychotherapy does not address the symptoms or underlying causes of ADHD, but may help your child if he or she has difficulty liking and accepting him- or herself. Psychotherapy might also be used to bring other family members to accept and value him or her for who he or she is. The therapist will encourage the family to discuss upsetting thoughts and feelings, explore self-defeating patterns of behavior, and learn alternative ways to handle emotions. The therapist will also try to help family members understand how they can change to better cope with ADHD.

Behavioral therapy helps people develop more effective ways to deal with issues. Rather than helping your child understand his or her feelings and actions, behavioral therapy works directly to change his or her thinking and develop coping skills. The support might be practical assistance, such as helping him or her organize tasks or schoolwork, or deal with emotionally charged events. Behavioral therapy might also help him or her monitor his or her own behavior and give him- or herself praise or rewards for acting in a desired way, such as controlling anger or thinking before acting.

Social skills training works to help your child develop the skills needed to play and work with other children. In social skills training, the therapist discusses and models appropriate behaviors important in developing and maintaining social relationships, like waiting for a turn, sharing toys, asking for help, or responding to teasing, then gives him or her a chance to practice. For example, he or she might learn to *read* other people's facial expression and tone of voice in order to respond appropriately.

Support groups help parents connect with other people, who have similar problems and concerns with their ADHD children. Many online support groups can be found now that allow parents to gain insight and share their experiences with a wide range of people across the nation or the world. While online groups offer 24-hour convenience, many people prefer face-to-face meeting with other parents of ADHD children. Most communities have support groups that meet on a regular basis (such as monthly) to hear lectures from experts on ADHD, share frustrations and successes, and obtain referrals to qualified specialists and information about what works. There is strength in numbers, and sharing experiences with others who have similar problems helps people know that they are not alone.

Parenting skills training teaches tools and techniques for managing your child's behavior. One such technique is the use of token or point systems for immediately rewarding good behavior or work. Another is the use of *time-out* or isolation to a chair or bedroom when he or she becomes too unruly or out of control. During time-outs, he or she is removed from the agitating situation and is made to sit alone quietly for a short time to calm down. You may also be taught to give him or her *quality time* each day to share a pleasurable or relaxing activity. During this time together, you can look for opportunities to notice and point out things he or she does well and praise his or her strengths and abilities.

This system of rewards and penalties can be an effective way to modify your child's behavior. You can identify a few desirable behaviors that your child wants to encourage, such as asking for a toy instead of grabbing it or completing a simple task. The technique is fairly uncomplicated and straightforward; you merely tell him or her exactly what he or she needs to do to earn a reward, and give him or her the reward when he or she performs the desired behavior or a mild penalty when he or she does not. The reward can be small, such as a token that can be exchanged for special privileges, but it should be something he or she wants and is eager to earn. The penalty might be removal of a token or a brief time-out. Make an effort to find him or her being good. The goal, over time, is to help him or her learn to control his or her own behavior and to choose the more desired behavior. The technique works well with all children, although children with ADHD may need more frequent rewards.

In addition, you may learn to structure situations in ways that will allow your child to succeed. This may include allowing only one or two playmates at a time, so that he or she does not become too stimulated. If your child has trouble completing tasks, you may learn to help him or her divide a large task into small steps, praising him or her as each step is completed. Regardless of the specific techniques you may use to modify your child's behavior, some general principles appear to be useful for most children with ADHD. These include

- providing frequent and immediate feedback, punishments, and rewards;
- structuring activities to avoid potential problem situations; and
- providing greater supervision and encouragement to him or her during *boring* or tedious activities.

You may also learn to use stress management methods, such as meditation, relaxation techniques, and exercise, to increase your own tolerance for frustration so that you can respond more calmly to your child's behavior.

FOOD ADDITIVES AND SUGAR

It has been suggested that attention disorders are caused by refined sugar or food additives, or that symptoms of ADHD are exacerbated by sugar or food additives. The NIH has found that diet restrictions do help up to 5 percent of children with ADHD, mostly young children with food allergies.[8] If this number is correct, then about one in twenty children will show improvement when placed on dietary restrictions. However, the improvement your child might experience from a dietary restriction may not be enough to warrant taking him or her off of medication therapy.[9] As always, discuss any changes you plan to make in your child's diet or medications with your family physician or pediatrician.

In addition, it may be possible that parents overrate the effect of sugar on their child. In one study, children whose mothers felt they were sugar sensitive were given aspartame as a substitute for sugar.[10] Half the mothers were told their children were given sugar and half that their children were given aspartame. The mothers who thought their children had received sugar rated them as more hyperactive than the other children, and were more critical of their behavior.

Another study found that eating sugar had no significant effects on an ADHD child's behavior or learning. The children used sugar some days and a sugar substitute on other days, and the parents and staff could not guess with any degree of accuracy which substance the children had consumed on any given day.[11]

Of course, it is imperative that all children receive a well-balanced diet that includes breakfast, and it is a good idea to limit the amount of sugar the child eats. Processed products high in sucrose and other sugars are usually lacking in protein and other nutrients your child needs, and a diet high in sugar could increase the chances of obesity and its associated health conditions later in life.

CONCLUSION

Deciding to place your child on a medication regimen is a sensitive and personal issue that should only be entered into with a good deal of thought and research. Discuss every aspect of the drug therapy with your physician, and be sure that you mention any other medications or therapies that your child is taking, even herbal or homeopathic remedies. Many *natural* supplements or remedies have adverse side effects when combined with prescription medications.

11

COMORBID CONDITIONS

Nancy Edison certainly had her hands full with young Al Edison. Al was not just hyperactive, he was downright dangerous too. He burned down the family barn. He fell into a canal and nearly drowned. He almost suffocated after falling into an elevator full of grain. He had a fingertip chopped off with an axe. A ram attacked him in a field while he was daydreaming. (He barely managed to escape by climbing over a fence.) He accidentally started a chemical fire on a train. No doubt, young Al Edison was trouble.

Increased risk of injuries is an all too common trait of tangential thinkers. These children are sometimes so excited at their plans that they fail to consider risks. Other times they are simply lost in their thoughts and do not recognize dangerous situations.

Nancy also had to contend with Al's frequent illnesses in addition to his propensity for accidents and injury. His loss of hearing, in fact, may have been due to an early attack of scarlet fever. Al's accident-prone nature and partial deafness are examples of *comorbid conditions*, or conditions that occur in conjunction with attention deficit hyperactivity disorder (ADHD). About half of children with ADHD referred to clinics have other behavior disorders in addition to ADHD.[1]

Increased injuries, strained peer relationships, dyslexia, Tourette's syndrome (TS), obsessive-compulsive disorder (OCD), childhood bipolar disorder, autism spectrum disorders (ASDs), and childhood depression are some of the common conditions shared by ADHD children. It is important to screen every child with ADHD for other disorders and problems because of the significant challenges that may result from having ADHD combined with another disorder.

The symptoms caused by comorbid conditions can mask the symptoms of ADHD, making the diagnosis and treatment of ADHD very difficult. ADHD, on the other hand, may also mask symptoms of a comorbid condition, and cause it to go undiagnosed and untreated. For example, a comorbid condition such as dyslexia (discussed later in this chapter) can cause a child to have reading troubles that are unrelated directly to ADHD, but ADHD may be the *attention-getting* condition that takes the blame for the child's poor reading skills. "She's just not paying attention," the teacher might say, "and that's why she falls behind in her reading."

Comorbid conditions can also complicate treatment of ADHD (and vice versa), especially with medications that may help ADHD but aggravate another condition. One father, for example, told me that his son's behavior and grades at school improved dramatically after beginning ADHD medication therapy, but the side effects aggravated the boy's bipolar disorder too much to continue their use.

Properly diagnosing a comorbid disorder can result in a liberating feeling. For example, one mother exclaimed to me that finding out her son had dyscalculia (a condition which makes numbers difficult to understand) gave both her and her son a feeling of relief. Just knowing what the problem was eased their minds and gave them a starting point to hunt for solutions.

The nature and course of treatment for ADHD and various comorbid conditions may very well be different, and you may have to obtain help from several different types of providers. Do not be afraid to ask your health-care professionals for appropriate referrals; you may have to go to a specialist who has had experience dealing with your child's particular combination of comorbid conditions.

Listed below are some of the more common comorbid conditions experienced by children with ADHD.

CONDUCT DISORDER

Children with conduct disorder (CD) display behavior problems that last 6 months or longer, such as defiant, impulsive, or antisocial behavior, and drug use or criminal activity.[2]

CD is a *disruptive behavior disorder* because of its impact on children and their families, neighbors, and schools.[3] However, because many of the qualities necessary to make the diagnosis (such as *defiance* and *rule breaking*) can be subjective, it is hard to know how common the disorder really is. For accurate diagnosis, the behavior must be far more extreme than simple adolescent rebellion or childish exuberance.[2]

Symptoms of CD include

- aggressive behavior that harms or threatens other people or animals;
- destructive behavior that damages or destroys property;
- lying or theft;
- truancy or other serious violations of rules;
- early tobacco, alcohol, and substance use and abuse; and
- precocious sexual activity.

CD affects 1−4 percent of 9-to-17-year-old children, depending on exactly how the disorder is defined.[3] The disorder appears to be more common in boys than in girls, and more common in cities than in rural areas.

Research shows that some cases of CD begin in early childhood, often by the preschool years.[3] In fact, some infants who are especially *fussy* appear to be at risk for developing CD. Other factors that may make a child more likely to develop CD include

- early maternal rejection;
- separation from parents, without an adequate alternative caregiver;
- early institutionalization;
- family neglect;
- abuse or violence;
- parental mental illness;
- parental marital discord;
- large family size;
- crowding; and
- poverty.

Although CD is one of the most difficult behavior disorders to treat, young people often benefit from a range of services that include

- training for parents on how to handle child or adolescent behavior;
- family therapy;
- training in problem-solving skills for children or adolescents; and
- community-based services that focus on the young person within the context of family and community influences.

Some child and adolescent behaviors are hard to change after they have become ingrained. Therefore, success is more likely when the CD is diagnosed and treated as early as possible.

OPPOSITIONAL DEFIANT DISORDER

Another disruptive behavior disorder, called oppositional defiant disorder (ODD), may be a precursor of CD.[2] ODD is a pattern of disobedient, hostile, and defiant behavior toward authority figures.[4] This pattern must persist for at least 6 months and must go beyond the bounds of normal childhood misbehavior.

ODD is one of the most common comorbid conditions in ADHD children. This behavior may start as early as the preschool years, and onset typically occurs by age 8. CD, in contrast, is generally diagnosed when children are older.

Common symptoms of ODD include

- having frequent arguments with adults;
- showing loss of temper;
- being angry and resentful of others;
- defying adults' requests actively;
- showing spiteful or vindictive behavior;
- blaming others for their own mistakes;

- being touchy or easily annoyed;
- having few or no friends or loss of previous friends; and
- having constant trouble in school.

Children with CD or ODD may experience

- higher rates of depression, suicidal thoughts, suicide attempts, and suicide;
- academic difficulties;
- poor relationships with peers or adults;
- sexually transmitted diseases;
- difficulty staying in adoptive, foster, or group homes; and
- higher rates of injuries, school expulsions, and problems with the law.

Parents or other caregivers who notice signs of CD or ODD in a child or adolescent should

- pay careful attention to the signs, try to understand the underlying reasons, and then try to improve the situation;
- talk with a mental health or social services professional, such as a teacher, counselor, psychiatrist, or psychologist specializing in childhood and adolescent disorders;
- get accurate information from libraries, hotlines, or other sources;
- talk to other families in their communities; and
- find family network organizations.

Address any concerns you have about the mental health services your child or the rest of the family receives with your provider immediately. Do not be afraid to ask for more information or seek help from other sources.

ADHD AND RISK OF INJURIES

The main traits of ADHD—inattention, impulsiveness, and hyperactivity—may place a child with ADHD at risk for frequent and severe injuries. Head injuries, injuries to more than one part of the body, hospitalization, and accidental poisoning occur at above-average rates with ADHD children. Children with ADHD also enter intensive care units or have an injury result in disability more frequently than other children.[5]

Parents love the joy of taking their child to a playground. Unfortunately, playgrounds can be a dangerous place for children. Each year in the United States, emergency departments treat more than 200,000 children of age 14 and younger for playground-related injuries[6]:

- About 45 percent of playground-related injuries are severe, such as fractures, internal injuries, concussions, dislocations, and amputations.
- About 75 percent of nonfatal injuries related to playground equipment occur on public playgrounds. Most occur at schools and day care centers.

- Between 1990 and 2000, 147 children of age 14 and younger died from playground-related injuries. Of them, 82 (56%) died from strangulation and 31 (20%) died from falls to the playground surface. Most of these deaths (70%) occurred on home playgrounds.

Unsurprisingly, health care costs for ADHD children may be more than twice as high as medical costs for children without ADHD.[5]

This high risk of injury does not end when they become teenagers, as teens with ADHD have more traffic violations and accidents and are twice as likely to have their driver's licenses suspended than drivers without ADHD.

Common steps taken to prevent injury may be particularly useful for people with ADHD, such as

- ensure bicycle helmet use;
- remind children as often as necessary to watch for cars and to avoid unsafe activities;
- supervise children when they are involved in high-risk activities or are in risky settings, such as when climbing or when in or around a swimming pool;
- keep potentially harmful household products, tools, equipments, and objects out of the reach of young children;
- teens with ADHD may need to limit the amount of music listened to in the car while driving, drive without passengers and/or keep the number of passengers to a chosen few, plan trips well ahead of time, avoid alcohol, and drug use and cellular phone usage; and
- parents may want to consider enrolling their teens in additional driving safety courses before they get their driver's license.

PEER RELATIONSHIPS AND ADHD

Children with ADHD may find it difficult to develop close friendships, play with groups of friends, or engage in after-school activities. They may also have trouble getting along with other children or find themselves *picked on* at school.[7] Peers may perceive children with predominantly inattentive ADHD as shy or withdrawn, or see children with impulsiveness or hyperactivity as too aggressive.

The ability to develop close friendships is very important and contributes to your child's immediate happiness, as well as his or her long-term development. Children that are unable to develop these close friendships are at higher risk for anxiety, behavioral and mood disorders, substance abuse, and delinquency as teenagers.[7]

Of course, not everyone with ADHD has difficulty getting along with others. For those who do, many things can be done to improve the person's relationships. As always, early detection and intervention leads to the most successful treatment.

Although researchers have not provided definitive answers, some things parents might consider as they help their child build and strengthen peer relationships are

- Recognize the importance of healthy peer relationships for children. These relationships can be just as important as grades to school success.
- Maintain ongoing communication with people who play important roles in your child's life (such as teachers, school counselors, after-school activity leaders, health care providers, etc.).
- Keep updated on your child's social development in community and school settings.
- Involve your child in activities with his or her peers.
- Communicate with other parents, sports coaches, and other involved adults about any progress or problems that may develop with your child.

DYSLEXIA

Dyslexia is a common disorder that causes 10–17 percent of the U.S. population to have difficulties with word recognition.[8] A dyslexic child might have trouble distinguishing the letter "b" from the letter "d," for example. About 30 percent of dyslexics see letters, words, or entire sentences in a backward or garbled form. Others may have learned to read by sight memorization rather than using phonics.

Dyslexic children often benefit from modified teaching methods that stress phonics or use multisensory teaching methods:

- Teaching phonics may include breaking words apart into smaller segments called phonemes. Next, they map these phonemes to the printed words on a page. Once children have mastered these steps, they can then receive training to help them read fluently and comprehend what they read.[9]
- Multisensory teaching methods include letting a child handle three-dimensional or textured (i.e., sandpapered) letters such as "b" and "d" so that they can *feel* the difference between the two.

A child with poor reading skills may feel unintelligent, inferior, and unconfident. However, research has shown that many dyslexic individuals have normal or above-average intelligence.

Dyslexia does not always manifest itself the same in every child; it produces a number of different symptoms with varying degrees of severity. Therefore, your child must have a customized remediation program developed specifically for his or her individual set of symptoms. As with most conditions, early diagnosis generally yields higher success. It is also important that you develop a strong support group of family and friends to build up your child's self-confidence and sense of acceptance.

Studies have shown that up to 50 percent of children of dyslexic parents have dyslexia themselves, indicating that it may be a hereditary condition and thus have a genetic cause. This genetic cause may include variations in a gene called *DCDC2*, which disrupt the normal formation of brain circuits necessary for fluent reading. One day in the future, genetic screening for these variations could identify affected children early in their lives and possibly prevent the misdiagnosis of other learning disabilities that resemble dyslexia.

TOURETTE'S SYNDROME

TS is a neurological disorder characterized by repetitive, stereotyped, involuntary movements and vocalizations called *tics*.[10] The disorder is named for Dr. Georges Gilles de la Tourette, the pioneering French neurologist who in 1885 first described the condition in an 86-year-old French noblewoman.

The early symptoms of TS are usually noticed first in childhood, with the average onset between the ages of 7 and 10 years. TS occurs in people from all ethnic groups, with males affected about three to four times more often than females. It is estimated that 200,000 Americans have the most severe form of TS, and as many as 1 in 100 exhibit milder and less complex symptoms, such as chronic motor or vocal tics or transient tics of childhood. Although TS can be a chronic condition with symptoms lasting a lifetime, most people with the condition experience their worst symptoms in their early teens, with improvement occurring in the late teens and continuing into adulthood.

Tics may be either motor or vocal, and each type may be simple or complex:

- Simple motor tics are sudden, brief, repetitive movements that involve a limited number of muscle groups. Some of the more common simple tics include eye blinking and other vision irregularities, facial grimacing, shoulder shrugging, and head or shoulder jerking.
- Simple vocal tics may include throat clearing, sniffing/snorting, grunting, or barking.
- Complex motor tics are distinct, coordinated patterns of movements involving several muscle groups. Complex motor tics might include facial grimacing combined with a head twist and a shoulder shrug. Other complex motor tics may actually appear purposeful, including sniffing or touching objects, hopping, jumping, bending, or twisting.
- Complex vocal tics include words or phrases, including coprolalia (uttering swear words) or echolalia (repeating the words or phrases of others).

The most dramatic and disabling motor tics may involve self-harm, such as punching oneself in the face.

An urge or sensation (commonly described as an *itch* or a *tickle*) in the affected muscle group may precede some tics. These sensations are known as *premonitory urges*. Some with TS will describe a need to complete a tic in a certain way or a certain number of times in order to relieve the urge or decrease the sensation.

Tics are often less prominent during calm, focused activities but worse when the child is excited or anxious.

Certain physical experiences can trigger or worsen tics, such as tight collars triggering neck tics or hearing another person sniff or throat clear may trigger similar sounds. Tics do not go away during sleep but are often significantly diminished.

Tics come and go over time, varying in type, frequency, location, and severity. The first symptoms usually occur in the head and neck area, and may progress to include muscles of the trunk and extremities. Motor tics generally precede the development of vocal tics, and simple tics often precede complex tics. Most patients experience peak tic severity before the mid-teen years, with improvement for the majority of patients in the late teen years and early adulthood. Approximately 10 percent of those affected have a progressive or disabling course that lasts into adulthood.

Although the symptoms of TS are involuntary, some people can sometimes suppress, camouflage, or otherwise manage their tics in an effort to minimize their impact on functioning. However, people with TS often report a substantial buildup in tension when suppressing their tics to the point where they feel that the tic must be expressed. Tics in response to an environmental trigger can appear to be voluntary or purposeful but are not.

TS is a diagnosis that doctors make after verifying that the patient has had both motor and vocal tics for at least 1 year. The existence of other neurological or psychiatric conditions, such as childhood-onset involuntary movement disorders such as dystonia, or psychiatric disorders characterized by repetitive behaviors/movements (for example, stereotypic behaviors in autism and compulsive behaviors in OCD), can also help doctors arrive at a diagnosis.

Many TS sufferers obtain a formal diagnosis of TS only after symptoms have been present for some time. The reasons for this are many. Families who do not understand TS often overlook mild and even moderate tic symptoms, considering them inconsequential, part of a developmental phase, or the result of another condition. For example, parents may think that eye blinking is related to vision problems or that sniffing is related to seasonal allergies. Many patients are self-diagnosed after they, their parents, other relatives, or friends read or hear about TS from others.

Because tic symptoms do not often cause impairment, the majority of people with TS require no medication for tic suppression. However, effective medications are available for those whose symptoms interfere with functioning. Neuroleptics are the most consistently useful medications for tic suppression; a number of medications are available but some are more effective than others (for example, haloperidol and pimozide). Unfortunately, there is no one medication that is helpful to all people with TS, nor does any medication completely eliminate symptoms.

Neuroleptics, like all medications, have side effects. Most can be managed by initiating treatment slowly and reducing the dose when side effects occur. The most common side effects of neuroleptics include sedation, weight gain, and cognitive dulling. Less common side effects may include tremor, twisting movements or postures, parkinsonian-like symptoms, and involuntary movements.

Discontinuing neuroleptics after long-term use must be done slowly to avoid rebound increases in tics and other withdrawal symptoms.

Other medications may also be useful for reducing tic severity, but most have not been as extensively studied or shown to be as consistently useful as neuroleptics. Additional medications with demonstrated efficacy include alpha-adrenergic agonists, such as clonidine and guanfacine. These medications are used primarily for hypertension, but are also used in the treatment of tics. Their most common side effect is sedation.

Psychotherapy may also be helpful, even though psychological problems do not cause TS. Psychotherapy can help the person with TS better cope with the disorder, and deal with the secondary social and emotional problems that sometimes occur. More recently, specific behavioral treatments that include awareness training and competing response training, such as voluntarily moving in response to a premonitory urge, have shown effectiveness in small, controlled trials.

Evidence from twin and family studies suggests that TS is an inherited disorder. Genetic studies also suggest that some forms of ADHD and OCD are genetically related to TS, but there is less evidence for a genetic relationship between TS and other neurobehavioral problems that commonly co-occur with TS. It is important for families to understand that genetic predisposition may not necessarily result in full-blown TS; instead, it may express itself as a milder tic disorder or as obsessive-compulsive behaviors. It is also possible that the gene-carrying offspring will not develop any TS symptoms.

The sex of the person also plays an important role in TS gene expression. At-risk males are more likely to have tics, and at-risk females are more likely to have obsessive-compulsive symptoms.

People with TS may have genetic risks for other neurobehavioral disorders, such as depression or substance abuse. Genetic counseling of individuals with TS should include a full review of all potentially hereditary conditions in the family.

Although there is no cure for TS, the condition in many individuals improves in the late teens and early 20s. As a result, some may actually become symptom free or no longer need medication for tic suppression. Although the disorder is generally lifelong and chronic, it is not a degenerative condition. Individuals with TS have a normal life expectancy. TS does not impair intelligence. Although tic symptoms tend to decrease with age, it is possible that neurobehavioral disorders such as depression, panic attacks, mood swings, and antisocial behaviors can persist and cause impairment in adult life.

Although students with TS often function well in the regular classroom, ADHD, learning disabilities, obsessive-compulsive symptoms, and frequent tics can greatly interfere with academic performance or social adjustment. After a comprehensive assessment, students should be placed in an educational setting that meets their individual needs. Students may require tutoring, smaller or special classes, and in some cases special schools.

All students with TS need a tolerant and compassionate setting that encourages them to work to their full potential and is flexible enough to accommodate their special needs. This setting may include a private study area, exams outside the regular classroom, or even oral exams when the child's symptoms interfere with his or her ability to write. Untimed testing reduces stress for students with TS.

OBSESSIVE-COMPULSIVE DISORDER

OCD is an anxiety disorder characterized by recurrent, unwanted thoughts (obsessions) and/or repetitive behaviors (compulsions).[11] Repetitive behaviors such as hand washing, counting, checking, or cleaning are often performed with the hope of preventing obsessive thoughts or making them go away. Performing these so-called *rituals*, however, provides only temporary relief, and not performing them markedly increases anxiety.

People with OCD may be plagued by persistent, unwelcome thoughts or images, or by the urgent need to engage in certain rituals. They may be obsessed with germs or dirt, and wash their hands repeatedly. *Doubt* is a constant companion to someone with OCD, making him or her feel the need to check things repeatedly.

Most children develop some superstitious or semicompulsive behaviors, known as *developmental rituals*. These behaviors are common between the ages of 2 and 8, and seem to console children by empowering them with imagined control over their environment. *Lucky* numbers and rhymes, such as "step on a crack, break your Momma's back," help to bring about a sense of control and mastery. As they mature and develop into adulthood, most of these ritualistic behaviors disappear on their own. In contrast, rituals of the child with OCD persist well into adulthood. Instead of giving the child a feeling of control, these rituals result in feelings of shame and isolation. Attempts to stop doing the rituals result in extreme anxiety.[12]

It can be sometimes difficult to make a distinction between tics caused by a tic disorder, such as TS, and OCD. Common tics such as tapping, eye blinking, throat clearing, spitting, nose twitching, shoulder shrugging, and licking can also occur in a child with OCD; however, the child with OCD performs these behaviors for a different reason than the child with a tic disorder. If the behavior is caused by OCD, an unpleasant thought will have most likely preceded it. (For example, the child may tap his or her knee four times to decrease the fear of shouting out a swear word; the tapping decreases the anxiety associated with the fear of swearing.)

Cognitive behavioral therapy (CBT) and/or medications are usually effective treatments for the majority of children. You will need to consult a physician, psychiatrist, or psychologist to tailor the therapy to meet your child's needs.

CBT operates on the idea that children with OCD perform repetitive behaviors/compulsions to alleviate the anxiety associated with a bad thought/obsession. For example, both a normal child and an OCD child may experience anxiety when they see a dirty toilet seat. However, the normal child may feel relief from the anxiety by merely looking away or leaving the bathroom. The OCD child, by contrast, cannot stand feeling uncomfortable even for a few seconds, and so he or she washes his or her hands in order to decrease his or her anxiety level. Unfortunately, this hand washing actually increases his or her anxiety level. This increased anxiety leads to more hand washing, setting up a vicious cycle in which he or she becomes stuck.

In CBT, the child slowly encounters objects that cause anxiety, gradually learning to resist the urge to perform a compulsion. Eventually, the child grows desensitized to the feared object and thus no longer feels the need to perform the compulsion.

CBT is not suitable for every child. Young children may not have the insight or cognitive capabilities to participate in this type of therapy. Additionally, some children have symptons that are resistant to CBT. (This includes children who only have obsessions or children with mental compulsions.)

The selective serotonin reuptake inhibitors (SSRIs) are the medical treatment of choice for OCD. These drugs are effective, yet have few side effects. They work by increasing the amount of serotonin in the brain, which corrects the chemical imbalance that is causing the child's symptoms. There are a number of SSRIs approved for use in children by the Food and Drug Administration: sertraline (Zoloft), fluvoxamine (Luvox), and fluoxetine (Prozac). Each one of these drugs has a slightly different formula; therefore, if one medication does not help your child, it is a good idea to try another one. However, it is important to keep in mind that these medications can take 8–10 weeks to have an effect; it is preferable to avoid switching medications before this point. The tricyclic antidepressant clomipramine (Anafranil) may also treat OCD effectively. However, this drug has more side effects than the SSRIs, and therefore the SSRIs are usually tried first. More than 80 percent of children with OCD will respond to clomipramine or SSRI treatment with a reduction in symptom severity.

On average, 2–3 percent of children are OCD by late adolescence. The number of children that develop the disorder peaks at puberty and then again during early adulthood, and boys tend to have an earlier age of onset than do girls.

According to a comprehensive review of literature on OCD, 10–50 percent of children with pediatric OCD have a complete remission of symptoms by late adolescence. A majority of children that continue to experience OCD are able to manage their symptoms with medications and behavioral therapy.

Cautionary Note

Pediatric autoimmune neuropsychiatric disorders associated with streptococcal infections (PANDAS) can cause a child (prepuberty) to develop OCD or a tic disorder, following a strep infection.[13]

The typical PANDAS child will contract a strep infection and shortly thereafter develop sudden onset of OCD and/or tics. These children may also develop separation anxiety, sleep problems, an increase in urinary frequency, a sudden onset of bed-wetting, hyperactivity/inability to pay attention, difficulties with fine motor control, and a marked increase in irritability. Eventually, these symptoms will remit until the child has another strep infection, and then the cycle will begin again.

If you believe that your child may fit the PANDAS criterion, please visit the following Web site for more information: http://intramural.nimh.nih.gov/ research/pdn/gen_info.htm.

CHILDHOOD OR ADOLESCENT DEPRESSION

Only in the past two decades has depression in children been taken very seriously.[14] The depressed child may pretend to be sick, refuse to go to school, cling to a parent, or worry that the parent may die. Older children may sulk, get into trouble at school, be negative, grouchy, and feel misunderstood.

Because normal behaviors vary from one childhood stage to another, it can be difficult to tell whether a child is just going through a temporary *phase*, or is suffering from depression. Sometimes the parents or a teacher becomes worried about how the child's behavior has changed, often saying that the child "doesn't seem to be himself." In such a case, if a visit to the child's pediatrician rules out physical symptoms, have the child evaluated by a psychiatrist who specializes in the treatment of children.

Treatment for depressive disorders in children and adolescents often involve short-term psychotherapy and/or medication.[15] In addition, targeted changes may need to occur in the home or school environment.

Recent research shows that certain types of short-term psychotherapy, particularly CBT, can help relieve depression in children and adolescents. CBT operates on the premise that people with depression have cognitive distortions in their views of themselves, the world, and the future. CBT, designed to be a time-limited therapy, focuses on changing these distortions. A National Institute of Mental Health supported study that compared different types of psychotherapy for major depression in adolescents found that CBT led to remission in nearly 65 percent of cases, a higher rate than either supportive therapy or family therapy.

Research clearly demonstrates that antidepressant medications, especially when combined with psychotherapy, can be very effective treatments for depressive disorders in adults. Using medication to treat mental illness in children and adolescents, however, has caused controversy. Many doctors have been understandably reluctant to treat young people with psychotropic medications because, until fairly recently, little evidence was available about the safety and efficacy of these drugs in youth.

In the last few years, however, researchers have been able to conduct randomized, placebo-controlled studies with children and adolescents. Some of the newer antidepressant medications, specifically the SSRIs, have been shown to be safe and efficacious for the short-term treatment of severe and persistent depression in young people, although large-scale studies in clinical populations are still needed.

CHILD AND ADOLESCENT BIPOLAR DISORDER

Research findings, clinical experience, and family accounts provide substantial evidence that bipolar disorder, also called manic–depressive illness, can occur in children and adolescents.[16] However, bipolar disorder in children does not fit precisely the symptom criteria established for adults, making it difficult to recognize and diagnose in youth. Its symptoms can also resemble or co-occur with those of other common childhood-onset mental disorders. For example, symptoms of bipolar disorder may be initially mistaken for normal emotions and behaviors of children and adolescents. However, unlike normal mood changes, bipolar disorder significantly impairs functioning with peers at school and at home with family.

Effective treatment depends on appropriate diagnosis of bipolar disorder in children and adolescents. There is some evidence that using antidepressant medication *without* a mood stabilizer to treat bipolar disorder may induce manic symptoms. In addition, using stimulant medications to treat ADHD or ADHD-like symptoms in a child with bipolar disorder may worsen manic symptoms. A family history of bipolar disorder can increase this tendency to become manic. If manic symptoms develop or markedly worsen during antidepressant or stimulant use, consult a physician immediately.

Bipolar disorder is a serious mental illness characterized by recurrent episodes of depression, mania, or a mixture of the two states. These episodes cause unusual and extreme shifts in mood, energy, and behavior, which interfere significantly with normal, healthy functioning.

Manic symptoms include:

- severe changes in mood, either extremely irritable or overly silly and elated;
- overly inflated self-esteem, grandiosity;
- increased energy;
- decreased need for sleep, ability to go with very little or no sleep for days without tiring;
- increased talking, talks too much, too fast; changes topics too quickly; cannot be interrupted;
- distractibility, attention moves constantly from one thing to the next;
- hypersexuality, increased sexual thoughts, feelings, or behaviors; use of explicit sexual language;
- increased goal-directed activity or physical agitation; and
- disregard of risk, excessive involvement in risky behaviors or activities.

Depressive symptoms include

- persistent sad or irritable mood;
- loss of interest in activities once enjoyed;

- significant change in appetite or body weight;
- difficulty sleeping or oversleeping;
- physical agitation or slowing;
- loss of energy;
- feelings of worthlessness or inappropriate guilt;
- difficulty concentrating; and
- recurrent thoughts of death or suicide.

Symptoms of mania and depression in children and adolescents may manifest themselves through a variety of different behaviors. When manic, children and adolescents, in contrast to adults, are more likely to be irritable and prone to destructive outbursts than to be elated or euphoric. When depressed, there may be many physical complaints, such as headaches, muscle aches, stomachaches, or tiredness; frequent absences from school or poor performance in school; talk of or efforts to run away from home; and irritability, complaining, unexplained crying, social isolation, poor communication, and extreme sensitivity to rejection or failure. Other manifestations of manic and depressive states may include alcohol or substance abuse and difficulty with relationships.

A child or adolescent who appears to be depressed and exhibits ADHD-like symptoms that are very severe, with excessive temper outbursts and mood changes, should be evaluated by a psychiatrist or psychologist with experience in bipolar disorder, particularly if there is a family history of the illness. This evaluation is especially important since psychostimulant medications, often prescribed for ADHD, may worsen manic symptoms.

The essential treatment for this disorder involves the use of appropriate doses of mood stabilizers, most typically lithium and/or valproate, which are often very effective for controlling mania and preventing recurrences of manic and depressive episodes. Research on the effectiveness of these and other medications in children and adolescents with bipolar disorder is ongoing. In addition, studies are investigating various forms of psychotherapy, including CBT, to complement medication treatment for this illness in young people.

Cautionary Note: Valproate Use

According to studies conducted in Finland in patients with epilepsy, valproate may increase testosterone levels in teenage girls and produce polycystic ovary syndrome in women who begin taking the medication before age 20.5. Increased testosterone can lead to polycystic ovary syndrome with irregular or absent menses, obesity, and abnormal growth of hair. Therefore, young female patients taking valproate should be monitored carefully by a physician.

AUTISM

Autism is a complex biological disorder of development that lasts throughout a person's life.[17] People with autism have problems with social interaction and communication. They may have trouble having a conversation with you, for example, or they may not look you in the eye. They sometimes have behaviors that they have to do or that they do repeatedly, like not being able to listen until their pencils are lined up or saying the same sentence again and again. They may flap their arms to tell you they are happy, or they might hurt themselves to tell you they are not.

One person with autism may have different symptoms, show different behaviors, and come from different environments than others with autism. Because of these differences, doctors now think of autism as a *spectrum* disorder, or a group of disorders with a range of similar features. Doctors classify people with ASD on the basis of their autistic symptoms. A person with mild autistic symptoms is at one end of the spectrum, while a person with more serious symptoms of autism is at the other end of the spectrum.

The prevalence of autism estimates run from approximately 1 in 500 children to 1 in 1,000 children.

Diagnosis of autism may begin before the age of 3. Parents and expert clinicians can usually detect symptoms during infancy, although a formal diagnosis is generally not made until the child fails to develop functional language by age 2. Approximately 20 percent of children with autism reportedly experience a *regression*; that is, they have apparently normal development followed by a loss of communication and social skills.

Autism is three to four times more likely in boys than in girls. Autism occurs in all racial, ethnic, and social groups.

Although there is currently no known cure for autism, autism is treatable. Persons with autism can make progress if they receive appropriate, individual intervention. Preschool children who receive intensive, individualized, behavioral interventions show remarkable progress.

Many children with behavioral or developmental impairments, such as autism, are missing vital opportunities for early detection and intervention.[18]

In the United States, 17 percent of children have a developmental or behavioral impairment, such as autism, mental retardation, and ADHD; in addition, many children have delays in language or other areas, which also impact school readiness. However, less than 50 percent of these children are identified as having a problem before starting school, by which time significant delays may have already occurred and opportunities for treatment have been missed.

Recent surveys indicate that parents want information and guidance from their health care provider about their child's development, but studies sponsored by the American Academy of Pediatrics show that 65 percent of pediatricians feel inadequately trained in assessing children's developmental status.

Developmental screening—a brief assessment designed to identify children who should receive more intensive diagnosis or assessment—can improve child health and well-being, especially for children with autism and other developmental disabilities or delays.

Research has demonstrated that early detection of developmental disabilities and appropriate intervention can significantly improve functioning and reduce the need for lifelong interventions. For example, children with autism identified early and enrolled in early intervention programs show significant improvements in their language, cognitive, social, and motor skills, as well as in their future educational placement.

The Centers for Disease Control and Prevention has established the following goals to help children reach their full potential:

- Develop and test community-based model programs in primary care settings (and potentially other settings that care for young children) to screen children early on, identify those with autism and other developmental disabilities or delays, and ensure that children with these conditions receive appropriate care.
- Increase health care providers' knowledge and skills in developmental screening by incorporating developmental screening into professional health care training.
- Monitor the use of screening for autism and other developmental disabilities or delays in primary care settings.
- Raise awareness about the need for and benefits of developmental screening to identify and care for children with autism and other developmental disabilities or delays.

Do Vaccines Cause Autism?

Some parents and families of children with autism believe that the measles/mumps/rubella (MMR) vaccine caused their children's autism.[19] These parents report that their children were *normal* until they received the MMR vaccine. Then, after getting the vaccine, their children started showing symptoms of autism. Because the symptoms of autism begin to occur around the same time as the child's MMR vaccination, parents and families see the vaccine as the cause of the autism. However, just because the events happen around the same time does not mean that one caused the other.

To date, there is no definite, scientific proof that any vaccine or combination of vaccines can cause autism.

ASPERGER'S SYNDROME

Asperger's syndrome (AS) is an ASD in which children retain their early language skills.[17]

The most distinguishing symptom of AS is a child's obsessive interest in a single object or topic to the exclusion of any other. Children with AS want to know everything about their topic of interest, and their conversations with others will be about little else. Their expertise, high level of vocabulary, and formal speech patterns make them seem like little professors. Other characteristics of AS include repetitive routines or rituals; peculiarities in speech and language; socially and emotionally inappropriate behavior and the inability to interact successfully with peers; problems with nonverbal communication; and clumsy and uncoordinated motor movements.

Children with AS often find themselves isolated because of their poor social skills and narrow interests. They may approach other people, but make normal conversation impossible by inappropriate or eccentric behavior, or by wanting to talk about only their singular interest. Children with AS usually have a history of developmental delays in motor skills, such as pedaling a bike, catching a ball, or climbing outdoor play equipment. They are often awkward and poorly coordinated with a walk that can appear either stilted or bouncy.

Treatment for AS should address the three core symptoms of the disorder:

1. poor communication skills;
2. obsessive or repetitive routines; and
3. physical clumsiness

There is no single best treatment package for all children with AS, but most professionals agree that the earlier the intervention, the better.

An effective treatment program builds on the child's interests, offers a predictable schedule, teaches tasks as a series of simple steps, actively engages the child's attention in highly structured activities, and provides regular reinforcement of behavior. It may include social skills training, CBT, medication for coexisting conditions, and other measures.

With effective treatment, children with AS can learn to cope with their disabilities, but they may still find social situations and personal relationships challenging. Many adults with AS are able to work successfully in mainstream jobs, although they may continue to need encouragement and moral support to maintain an independent life.

12

GETTING BOTH PARENTS ON THE SAME TRACK

Nancy Edison stubbornly maintained her faith in young Al's ability to learn, even after the teachers at his school declared him to be unteachable. Unfortunately, Al's father was skeptical that Al would be able to learn. Samuel Edison may have been remembering the doctor's proclamation at Al's birth that the boy was probably mentally retarded. Although Al's industrious nature eventually impressed his father, it appears that Samuel was not surprised that Al did poorly at school. It is possible that Al could have remained illiterate and uneducated if not for Nancy's insistence that he was an intelligent and teachable child.

Sadly, this situation appears to be all too common today, as many parents of attention deficit hyperactivity disorder (ADHD) children do not agree on their child's diagnosis and treatment.

More often than not, it seems that the father is the one who does not understand or accept the diagnosis of ADHD. As one mother explained to me, "It is very normal that husbands just aren't as involved and usually are in denial for a while after diagnosis. Even then, they tend to gloss over it all and think it isn't as big of a deal as it is."

The tendency for fathers to discount a diagnosis of ADHD or other learning difference may be due to a number of reasons, such as

- Mothers usually spend more time than the fathers do in direct contact with young children. The mother therefore may be more cognizant of the child's behavior than the father is, making it easier for mom to accept the diagnosis of ADHD. As one mother described it, "My husband works at night during the week, so he is not around to see our son in action and learn what our son can control and what he can't."
- Fathers may feel that a child's ADHD behavior is simply a discipline problem. Of course, this inevitably leads to the child being punished for behavior that he or she cannot control. One mother in Missouri describes her dilemma: "My son has a problem, and all the punishment in the world will not change him, but my husband's answer is always corporal punishment."

- The father may have had an undiagnosed learning disorder as a child, which he has now passed on to his son or daughter. One mother expressed her frustration that "since he (the father) made it through without intervention, he feels that our son should also be able to make it on his own."
- Men are very visually oriented, and it is sometimes difficult for them to accept things they cannot see. A man will feel compassion immediately when he sees a child confined to a bed or a wheelchair, but if a child has ADHD, dyslexia, or depression, he cannot see it; it is therefore harder to believe.
- Men may misunderstand the nature of a learning disorder, and think that it will label the child as unintelligent or *abnormal.*

Sometimes this situation is further complicated by the parents' divorce or separation, making it even harder for both parents to agree on their child's diagnosis and treatment.

One mother described her situation to me after a divorce, saying that her ex-husband was having great difficulty accepting the fact that his only son had a learning disorder. Rather than accepting the diagnosis, he chose to blame his ex-wife for his son's behavior and school problems. Essentially, this father found it easier to accept the belief that his ex-wife was a bad mother than to think that his child was *abnormal.*

Regardless of your home's marital status, it is imperative that the father be actively involved in your child's education. Wade F. Horn, Ph.D., Assistant Secretary for Children and Families, claims that a father's involvement is both unique and irreplaceable. As Dr. Horn explains,[1]

Children do best in life when they grow up with the active, positive involvement of both a mother and father. Whatever the measure—physical and emotional health, educational achievement, behavior, substance abuse, crime or delinquency—children are more likely to lead healthy, productive lives when both their mother and father are actively involved in their lives in positive ways. This is because moms and dads tend to parent differently, at least in some important ways, and their complementary parenting skills and attitudes combine to give children the best environment in which to grow up healthy and successful.

Despite the fathers' importance in their children's education, the U.S. Department of Education has called fathers the "hidden parent."[2] Until recently, most federal agencies and programs that dealt with family issues focused almost exclusively on mothers and their children. It has only been since 1995 that federal programs began to make a concerted effort to include fathers in their programs, policies, and research programs.

FATHER'S INVOLVEMENT IN EDUCATION

There is a great need to get fathers more involved in education for kids of all ages. A 1997 report from the U.S. Department of Education shows that fathers are much less likely than mothers in two-parent families to be highly involved in their children's schools.[3] Fathers who headed single-parent families were the only ones to show high participation levels, comparable to that of most mothers.

The good news is that fathers who do get involved in school are also more likely to become involved with education at home. Kids whose fathers are highly involved in their schools are more likely to have been told a story by their fathers in the past week, or to have visited a museum or historical site with their fathers in the past month.

Mothers who wish to get their husbands involved in school should note that fathers are more likely to be highly involved in school if the mother is already involved (and vice versa).

Having fathers involved in school greatly increases the likelihood that their children's grades will be mostly "A's." In addition, the children are more likely to enjoy school and less likely to have to repeat a grade.[4]

Research shows that even very young children who have experienced high father involvement show an increase in curiosity and problem-solving capacity. Fathers' involvement seems to encourage children's exploration of the world around them and confidence in their ability to solve problems.

Highly involved fathers also contribute to increased mental dexterity in children, increased empathy, less stereotyped sex-role beliefs, and greater self-control. Children with actively involved fathers are even more likely than other children to have solid marriages later in life.

Getting the father involved early is especially important; children who have an involved father in their lives in the early years show up for school with more of the qualities needed for learning. They are more patient, curious, and confident, and are better able to remain in their seats, wait patiently for their teacher, and maintain interest in their own work. This higher level of self-control in schoolchildren with involved fathers is also associated with many other healthy qualities, such as improved general life skills, self-esteem, and higher social skills.

Fathers who do not live with their children are much less likely than fathers in two-parent families to be involved in school. This is particularly troubling, since the involvement of a nonresident father appears to reduce the likelihood of a child ever being suspended or expelled from school or repeating a grade.[5]

RECOMMENDATIONS TO GET FATHER INVOLVED

At home, one of the most important things a father can do is read with his child.[6] The ability to read well is known to be one of the most critical skills a child needs to be successful.

Dad can also help to cultivate reading by taking frequent trips to the library with the child to check out books and get to know the children's librarian and children's library programs.

Fathers can also help establish and support a daily routine with a set time for homework, chores, and other activities. Limiting television-viewing time to

2 hours a day (or less) can help ensure that homework is completed and time remains for more healthy activities.

Helping the child complete homework and special projects can be another great way for dad to be involved. Even though father may not always have in-depth knowledge about a particular subject, he can always provide much-needed encouragement to the child.

Bedtime is a terrific opportunity for fathers to connect with their children. Bedtime usually has few distractions, giving dad a great chance to discuss the day's events or tell a story. Every moment he spends and every word he says helps build that all-important relationship with his child.

At school, fathers can attend parent–teacher conferences, Parent–Teacher Association meetings, individualized education programs (IEPs), and school or class events such as *open-house* nights.[7] Volunteering is another important activity, such as

- speaking on a career day;
- coaching a game or sport that they enjoy;
- offering to tutor other children;
- chaperoning a field trip, social activity, or athletic event; and
- pitching in to help meet school and program needs, such as installing new playground equipment, cooking at a school picnic, or painting and repairing school property.

It is important on any evaluation or IEP meeting to have both parents present, so that they are equally aware of the concerns, and each can have his or her questions answered.

Getting a father to pay more attention or become more involved may be as simple as reading to him. One mother told me that even though her husband can read well, he would usually ignore her requests to read articles about parenting or learning disorders. She found that he was too polite to not listen to her when she offered to read the article aloud to him.

One message I heard from several mothers: Do not give up on your husband, but do not push him away with expecting too much too soon either. Working together to bridge the gap can strengthen a marriage and teach the children a priceless message.

If necessary, ask your physician or another professional help to get the father involved. He may accept the doctor's authoritative word if it is given to him on a one-to-one basis.

Sadly, some parents may have to accept the fact that their partner will not get involved in their child's education. One mother lamented to me that she eventually realized that her husband was not going to help her with her son's education. She, like Nancy Edison, was going to have to be the sole advocate for her child.

13

Local Resources

Local resources are listed according to the state in which they are located. While many attorneys and advocates practice in multiple states, their listings will appear only in their home state. Please check the listings of your neighboring states for nearby providers if you are close to a border.

Note on Technical Assistance Centers: Each state or territory has at least one organization designated as a regional Technical Assistance Center (TAC) location. TACs develop, assist, and coordinate Parent Training and Information (PTI) projects and Community Parent Resource Centers (CPRC) under the Individuals with Disabilities Education Act (IDEA). The U.S. Department of Education, Office of Special Education Programs, contributes funds to each TAC, and many services have little to no cost to the parent. TAC resource centers may provide advocacy services or refer parents to special education advocates.

Note on Protection and Advocacy System: Organizations designated as Protection and Advocacy (P&A) centers receive federal funds to help protect the rights of disabled persons. P&A centers provide disability rights information, referrals, education, and training to individuals and groups. Individual case advocacy and legal services may be available for eligible individuals.

ALABAMA

Alabama Disabilities and Advocacy Program (ADAP) in Tuscaloosa is part of the federally mandated P&A system.
Phone: (205) 348-4928
www.adap.net.

Behavioral Assessment Clinic is part of the Civitan-Sparks Clinics in Birmingham, providing evaluation and treatment programs for a wide range of childhood disorders including attention deficit hyperactivity disorder (ADHD) and associated disorders such as oppositional defiant disorder (ODD)/conduct disorder (CD) or learning disability (LD). A Summer ADHD Treatment Program is also available.

Phone: (205) 934-5471 or (800) 822-2472
www.circ.uab.edu/Sparks/ADHD.

Susan Shirock DePaola, Attorney at Law, acts as an educational advocate for special needs children. Her office is in Montgomery.
Phone: (334) 262-1600
www.specialeducationattorney.com.

Parents as Partners is a TAC resource with offices in Birmingham, Mobile, Montgomery, and Madison.
Phone: (251) 478-1208 or (800) 222-7322
http://home.hiwaay.net/~seachsv/.

ALASKA

Alaska Youth and Family Network, or AYFN, supports and teaches family members with emotionally or behaviorally disturbed children. AYFN provides phone and e-mail consultations as well as in-person services, and may render some services at no cost.
Phone: (907) 770-4979 or (888) 770-4979
www.ayfn.org.

Denali Family Services in Anchorage provides individual, family, and group psychotherapy services. It serves the Anchorage and the Matanuska-Susitna Valley areas.
Phone: (907) 274-8281 or (888) 337-6525
www.denalifs.org.

Disability Law Center of Alaska in Anchorage is an independent nonprofit organization that provides legal advocacy services for people with disabilities anywhere in Alaska. Disability Law Center is the current federally designated P&A agency for Alaska.
Phone: (907) 565-1002
www.dlcak.org.

National Alliance for the Mentally Ill, or NAMI Alaska, is a nonprofit support and advocacy center based in Anchorage with local affiliates throughout the state. NAMI Alaska may render some services at no cost.
Phone: (907) 277-1300 or (800) 478-4462
www.nami-alaska.org.

Parents, Inc., is a partnership of Alaska families containing children with disabilities. It provides support, training resources, and advocacy statewide. Offices are in Anchorage, Juneau, and Fairbanks, and they may render some services at no cost. Parents, Inc., is a TAC resource.
Phone: (800) 478-7678 or (907) 337-7678
www.parentsinc.org.

Providence Behavioral Medicine Group (PBMG)–North Clinic in Anchorage and Wasilla provides assessment and treatment for ADHD and other LDs.
Phone:
Anchorage office: (907) 561-0044
Wasilla office: (907) 373-8080
www.providence.org/alaska/bhs/bmgnorth.htm.

AMERICAN SAMOA

Client Assistance Program and Protection & Advocacy is American Samoa's federally funded P&A organization. Based in Pago Pago.
Phone: 011-684-633-2441
E-mail: pt_tauanuu@yahoo.com.

CPRC in American Samoa hosts outreach programs and assists parents with participating effectively in their child's individualized education program (IEP). Based in Pago Pago.
Phone: (684) 699-6621
www.taalliance.org/ptis/amsamoa/.

ARIZONA

Arizona Center for Disability Law is the designated P&A center for Arizona.
Phone:
Tucson Office: (520) 327-9547 or (800) 922-1447
Phoenix Office: (602) 274-6287 or (800) 927-2260
www.azdisabilitylaw.org.

Clinical Psychology Center (CPC) at Arizona State University Tempe offers ADHD therapy for children, adolescents, and adults, as well as evaluation, behavioral intervention, and social skills for children.
Phone: (480) 965-7296
http://asu.edu/clas/psych/cpc/.

Jeri Goldstein, LPC, in Phoenix is a special education advocate.
Phone: (480) 753-5045
E-mail: jeri123@aol.com.

Sandra L. Massetto, Esquire, is an attorney in Phoenix who accepts special education cases.
Phone: (603) 242-9798
E-mail: massetto@mindspring.com.

Oak Creek Ranch School in Sedona is an accredited private school for children with ADHD in grades 6–12. Residential and summer school programs are offered.
Phone: (928) 634-5571
www.ocrs.com/.

Raising Special Kids is a nonprofit TAC resource serving families of children with disabilities and special health care needs in central and northern Arizona. Many programs and services may have no cost, including special education information, individual IEP consultation, training, and problem-solving support. Based in Phoenix.
Phone: (602) 242-4366 or (800) 237-3007
www.raisingspecialkids.org.

Faith G. Thaw is a special education advocate in Scottsdale.
Phone: (489) 560-8696
E-mail: faithsped@cox.net.

Kim Yamamoto is a special education advocate in Glendale.
Phone: (602) 471-0346
E-mail: jyamamoto@cox.net.

ARKANSAS

Arkansas PTI Center is a TAC resource that provides information, support, and training throughout the state.
Phone:
Little Rock office: (501) 614-7020 or (800) 223-1330
Jonesboro office: (870) 935-2750 or (888) 217-3843
Springdale office: (501) 927-1004 or (800) 759-8788
www.adcpti.org.

Disability Rights Center (DRC) is a private, nonprofit agency with offices in Little Rock. DRC is the designated P&A center for Arkansas.
Phone: (501) 296-1775 or (800) 482-1174
www.arkdisabilityrights.org.

Becky Taylor is a special education advocate in Harrison.
Phone: (870) 743-9881
E-mail: kids_first_harrison@hotmail.com.

CALIFORNIA

Access Center for Education (ACE) provides direct advocacy and educational support services to parents and guardians of special education students in Los Angeles and Orange Counties. ACE helps parents participate in the special education IEP process and conducts parent advocacy training.
Phone: (949) 370-1186
www.ace-ca.org.

ADHD Clinic at Cedars-Sinai Hospital in Los Angeles provides assessments, treatment, and support for ADHD patients of all ages.

Phone: (310) 423-3411
www.csmc.edu/1668.

Advocate 4 U is a group of special education advocates based in Ramona. Services may be available statewide via telephone and e-mail.
Phone: (760) 415-4872
www.advocate4u.org.

Advocates for Education, based in Saratoga, is a professional advocacy service operated by Elizabeth Essner.
Phone: (408) 741-1404

Neil Steven Alex, M.D., is a San Diego doctor who specializes in ADHD.
Phone: (619) 221-6101
www.edutechsbs.com/adhd.

Alternative Horizons is a group of special education advocates based in Brea.
Phone: (714) 774-7755
www.alternativehorizons.com.

Susan Bardet, attorney at law, takes special education cases, and is based in San Mateo.
Phone: (650) 340-9243
E-mail: sbarder@gmail.com.

Marilyn Barraza is a special education advocate based in Manhattan Beach.
Phone: (310) 871-3255
E-mail: mar41349@aol.com.

Arlen Bell, M.A., J.D., is an attorney dedicated to Special Education Law. Ms. Bell has a Master of Arts Degree in special education and 14 years of teaching experience. She has offices in Santa Monica and Granada Hills.
Phone: (310) 829-2029
www.arlenebell.com; www.advocatesforeducation.com.

Bruce E. Bothwell, Esquire, is an attorney taking special education cases. Based in Long Beach.
Phone: (562) 435-0818
E-mail: brucebothwell@yahoo.com.

Linda J. Boyd, Esquire, is an attorney accepting special education cases. Based in Ventura.
Phone: (805) 201-2879
E-mail: lboyd56@earthlink.net.

Cindy Brining is a special education advocate working in the Law Office of Carol Graham in Santa Monica.
Phone: (310) 393-7160
www.grahamspecialedlaw.com.

Ed Brostoff is a special education advocate in Los Angeles.
Phone: (323) 664-9312
www.specialedhelp.com.

Susan J. Burnett, Ph.D., is a special education advocate in Yorba Linda.
Phone: (714) 985-0922
E-mail: drburnett@adelphia.net.

Carol M. Burton, M.A., and Associates in Temple City provide educational
therapy, special education teaching, tutoring, and assessment. They specialize
in LDs, math skills, study skills, social skills, and reading/writing for children,
adolescents, and adults. They also consult for assistive technology and participate in IEP advocacy.
Phone: (626) 582-8842
http://edtherapytutor.com.

California Comprehensive Psychological Services, Inc., in West Los Angeles, offers psychological assessment, therapy, and behavioral management
for persons with LDs.
Phone: (310) 445-4100
www.ccpsychological.com.

Gwen E. Campbell is a special education advocate in Westlake Village.
Phone: (818) 706-8801
E-mail: gc8801@sbcglobal.net.

Childrens Hospital of Los Angeles provides outpatient psychiatric evaluation and therapy for children with ADHD.
Phone: (323)660-2450
www.childrenshospitalla.org.

Chinese Parents Association for the Disabled is a nonprofit TAC resource
based in San Gabriel. Parent volunteers share their knowledge and experiences in raising children with disabilities, provide information about various
disabilities, suggest referrals to appropriate community resources, and offer
interpreter/translation assistance.
Phone: (626) 307-3837
www.cpad.org.

Janice S. Cleveland is an attorney accepting special education cases. Based
in Riverside.
Phone: (951) 680-9195
E-mail: jsclev@charter.net.

Annie P. Cox is an attorney focusing on special education cases. Based in
Loomis.
Phone: (916) 652-9797
E-mail: sels1@sbcglobal.net.

Roxana Cruz is a special education advocate based in Los Angeles.
Phone: (323) 269-2375
E-mail: rvcruz82@hotmail.com.

Disability Rights Education and Defense Fund, Inc. (DREDF) protects and advances the civil rights of people with disabilities through legislation, litigation, advocacy, technical assistance, and education and training of attorneys, advocates, persons with disabilities, and parents of children with disabilities. DREDF is the Parent Training and Information (PTI) center for Alameda, Contra Costa, and Yolo counties in northern California. Parent-advocates provide guidance to help parents through the special education process. Based in Berkeley.
Phone: (510) 644-2555 or (800) 466-4232
www.dredf.org.

Rebecca Dodge, Ph.D., is an academic therapist in Ramona, specializing in LD evaluation, assessment, counseling, and IEP advocacy.
Phone: (760) 787-5844
E-mail: bruinbecky1@excite.com.

Excell Tutoring and Educational Consultants in Escondido specialize in helping persons improve Scholastic Assessment Test (SAT) verbal and writing skills.
Phone: (760) 743-7433
E-mail: smarttutor1@aol.com.

Exceptional Parents Unlimited is a nonprofit TAC resource based in Fresno and serving Central California. Its services include parent support groups, teen and young adult groups, hospital support, advocacy, workshops and training, a resource center library, and IEP clinics. Many services have no cost.
Phone: (559) 229-2000
www.exceptionalparents.org.

Mandy Favaloro is an attorney focusing on special education cases and is based in Pacific Palisades.
Phone: (310) 573-1430
E-mail: mandy@a2zedad.com.

Fiesta Educativa is a Los-Angeles-based nonprofit CPRC that informs and assists Latino families in obtaining services and caring for their children with special needs.
Phone: (323) 221-6696
www.fiestaeducativa.org.

Paula Flower is a child advocate serving Santa Clara County. Paula may perform work on a sliding fee scale based on the parent's ability to pay, and may offer a free initial consultation.
E-mail: Flowerpowerof3@cs.com.
www.geocities.com/pflowerett.

Susan Foley, attorney at law, provides consultations, IEP meetings, mediations, and due process hearing services in the San Francisco Bay Area. Ms. Foley may offer a free initial consultation.
Phone: (650) 345-2300
www.susanfoley.com.

Foundation for Mexican American Services in Moreno Valley offers special education advocacy.
Phone: (951) 485-3394
E-mail: victoriabaca@verizon.net.

Eric B. Freedus, Esquire, is an attorney focusing on special education cases. Based in Oceanside.
Phone: (760) 726-9919
E-mail: efreedus@specialed.law.pro.

Dr. Susan Gamble is a psychologist in Pasadena, specializing in LD assessment and counseling.
Phone: (626) 319-3258
www.drsusangamble.com.

Linda Geller is a special education advocate in Vacaville.
Phone: (707) 446-3259
E-mail: valleyoak@aol.com.

Hallowell-West Medical Center offers a variety of services for adults, adolescents, and children with learning disabilities, specializing in a positive approach to ADHD. Located in Solana Beach.
Phone: (858) 350-4595
www.hallowellwest.com.

Herman & Associates is a corporation of psychologists in South Pasadena, specializing in LD assessment and counseling.
Phone: (323) 344-0123
www.docherman.com.

Bruce Hirsch, Ph.D., is a psychologist in Pasadena specializing in LD assessment and counseling.
Phone: (626) 395-7833
E-mail: drbruce@sbcglobal.net.

Hyperactivity, Attention and Learning Problems (HALP) Clinic at the University of San Francisco Langley Porter Hospital evaluates, identifies, and treats ADHD and other disruptive behavior and learning problems.
Phone: (415) 476-7231
http://psych.ucsf.edu/Patients/halp.asp.

Sholeh Iravantchi is a special education advocate in Los Alamitos.
Phone: (562) 460-3763
E-mail: sholeh_ir@yahoo.com.

Douglas Jacobs is an attorney and former public school teacher, offering special education advocacy. Based in Vista.
Phone: (760) 295-2255
www.thejacobslawoffice.com.

Jodie Knott, Ph.D., is a psychologist in Newport Beach, specializing in ADD/ADHD, LD assessment, and IEP consulting.
Phone: (714) 490-3428
http://drjodieknott.com.

KPS4Parents, Inc., is a nonprofit organization with teams in Orange, Los Angeles, Ventura, and Santa Barbara counties. "Intake specialists" review the child's situation with the parents and recommend appropriate services and types of support. Sliding scale fees may apply for qualified families.
Phone: (877) 536-5940
www.kps4parents.org.

Joanne Kraenzel is a special education advocate based in Granite Bay.
Phone: (916) 769-9268
E-mail: specialaid@surewest.net.

Sally S. Kirk is a special education advocate based in San Rafael.
Phone: (415) 472-5777
E-mail: marinkirks@comcast.net.

Ron Lackey, Ed.D., is a special education advocate based in Monarch Beach.
Phone: (949) 388-3025
http://dreamteamnetwork.org.

Debra D. Lamb is a special education advocate based in Sacramento.
Phone: (916) 348-8668
E-mail: iepconsult@yahoo.com.

Lance Landre is a special education advocate based in Fresno.
Phone: (559) 977-8471
E-mail: lancelandre@sbcglobal.net.

LD Advisor Coaching is operated by Jennifer Hart and is based in Granite Bay. Ms. Hart offers coaching over the phone or via e-mail.
Phone: (916) 797-9899
www.LDadvisor.com.

LD/ADHD Evaluation is an assessment center in Encino operated by Dr. Ghassemi and Dr. Sellwood, clinical psychologists.
Phone: (818) 907-5494
www.ldevaluation.com.

Dana Lear, Ph.D., is a special education advocate based in Albany and serving the Bay Area.
Phone: (510) 528-8942
www.negotiatingthemaze.org.

Legal Aid Society of San Mateo County helps disadvantaged persons obtain equal access to justice, including special education needs.
Phone: (650) 558-0915
www.legalaidsmc.org.

Loving Your Disabled Child (LYDC) is a Los-Angeles-based nonprofit CPRC established to provide parent friendly support in a Christian setting. LYDC provides a library, support groups, workshops, and telephone support.
Phone: (323) 299-2925
www.lydc.org.

Claudia Lowe, BS, JD, SENC, is a Special Educational Needs Consultant counseling students and their families on educational strategies and provisions for an appropriate IEP or 504 plan. Based in El Dorado Hills.
Phone: (916) 939-3492
www.advocacyiep504.com.

Marilyn Maggio is a special education advocate based in El Dorado Hills.
Phone: (916) 941-0983
E-mail: marilynmaggio@comcast.net.

Marina Psychological Services, Inc., offers evaluations, counseling, and psychotherapy to children and adults with LDs. Based in Marina del Rey.
Phone: (310) 822-0109
www.iser.com/marina.html.

Matrix Parent Network & Resource Center is a parent-run information and resource center in Novato, helping families in Marin, Napa, Solano, and Sonoma counties. All four counties have bilingual and bicultural staff available to serve Latino families.
Phone: (415) 884-3535 or (800) 578-2592
www.matrixparents.org.

Linda McNulty is a special education advocate based in Morgan Hill.
Phone: (408) 569-6530
E-mail: linmcnulty@aol.com.

The Neurodevelopmental Academy in San Dimas both identifies a child's learning differences and develops a remediation plan to help the child achieve improved academic performance.
Phone: (626) 339-4400
www.youcanlearn.org.

Kristina Nicole is a special education advocate based in Anaheim.
Phone: (714) 991-9357
E-mail: kristinanicolejd@gmail.com.

Parents Helping Parents of Santa Clara is a nonprofit family resource center that benefits children with special needs.

Phone: (408) 727-5775
www.php.com

Parents of Watts is a CPRC in Los Angeles.
Phone: (323) 566-7556
E-mail: pow90059@yahoo.com.

Protection & Advocacy, Inc., is a nonprofit disability rights advocacy organization designated as California's P&A center. Free advocacy services are provided for eligible residents.
Phone:
Sacramento Regional Office: (916) 488-9950 or (800) 719-5798
Bay Area Regional Office: (510) 267-1200 or (800) 649-0154
Los Angeles Regional Office: (213) 427-87471 or (800) 781-4546
San Diego Regional Office: (619) 239-7861 or (800) 576-9269
www.pai-ca.org.

Rady Children's Institute of Behavioral Health, part of the San Diego Children's Hospital, evaluates children for ADHD and makes appropriate referrals.
Phone: (858) 966-5832
www.chsd.org.

Roberts & Adams is a law firm in Huntington Beach that works with disability and special education cases.
Phone: (714) 698-0239
www.edattorneys.com.

Dr. Keri Ross is a clinical psychologist in Santa Clarita, specializing in LD or mood disorder assessment and IEP reviews.
Phone: (661) 287-3751
E-mail: drkeriross@yahoo.com.

Rowell Family Empowerment of Northern California (RFENC) is a CPRC in Redding. RFENC offers family support, workshops, and a lending library for families of children with special needs.
Phone: (530) 226-5129 or (877) 227-3471
www.rfenc.org.

San Diego ADHD is part of the San Diego ADHD project, a quality improvement initiative to improve identification and treatment of children with ADHD in the San Diego Community.
www.sandiegoadhd.org.

David Sherman, Esquire, is a special education attorney, with offices in Petaluma and San Francisco.
Phone: (415) 924-1300
www.aboutautismlaw.com.

Jeanne M. Shockley is a special education advocate based in Madera.
Phone: (559) 822-6246
E-mail: jshockley@netptc.net.

Special Education Consulting in Calabasas offers an advocate service for children with special needs.
Phone: (818) 253-6795
www.sped-law.com.

Stockdale Learning Center serves students in Kern County who have learning disabilities, offering services for dyslexia, ADHD, and other learning disorders. They are based in Bakersfield.
Phone: (661) 326-8084
www.stockdalelearningcenter.net.

Support for Families of Children with Disabilities offers information, education, and parent-to-parent support to families of children with any kind of disability or special health care need in San Francisco. Many services may come at no cost.
Phone: (415) 282-7494
www.supportforfamilies.org.

Team of Advocates for Special Kids (TASK) operates nonprofit PTI centers in San Diego and Anaheim that serve southern California. TASK offers assistance in seeking and obtaining early intervention, educational help, and medical and therapeutic support services for children. It also offers advocacy information and workshops in English, Spanish, and Vietnamese.
Phone:
San Diego office: (858) 874-2386
Anaheim office: (714) 533-8275
www.taskca.org.

Testing & Treatment Specialists operates testing and assessment centers in Los Angeles and Orange counties. The test report includes recommendations for accommodations and remediation. On-staff educational therapists are available to work on weaknesses identified in the report.
Phone: (800) 794-0062
www.privatetesting.com.

University Psychological Associates provides assessments, using standardized tests of intellectual ability, achievement, memory process, emotional and social functioning, and motor skills in Sacramento.
Phone: (916) 290-3994 or (916) 290-3995
http://home.earthlink.net/~mcmahonpsy.

Lori Waldinger, M.A., is a special education advocate based in La Crescenta.
Phone: (818) 957-8115
E-mail: loris@earthlink.net.

Betty L. Willdorff, M.Ed., is an education specialist and professional IEP advocate in Los Altos. She specializes in the assessment and the diagnosis of LDs.
Phone: (650) 917-0466
E-mail: ldspec1@yahoo.com.

COLORADO

Louise Bouzari is a special education attorney based in Englewood.
Phone: (303) 228-1616
E-mail: lbouzari@msn.com.

Child Development Unit of Children's Hospital in Denver provides evaluation, treatment, and management of ADHD.
Phone: (303) 861-8888 or (800) 624-6553
www.thechildrenshospital.org.

Denver Parent Resource Center is a TAC resource, providing Denver families with information about family rights in the special education process and ways parents can help the school understand their children.
Phone: (303) 864-1900 or (800) 284-0251
www.peakparent.org.

The Learning Camp is a summer camp in Vail developed specifically for boys and girls ages 7–14 with learning disabilities, such as ADD, ADHD, dyslexia, and other challenges.
Phone: (970) 524-2706
www.learningcamp.com.

Learning Disabilities Association of Colorado is a special education advocacy group based in Franktown.
Phone: (303) 588-7625
E-mail: bobbi_neiss@yahoo.com.

The Legal Center is the designated P&A center for Colorado, offering a range of services to help ensure that students with disabilities receive a free, appropriate public education. General information about special education law is provided as well as technical assistance and direct representation for parents at IEP meetings and dispute resolution procedures.
Phone:
Denver office: (303) 722-0300 or (800) 288-1376
Grand Junction office: (970) 241-6371 or (800) 531-2105
www.thelegalcenter.org.

PEAK Parent Center is Colorado's federally designated PTI center, providing training, information, and technical assistance to families of children with disabilities. The Peak Parent Center serves the entire state with headquarters in Colorado Springs.

Phone: (719) 531-9400 or (800) 284-0251
www.peakparent.org.

Special Education and Disability Advocacy, LLC, is a special education advocacy organization in Denver.
Phone: (303) 233-4073
E-mail: slrj9557@comcast.net.

Desiree Vandelac is a special education advocate based in Englewood.
Phone: (303) 833-9216
E-mail: dvandelac@yahoo.com.

CONNECTICUT

ADHD Clinic at the UConn Health Center in Hartford provides evaluations for ADHD in adults and adolescents.
Phone: (860) 679-2890
http://psychiatry.uchc.edu.

Stephen M. Augeri is a special education advocate based in Middlefield.
E-mail: julieswan@comcast.net.

Nora Belanger is an attorney focusing on special education cases and is based in Norwalk.
Phone: (203) 854-8597
E-mail: norabelanger@gmail.com.

Meredith Braxton, Esquire, is an attorney focusing on special education cases and is based in Greenwich.
Phone: (203) 661-4610
E-mail: braxtonlaw@conversent.net.

Annamarie P. Briones is an attorney, practicing special education law in Fairfield.
Phone: (203) 259-5300
www.fnlslaw.com.

Collaborative Advocacy Associates, or CAA, is a professional advocacy service founded by Noreen J. O'Mahoney.
Phone: (203) 454-6630
www.collaborativeadvocacy.com.

Connecticut Educational Services (CES) diagnoses and treats ADHD and LDs. CES provides free educational seminars monthly to students and families of Connecticut.
Phone: 860-343-0227
www.CT-ED.com.

Connecticut Parent Advocacy Center, or CPAC, is a statewide nonprofit organization that offers information and support to families of children with any disability or chronic illness, age birth through 21.

Phone: (860) 739-3089 or (800) 445-2722
www.cpacinc.org.

Andrew A. Feinstein, Esquire, is an attorney focusing on special education cases, and is based in Bloomfield.
Phone: (860) 242-1238
E-mail: feinsteinandrew@sbcglobal.net.

Linda M. Gottlieb, M.A., CCC/SLP is a speech-language pathologist and special education advocate based in Woodbridge.
Phone: (203) 387-1779
E-mail: LmgRED@aol.com.

Catherine A. Hopgan, MSW, LCSW, is a special education advocate based in Milford.
Phone: (203) 877-8449
E-mail: cahogan@optonline.net.

Dana Johnson is an attorney focusing on special education cases, and is based in Ridgefield.
Phone: (203) 431-4757 or (203) 838-5485
www.dajllc.com; www.spedlawyers.com.

Helen A. Krueger is a special education advocate based in Newton.
Phone: (203)426-3541
E-mail: hkrueger@sbcglobal.net.

Debra Lauzier is a special education advocate based in Torrington.
Phone: (860) 482-8288
E-mail: ddeslauz@yahoo.com.

Jennifer D. Laviano, Esquire, is an attorney focusing on special education cases, and is based in Ridgefield.
Phone: (203) 431-4262
E-mail: lavlaw3@aol.com.

Law Offices of Anne I. Eason, LLC, in Norwalk performs work as an advocate for children with special needs. Ms. Eason is a coauthor of *IEP and Inclusion Tips for Parents and Teachers.*

Learning Disabilities Association of Connecticut, or LDACT, is a Hartford-based nonprofit organization of parents, professionals, and persons with LDs.
Phone: (860) 560-1711
www.ldact.org.

Jeen Melendez is a special education advocate in Cheshire. Jeen may offer a free initial consultation.
Phone: (203) 232-0031
www.webspawner.com/users/childadvocacy.

Office of P&A for Persons with Disabilities is the designated P&A center for Connecticut. Based in Hartford.

Phone: (860) 297-4300 or (800) 842-7303
www.state.ct.us/opapd.

Jennifer Weissman is a special education advocate based in Woodbridge.
Phone: (203) 843-4590
E-mail: ctedadvocate@yahoo.com.

Diane Willcutts is a special education advocate based in Hartford.
Phone: (860)256-4186
E-mail: dlk@toast.net.

DELAWARE

Community Legal Aid Society, Inc., is the designated P&A center for Delaware residents.
Phone: (302) 575-0660
www.declasi.org.

The Parent Information Center of Delaware, or PIC/DE, is a TAC resource. PIC/DE is a statewide nonprofit organization dedicated to providing information, support, and learning opportunities to students with disabilities or special needs and their families. They have offices in Wilmington and Georgetown.
Phone: (302) 999-7394 or (888) 547-4412
www.picofdel.org.

DISTRICT OF COLUMBIA

Advocates for Justice and Education is a TAC resource located in Washington, DC.
Phone: (202) 678-8060 or (888) 327-8060
www.aje-dc.org.

All Can Read LLC is a reading and math tutoring organization operated by Faune Watkins.
Phone: (202) 783-2211
www.allcanread.com.

Attention Program at Georgetown University Center for Child and Human Development performs evaluations, consultations, referrals, and medical management for children and adolescents with ADHD.
Phone: (202) 444-6619
http://gucchd.georgetown.edu.

Margaret A. Kohn, Esquire, is an attorney focusing on special education cases.
Phone: (202) 667-2330
E-mail: makohn@aol.com.

University Legal Services is a private, nonprofit organization that serves as the District of Columbia's federally mandated protection and advocacy system for the human, legal, and service rights of people with disabilities.
Phone: (202) 547-0198
www.uls-dc.org.

FLORIDA

Advocacy Center for Persons with Disabilities serves as the federally mandated center for protection and advocacy of persons with disabilities.
Phone:
Tallahassee office: (850) 488-9071 or (800) 342-0823
Tampa office: (813) 233-2920 or (866) 875-1794
Hollywood office: (954) 967-1493 or (800) 350-4566
www.advocacycenter.org.

Community Legal Services of Mid-Florida, Inc., provides free assistance to qualified persons, including special education advocacy.
Phone:
Orlando office: (407) 841-7777
Tavares office: (352) 343-0815
Kissimmee office: (407) 847-0053
Daytona office: (386) 255-6573
Cocoa office: (321) 636-3515
Palatka office: (386) 328-8361
Bunnell office: (386) 437-8485
Sanford office: (407) 322-8983
Ocala office: (352) 629-0105
Brooksville office: (352) 796-7238
Inverness office: (352) 726-8512 or (352) 568-0257
www.clsmf.org.

Extra Special Kids is an independent firm based in Coral Springs that provides educational consulting and parent training services. They offer several affordable *packages* of advocacy services, as well as customized services.
Phone: (954) 261-9226
www.extraspecialkids.com.

Family Network on Disabilities of Florida is located in Clearwater and provides statewide services. It is a TAC resource that provides or refers access to family driven support, education, information, resources, and advocacy.
Phone: (800) 825-5736
www.fndfl.org.

Florida School Partners is a Miami-based organization that works with children who struggle with all types of special needs, including autism spectrum

disorders, LDs, physical limitations, and ADHD. It is serving Palm Beach, Broward, and Miami-Dade counties.
Phone: (786) 423-1930
www.floridaschoolpartners.com.

Ford Center for Reading in Tampa specializes in educational therapy and tutoring for persons with dyslexia or other learning disabilities. Subjects include reading, fluency, comprehension, spelling, writing, attention difficulties, math, vocabulary, oral expression, handwriting, and critical thinking skills.
Phone: (813) 254-8393
www.thefordcenterforreading.com.

Kamleiter and Kirk law firm focuses on special education advocacy, mediation, and litigation (if necessary).
Phone:
St. Petersburg office: (727) 323-2555
Orlando office: (407) 401-9575
www.kamleiterlaw.com.

Legal Aid Society of Palm Beach County works to provide disadvantaged children, families, and individuals living in Palm Beach County with equal access to our judicial system.
Phone: (561) 655-8944
www.legalaidpbc.org.

Parent to Parent of Miami is a federally funded TAC CPRC, serving Miami-Dade and Monroe counties. It provides information, educational training, support, and emergency assistance to families who have children and adults with disabilities and/or special needs. Services are provided in English, Spanish, and Creole.
Phone: (305) 271-9797
www.ptopmiami.org.

Special Kids Law Center, LLC, is a law firm founded by Dennis and Minerva Bailey, parents of a special needs child. Based in Pembroke Pines.
Phone: (954) 437-3171
www.specialkidslawcenter.com.

The Vanguard School in Lake Wales is designed for students in grades 5 through 12, who are experiencing academic difficulties due to a learning disability.
Phone: (863) 676-6091
www.vanguardschool.org.

GEORGIA

Blue Ribbon Educational Consulting is an independent educational consulting agency available to assist parents, students, and education systems in

all aspects of education. It is based in Alpharetta and serving primarily the Atlanta area.
Phone: (678) 230-6985
www.blueribboned.com.

Center for Psychological & Educational Assessment in Marietta specializes in evaluation and counseling for persons with ADD/ADHD, dyslexia, Asperger's syndrome/autism spectrum disorders, and speech/language disorders.
Phone: (770) 352-9952
www.atlantachildpsych.com.

Kelly Fadeley is a special education advocate at Students First in Evans.
Phone: (706) 955-0535
www.studentsfirstaugusta.com.

Georgia Advocacy Office (GAO) is a private, nonprofit corporation in Decatur. GAO is designated as the agency to implement protection and advocacy within the State of Georgia.
Phone: (404) 885-1234 or (800) 537-2329
www.thegao.org.

K&L Solutions is operated by Linda Loff, a professional advocate. Although she primarily serves Metro Atlanta, Linda will consider travel throughout the State of Georgia. She is available for telephone, e-mail, and in-person consultations.
Phone: (404) 684-9361
www.klsolutions.org.

Parents Educating Parents & Professionals (PEPP) serves, supports, and advocates parents and families of individuals with disabilities. It is a TAC resource based in Douglasville and provides services across the State of Georgia.
Phone: (770) 577-7771 or (800) 322-7065
www.peppinc.org.

Carol Sadler is a special education consultant and advocate based in Woodstock. Carol offers phone and e-mail consultations, as well as in-person services.
Phone: (770) 442-8357
www.iepadvocate4you.com.

Torin D. Togut, Esquire, is an attorney who considers special education cases at Georgia Legal Services Program in Atlanta.
Phone: (678) 407-9512
E-mail: tandt@mindspring.com.

GUAM

Guam Legal Services in Hagatna is the federally mandated P&A center for persons with disabilities.

Phone: (671) 477-9811
E-mail: glsc@netpci.com.

Hawaii

Naomi Grossman is a special education advocate in Honolulu.
Phone: (808) 228-0122
E-mail: naomi_grossman@yahoo.com.

Hawaii Disability Rights Center (HDRC) is the designated P&A center for Hawaii residents with disabilities.
Phone: (808) 949-2922
www.hawaiidisabilityrights.org.

Hawaii Parent Training and Information Center serves families with children with learning disabilities and other special needs that interfere with learning by providing education advocacy, training, and support. Individual help is available (including advocacy), as well as workshops and telephone assistance. All islands are served from the Honolulu headquarters.
Phone: (808) 536-9684 or (800) 533-9684
www.ldahawaii.org.

Kahi Mohala Behavioral Health on the island of Oahu offers individual, family, and group therapy for persons with ADHD.
Phone: (808) 671-8511
www.kahimohala.org.

Carl Varady is an attorney, practicing special education law in Honolulu.
E-mail: carl@varadylaw.com.

Idaho

Comprehensive Advocacy, Inc. (Co-Ad) is a private, nonprofit legal services organization designated as the P&A center for the State of Idaho.
Phone: (208) 336-5396
http://users.moscow.com/co-ad.

Idaho Parents Unlimited (IPUL) is a statewide nonprofit PTI center based in Boise. IPUL offers information and workshops as well as one-on-one assistance by trained regional staff to families of children with disabilities from birth to age 21.
Phone: (208) 342-5884 or (800) 242-4785
www.ipulidaho.org.

Illinois

Bev Alfeld is a professional child advocate who lives in Crystal Lake and serves northwestern Illinois. Bev provides telephone, e-mail, and in-person services, and may offer a free initial consultation.

Phone: (815) 459-9518
http://tinyurl.com/3sgau.

Answers for Special Kids, or ASK, is an independent nonprofit organization directed by Marian Casey. ASK provides resources and support for families of children with special needs in Evanston and neighboring communities. Phone, e-mail, and in-person consultations are provided, and some services may be rendered at no cost.
Phone: (847) 733-1739
www.answersforspecialkids.org.

Carol Dimas is a special education advocate in Naperville.
Phone: (630) 624-3784
E-mail: etc_cd@sbcglobal.net.

Catherine Whitcher, M.Ed., is a special education advocate in Joliet.
Phone: (815) 302-1273
www.PrecisionEducation.com.

Children's Law Group is a law firm in Chicago, providing special education advocacy, mediation, and litigation (when necessary).
Phone: (312) 663-4426
www.childrenslawgroup.com.

Cognitive Solutions Learning Center is a practice of LD specialists, psychologists, and tutors based in Chicago. Assessment and evaluation services are also available.
Phone: (773) 755-1775
www.cognitivesolutionslc.com.

Designs for Change is a TAC resource with a Special Education Reform Program that helps families and educators create appropriate educational programs for Chicago students with disabilities.
Phone: (312) 236-7252
www.designsforchange.org.

Elizabeth Zavodny, Psy.D., is a special education advocate in Orland Park.
Phone: (708) 403-3200
E-mail: e.zavodny@comcast.net.

Equip for Equality is an independent, not-for-profit advocacy organization designated by the governor in 1985 to implement the federally mandated P&A system in Illinois. Equip for Equality provides self-advocacy assistance, legal services, and disability rights education.
Phone:
Chicago office: (312) 341-0022 or (800) 537-2632
Rock Island office: (309) 786-6868 or (800) 758-6869
Springfield office: (217) 544-0464 or (800) 758-0464
www.equipforequality.org.

Family Matters Parent Training and Information Center (FMPTIC) is a nonprofit organization run by Amanda Bain. Service area includes all ninety-four counties in Illinois that are not part of the greater eight "Chicagoland" counties. FMPTIC provides telephone, e-mail, and in-person consultations. FMPTIC is a TAC resource and may render some services at no cost.
Phone: (217) 347-5428 or (866) 436-7842
www.fmptic.org.

Family Resource Center on Disabilities (FRCD) is a TAC resource in Chicago, offering Family Support Project, providing individualized support and advocacy services for low-income Chicago families; Youth Advocacy Project, preparing Chicago youth for adulthood; and free seminars on the special education rights of children with disabilities.
Phone: (312) 939-3513
www.frcd.org.

Steven E. Glink, attorney at law, acts as an advocate for children with special needs, and is based in Northbrook.
Phone: (847) 480-7749
www.educationrights.com.

Lisa Hannum is a special education advocate in Schaumberg.
Phone: (847) 985-6437
E-mail: advocateidea@aol.com.

Hyperactivity, Attention Deficit, and Learning Problems Clinic at the University of Chicago's Comer Children's Hospital focuses on evaluation and treatment of learning disorders.
Phone: (773) 702-1000 or (888) 824-0200
www.uchicagokidshospital.org/specialties/psychiatry.

Thomas E. Kennedy, III, practices special education law in Alton.
Phone: (618) 474-5326
www.tkennedylaw.com.

Gary Michaels is a special education advocate in Peotone, serving the Chicagoland area and central Illinois.
Phone: (708) 258-6613
www.idea-advocacy.com.

MidAmerican Psychological Institute in Joliet serves Will, Cook, Lake, Kankakee, and Du Page counties. It provides psychological testing and therapy in addition to advocacy services.
Phone: (812) 735-0732
www.thempinstitute.com.

Monahan & Cohen is a law firm in Chicago, providing special education advocacy services and litigation.

Phone: (312) 419-0252
www.Monahan-Cohen.com.

Jennifer Olsen is a special education advocate in Chicago.
Phone: (312) 282-2350
E-mail: jennifer_olsen99@yahoo.com.

Gina Robuck is a special education advocate in Tinley Park.
Phone: (708) 805-3439
E-mail: glrobuck@yahoo.com.

Special Ed Advocacy Center (SEAC) is a nonprofit organization directed by Jill M. Dressner. SEAC provides free legal services to low-income parents and caregivers of children with disabilities seeking to obtain appropriate educational services for their children. The service area includes Cook, DuPage, Grundy, Kane, Kendall, Lake, McHenry, and Will counties.
Phone: (847) 736-8286
www.specialedadvocacycenter.org.

Jennifer M. Stonemeier, MJ, MT-BC, is a special education advocate in Grayslake.
Phone: (847) 772-6528
www.stonemeieradvocacy.com.

Helen Tosch is a special education advocate based in Wheaton, and is serving greater metropolitan area of Chicago, Illinois, including DuPage, Will, Cook, DeKalb, and Lake counties. She may consider travel to parts of northern Illinois or neighboring states on a case-by-case basis.
Phone: (630) 615-1567
E-mail: HelenTosch@thechildadvocate.com.

Janet M. Varchetto is a special education advocate in Elmhurst.
Phone: (630) 993-1937
E-mail: jmvarchetto@aol.com.

Voice Advocacy is an advocacy and legal organization in Frankfort that uses a "team approach" of consultation, advocacy, and parental training to produce the desired educational outcome.
Phone: (708) 717-8393
www.specialedadvocacy.org.

INDIANA

Julie Anne Burk is a special education advocate in Indianapolis.
Phone: (317) 862-7428
E-mail: julie500@comcast.net.

Nicole E. Goodson, Esquire, is an attorney focusing on special needs children and their parents, and is based in Indianapolis.

Phone: (317) 686-1156
www.geocities.com/ngoodsonlaw.

Pat Howey, advocate, author, and speaker, specializes in resolving special education disputes for parents.
E-mail: phowey@att.net.
www.pathowey.com.

The Indiana Parent Information Network (IPIN) is a TAC resource, providing support, training, and workshops to parents of special needs children.
Phone: (317) 257-8683 or (800) 964-4746

Indiana Protection and Advocacy Services is the designated P&A center for Indiana.
Phone: (317) 722-5555 or (800) 622-4845
www.in.gov/ipas.

Indiana Resource Center (IN*SOURCE) is a TAC resource for families with special needs, striving to provide parents and families the information and training necessary to assure effective educational programs and appropriate services for children and young adults with disabilities.
Phone: (574) 234-7101 or (800) 332-4433
www.insource.org.

Kyle A. Jones, Esquire, is an attorney focusing on special needs children and their parents, and is based in Indianapolis.
Phone: (317) 269-9330
E-mail: kjones@ncs-law.com.

Dorene Philpot is an Indianapolis attorney who represents children with special needs and their parents all over the State of Indiana.
Phone: (317) 486-4578
www.dphilpotlaw.com.

Sheila Wolfe is a special education advocate in Indianapolis.
Phone: (317) 573-9610
E-mail: sheilawolfe@sbcglobal.net.

IOWA

Access for Special Kids (ASK) is a TAC Family Resource Center for children and adults with disabilities and their families. Through its member organizations, the ASK Resource Center provides a broad range of information, advocacy, support, training, and direct services.
Phone: (515) 243-1713 or (800) 450-8667
www.askresource.org.

Iowa Protection and Advocacy Services, Inc., is the designated P&A center for Iowa. Part of its mission is to ensure that individuals with disabilities and/or mental illness obtain a free, appropriate public education.

Phone: (515) 278-2502 or (800) 779-2502
www.ipna.org.

KANSAS

Disability Rights Center of Kansas (DRC) is the designated P&A center for persons with disabilities in Kansas.
Phone: (785) 273-9661 or (877) 776-1541
www.drckansas.org.

Equal Chance Educational Consulting, LLC, offers special education training and advocacy. Based in Shawnee.
Phone: (913) 825-5286
www.equalchanceeducation.com.

Families Together is a statewide nonprofit TAC resource, serving families of children and young adults from birth to age 22 with all disabilities: physical, mental, learning, emotional, and attention deficit disorders. Families Together is the designated Kansas PTI center, serving the entire state with headquarters in Wichita.
Phone: (316) 945-7747 or (888) 815-6364
www.familiestogetherinc.org.

Key for Networking, Inc., is the designated CPRC for Kansas, serving the entire state from Topeka. Keys for Networking, Inc., is a nonprofit organization, providing information, support, and training to families in Kansas whose children have educational, emotional, and/or behavioral problems.
Phone: (785) 233-8732
www.keys.org.

Scott Wasserman & Associates, LLC, is a law firm, focusing on the rights of children and their parents or guardians. Based in Lenexa.
Phone: (913) 438-4636
www.yourchild1st.com.

KENTUCKY

Cindy Baumert is a special education advocate in Louisville.
Phone: (502) 741-1297
E-mail: cbaumert@bellsouth.net.

Family Information Network on Disabilities (FIND) of Louisville is a TAC resource that works to enhance the knowledge and skills of parents of children with disabilities. FIND primarily serves Jefferson County.
Phone: (502) 584-1239
www.findoflouisville.org.

Kentucky Protection and Advocacy is the designated P&A center for persons with disabilities in Kentucky.

Phone: (502) 564-2967 or (800) 372-2988
http://kypa.net.

Kentucky Special Parent Involvement Network is a TAC resource that provides families with the knowledge, skills, information, and support they need to obtain improved services for their children. It is based in Louisville but operates statewide. Many services are possibly provided at no cost.
Phone: (502) 937-6894
www.kyspin.com.

LOUISIANA

Advocacy Center is the designated P&A center for persons with disabilities in Louisiana.
Phone: (504) 522-2337 or (800) 960-7705
www.advocacyla.org.

Key Interdisciplinary Developmental Services (KIDS) at Shreveport's Christus Schumpert Health System offers both assessment and treatment of children with ADHD and other LDs.
Phone: (318) 681-4803 or (800) 494-0015
www.christusschumpert.org/services_kidsclinic.htm.

C.W. Lartigue Iv, Esquire, is an attorney who practices education law in Metairie.
Phone: (504) 836-8080
www.lartiguelaw.com.

Project PROMPT is a TAC resource that provides a variety of workshops, including training on Individuals with Disabilities Education Act (IDEA) and related federal and state laws.
Phone: (800) 766-7736
www.projectprompt.com.

MAINE

Disability Rights Center is Maine's P&A agency for people with disabilities. Based in Augusta.
Phone: (207) 626-2774 or (800) 452-1948
www.drcme.org.

Eddita Felt is a special education advocate living in Maine.
Phone: (207) 353-8648
www.TheParentsAdvocate.com.

The Maine Parent Federation is a statewide TAC resource that provides information, advocacy, education, and training to benefit all children.

Phone: (207) 623-2144 or (800) 870-7746
www.mpf.org.

Merrywing Corporation provides advocacy services for families in Maine, New Hampshire, and Massachusetts, and consultation to families in other states.
Phone: (207) 439-0382
www.merrywing.com

Richard L. O'Meara, Esquire, is an attorney practicing special education law in Portland with the Murray, Plumb, and Murray law firm.
Phone: (207) 773-5651
www.mpmlaw.com.

MARYLAND

Melissa Alexander is a special education advocate in Chaptico.
Phone: (301) 884-4662
E-mail: alexander@gmpexpress.net.

Bass Educational Services in Olney is an educational consulting service for adolescents with LDs. Operated by Judith Bass.
Phone: (240) 606-4996
www.collegeconsulting.info

Center for Development and Learning is an outpatient program for evaluation and treatment of children with learning difficulties. Part of the Kennedy Krieger Institute in Baltimore.
Phone: (443) 923-9400 or (888) 554-2080
www.kennedykrieger.org.

Brian K. Gruber is an attorney practicing special education law in Bethesda.
Phone: (301) 657-3777
E-mail: brian.gruber@bkgpc.com.

Dr. Sharon Hellman offers counseling, advocacy, and educational consulting for learning disabled children and teens in Rockville, Maryland.
Phone: (301) 468-6100
www.iser.com/counseling-MD.html.

Dr. Lawrence Andrew Larsen is a special education advocate in Towson.
Phone: (410) 296-8458
E-mail: larrylarsen@comcast.net.

Mark B. Martin, Esquire, practices special education law in Baltimore.
Phone: (410) 779-7770
www.markmartinlaw.com.

The Maryland Disability Law Center (MDLC) is a private, nonprofit organization staffed by attorneys and paralegals. MDLC is the P&A organization for persons with disabilities in Maryland. Based in Baltimore.

Phone: (410) 727-6352 or (800) 233-7201
www.mdlcbalto.org.

Jerrold Miller, Esquire, practices special education law in Bethesda.
Phone: (301) 986-4160
E-mail: jerroldmiller@yahoo.com.

Parents' Place of Maryland is a nonprofit TAC resource that includes parent educators who support and educate families on their rights in special education. It is located in Glen Burnie, but serves the entire state.
Phone: (410) 768-9100
www.ppmd.org.

Patrick Hoover Law Office practices special education law throughout Maryland and the District of Columbia. Based in Rockville.
Phone: (301) 424-5777
www.hooverlaw.com.

Dr. Lisa Schoenbrodt is a speech and language specialist in Ellicott City. She also helps in IEP development for children with learning differences.
Phone: (410) 241-0874
E-mail: lschoenbrodt@loyola.edu.

Tamieka A. Skinner, SEAC, LLC, is a special education advocate in Germantown.
Phone: (301) 540-6680
E-mail: spedteacher4life@yahoo.com.

Karen A. Snyder, M.S., is an advocate in Gaithersburg, Maryland. She is available to help in-person or over the phone.
Phone: (301) 315-2308, Fax: (301) 315-2309
www.ParentAdvocate.org.

Dr. Linda E. Spencer is a speech and language specialist in Ellicott City, offering assessment services and IEP consultation.
Phone: (410) 418-9275
E-mail: les4188@comcast.net.

Wayne Steedman, Esquire, is an attorney practicing special education law in Baltimore.
Phone: (410) 576-7606
www.callegarysteedman.com.

Rebecca Slade Yoshitani is an attorney practicing special education law in Clarksville.
Phone: (443) 812-5767
E-mail: rsyosh@aol.com.

MASSACHUSETTS

ADHD Clinic at UMass Memorial's Children's Medical Center in Worcester diagnoses and treats children with ADHD.
Phone: (508) 856-3028
www.umassmemorial.org/ummhc/hospitals/med_center/services/CMC/adhd.cfm.

Teri Bisbee is a special education advocate in Leominster.
Phone: (978) 227-5328
E-mail: tbadv@comcast.net.

Cape Cod Advocate is an advocacy service run by Christine Riley in Marstons Mills. Christine serves Cape Cod, the Islands, and south shore area of Massachusetts, and provides telephone, e-mail, and in-person consultations.
Phone: (508) 428-2288
www.capecodadvocate.com.

Lynne Carlson-Lefort is a special education advocate in West Boylston.
Phone: (508) 835-1188
E-mail: theadvocate1@comcast.net.

Center for Children with Special Needs at Tufts-New England Medical Center in Boston provides diagnosis and treatment of ADHD and other learning disorders.
Phone: (617) 636-7242
www.tufts-nemc.org/ccsn/home.

Andrea Chaitman is a special education advocate in Sandwich.
Phone: (508) 420-0436
E-mail: achaitman@msn.com.

Lucie Chansky is a special education advocate in Newton Center.
Phone: (617) 244-7310
E-mail: luciec@comcast.net.

Developmental Medicine Center at Boston Children's Hospital in Boston offers diagnosis and treatment of ADHD and other developmental disorders.
Phone: (617) 355-6501
www.childrenshospital.org.

Disability Law Center, Inc. (DLC) is the P&A agency for Massachusetts. DLC is a private, nonprofit organization responsible for providing protection and advocacy for the rights of Massachusetts residents with disabilities.
Phone:
Boston office: (617) 723-8455 or (800) 872-9992
Northampton office: (413) 584-6337 or (800) 222-5619
www.dlc-ma.org.

Education Consulting, Advocacy & Legal Services in Lynnfield offers special education advocacy, parental training, and legal representation (if necessary).
Phone: (781) 581-7266
www.educationandjuvenilelaw.com.

Educational Options, LLC, in Cambridge provides comprehensive educational planning for students with LD, ADHD, and behavioral/emotional issues.
Phone: (617) 864-8864
www.optionsined.com.

The Federation for Children with Special Needs is a TAC resource that provides information, support, and assistance to parents of children with disabilities, their professional partners, and their communities. Offices are in Boston and Worcester.
Phone: (617) 236-7210 or (800) 331-0688
www.fcsn.org.

Marie Feeney is a special education advocate in Winchester.
Phone: (617) 625-9600, ext 4
E-mail: mariefeeney@comcast.net.

Mary Fishman is a special education advocate in Sandwich.
Phone: (508) 477-5163
www.beyondexpectationsconsulting.com.

Pam Fitzgerald is a special education advocate in Northborough.
Phone: (508) 269-2032
E-mail: danielsmom94@hotmail.com

Suzanne Gervais is a special education advocate in Sharon.
Phone: (508) 284-7732
E-mail: suzanne.peyton@comcast.net.

Claudetter-Jean Girard is an attorney practicing special education law in Springfield.
Phone: (413) 739-1257
www.westernmasslaw.com.

Michael R. Goldberg, Esquire, practices special education law in Marblehead.
Phone: (781) 631-1255
www.mgoldberglaw.com.

Howard Learning Assessment Services is a diagnostic center evaluating and treating attention, learning, and memory disorders.
Phone:
Lexington office: (781) 860-7733
Newburyport office: (978) 465-2999

Portsmouth office: (603) 433-8954
Wellesley office: (781) 235-9972

Kotin, Crabtree & Strong, LLP, is a Boston law firm with experience in special education proceedings at local and state levels and in the state and federal court systems.
Phone: (617) 227-7031
www.kcslegal.com/education.html.

Lois M. Kraus is a special education advocate in Delham.
Phone: (781) 329-6874
E-mail: lois.kraus@rcn.com.

Law office of Michael L. Rich concentrates on children's and family law in Arlington.
Phone: (781) 641-3472

Stephanie LeBlanc is a special education advocate specializing in autism spectrum disorders, and is based in Hopkinton.
Phone: (781) 439-5787
www.autismspectrumadvocacy.com.

Carla C. Leone, Esquire, is an attorney practicing special education law in Arlington.
Phone: (781) 648-4006
www.leonelaw.com.

Stephen Lowe, Ph.D., is a special education advocate in Acton.
Phone: (978) 263-9725
E-mail: advocate@paragon-c.com.

Joseph McDonald is a special education advocate in East Taunton.
Phone: (508) 823-0909
E-mail: jmcdonald98@comcast.net.

Metrowest Educational Advocates offers special educational advocacy services to families of children with special needs, and is serving the areas around Holliston.
Phone: (508) 429-0962
www.metrowestadvocates.com.

Melody Ann Orfei is a special education advocate in Concord.
Phone: (978) 371-2182
http://concordspedpac.org.

Pediatric Psychology Assessment Center at the MassGeneral Hospital for Children offers assessment, diagnosis, and treatment of learning disorders.
Phone: (617) 726-3647
www.mgh.harvard.edu/mghfc.

Jaime Picariello is an attorney practicing special education law in Boston.
Phone: (781) 640-8169

Michael L. Rich, Esquire, practices special education law in Arlington.
Phone: (781) 641-3472
www.MichaelRichLaw.com.

Tim Sindelar, Esquire, is an attorney practicing special education law in
Cambridge.
Phone: (617) 871-2140
E-mail: sindelar@ahmslegal.com.

Anne Marie Smith, M.Ed., is a special education advocate in Sandwich.
Phone: (413) 789-0906
E-mail: fianafail1@comcast.net.

Speech Therapy Success in Southbridge offers educational consulting and
speech/language therapy.
Phone: (508) 764-1487
E-mail: rjsava60@aol.com.

Dena Steiling is a special education advocate in Chelmsford.
Phone: 978-2835
E-mail: capricolo@aol.com.

Allison Traxler, M.Ed., is a special education advocate in Newburyport.
Phone: (978) 462-1888
E-mail: traxlered@yahoo.com.

Marcia J. Tritter is a special education advocate in Jamaica Plain.
Phone: (617) 522-5252
E-mail: m.tritter@att.net.

Urban PRIDE is a community resource center founded to improve the availability of and access to culturally responsive disability-related support, information, and training for culturally and linguistically diverse families who have
children with disabilities and young adults with disabilities in urban Boston.
Phone: (617) 338-4453
www.urbanpride.org; www.michaelrichlaw.com.

MICHIGAN

Attention Camp is a summer day camp treatment program in Grand Haven
for children with ADHD.
Phone: (616) 842-4772
www.westernbehavioral.com.

Children's Hospital of Michigan provides diagnostic and consultation services for ADHD and Autism through their Department of Psychiatry/
Psychology. Located in Detroit.

Phone: (313) 745-5437 or (888) 362-2500
www.chmkids.org.

Citizens Alliance to Uphold Special Education (CAUSE) is the TAC PTI center for the State of Michigan. CAUSE is a statewide nonprofit coalition, providing information, referral, support, advocacy, and workshops to parents and professionals working with children with disabilities and special needs. CAUSE may provide some or all of its services at reduced or no cost.
Phone:
Lansing office: (517) 886-9167 or (800) 221-9105
Detroit office: (248) 424-9610 or (800) 298-4424
Grand Rapids office: (616) 455-8719 or (800) 715-5820
Munising office: (906) 387-2932 or (800) 628-5603
Sault Ste. Marie office: (906) 635-9573 or (800) 532-2873
www.causeonline.org.

Education Law Center, PLC, offers referral to legal services, as well as training on education law in Michigan to individuals and groups.
Phone: (810) 227-9850
www.michedlawcenter.com.

Michigan Protection and Advocacy Service is the designated P&A center for persons with disabilities in Michigan.
Phone:
Lansing office: (517) 487-1755 or (800) 288-5923
Livonia office: (248) 473-2990 or (866) 928-9148
Marquette office: (906) 228-5910 or (866) 928-5910
www.mpas.org.

Respect Ability Law Center offers special education legal services from Calvin and Patricia Luker in Royal Oak.
Phone: (248) 544-7223
E-mail: cluker360@comcast.net; tricialuker@comcast.net.

University of Michigan Health System in Ann Arbor diagnoses and treats ADHD of other LDs through its Department of Developmental and Behavioral Pediatrics.
Phone: (734) 936-4000
www.med.umich.edu/1libr/yourchild.

MINNESOTA

ADHD Clinic at the University of Minnesota in Minneapolis offers assessment and treatment of children with ADHD.
Phone: (612) 273-8710
www.med.umn.edu/psychiatry/clinics/adhdclinic.

Minnesota Disability Law Center (MDLC) is the designated P&A for person with disabilities in Minnesota. MDLC provides free civil legal assistance to individuals with disabilities on legal issues related to their disabilities. Based in Minneapolis.
Phone: (612) 332-1441 or (800) 292-4150
www.mndlc.org.

Parent Advocacy Coalition for Educational Rights (PACER) is a TAC PTI center that assists individual families and provides workshops, materials, and leadership in securing a free and appropriate public education for all children.
Phone: (952) 838-9000 or (800) 537-2237
www.pacer.org.

Regions Hospital Health and Wellness Program for Deaf and Hard of Hearing People offers diagnosis and treatment of ADHD in deaf and hard of hearing children and adults. Located in St. Paul.
Phone: (651) 254-3456 or (800) 627-3529
www.regionshospital.com.

MISSISSIPPI

EMPOWER Community Resource Center in Greenville is the state's TAC organization.
Phone: (662) 332-4852 or (800) 337-4852.

Mississippi Protection and Advocacy System, Inc., is the designated P&A center for persons in Mississippi with disabilities. Based in Jackson.
Phone: (601) 981-8207
www.mspas.com.

MISSOURI

Chackes, Carlson, Spritzer & Ghio is a St. Louis law firm, practicing special education law.
Phone: (314) 872-8420
www.vccs-law.com.

Children's Hospital St. Louis ADHD Program provides assessment and treatment for ADHD in children.
Phone: (314) 454-6069
www.stlouischildrens.org.

Dayna F. Deck, Esquire, is an attorney practicing special education law in St. Louis.
Phone: (314) 361-9900
E-mail: dayna.deck@sbcglobal.net.

Missouri Parents Act (MPACT) is a statewide TAC resource that assists parents to advocate for their children's educational rights and services. Headquarters are in Kansas City.
Phone: (816) 531-7070
www.ptimpact.com.

Missouri Protection & Advocacy (MO P&A) provides eight federally funded programs to protect the legal rights of persons with disabilities. Based in Jefferson City.
Phone: (573) 893-3333 or (800) 392-8667
www.moadvocacy.org.

Special Education Parent's Advocacy Link (SEPAL) is a network of special education advocates, serving parents in Missouri, Kansas, and Nebraska. SEPAL has experience serving the special needs of military families. Based in Kansas City.
Phone: (816) 680-0070
www.specialeducationrights.com.

University of Missouri Psychological Services Clinic in Columbia provides individual, family, and group therapy as well as assessment and treatment for LDs.
Phone: (573) 882-4677
http://psychology.missouri.edu/psychservicesclinic.php.

Val Lyons, RN-MA, is a certified paralegal offering special education advocacy and legal referral services, and is based in Chesterfield.
Phone: (636) 530-4661
www.FinishingStrong.org.

MONTANA

Montana Advocacy Program is the designated P&A center for persons in Montana with disabilities. Based in Helena.
Phone: (406) 449-2344 or (800) 245-4743
www.mtadv.org.

Parents Let's Unite for Kids (PLUK) is a private, nonprofit TAC resource formed in 1984 by parents of children with disabilities and chronic illnesses. PLUK provides information, support, training, and assistance from its headquarters in Billings.
Phone: (406) 255-0540 or (800) 222-7585
www.pluk.org.

NEBRASKA

ADHD Clinic at the University of Nebraska in Omaha offers comprehensive medical, psychological, academic, and other services, including follow-up activities taking place in school and in the community.

Phone: (402) 559-6403 or (800) 656-3937
www.unmc.edu/dept/mmi.

Nebraska Advocacy Service, Inc. (NAS) is the P&A center for persons with disabilities in the State of Nebraska. Based in Lincoln.
Phone: (402) 373-3183 or (800) 422-6691
www.nebraskaadvocacyservices.org.

Lynne M. Popp Educational Therapy, Inc., in Omaha specializes in children and adults with dyslexia and other learning disabilities. Parental training in educational rights is also offered.
Phone: (402) 498-8708
E-mail: slpopp1@cox.net

PTI Nebraska is a TAC resource providing training and information to families of children with disabilities and special health care needs. PTI Nebraska serves the entire state from headquarters in Omaha.
Phone: (402) 346-0525 or (800) 284-8520
www.pti-nebraska.org.

NEVADA

Deidre Hammon is a special education advocate in Reno.
Phone: (775) 544-9338
E-mail: djhammon@peoplepc.com.

Marianne Lanuti is an attorney in Henderson practicing special education law.
Phone: (702) 270-2346
E-mail: MLanuti@cox.net.

Nevada Disability Advocacy & Law Center, Inc. (NDALC) serves as Nevada's federally mandated P&A system for the human, legal, and service rights of individuals with disabilities.
Phone:
Las Vegas office: (702) 257-8150 or (888) 349-3843
Sparks office: (775) 333-7878 or (800) 992-5715
www.ndalc.org.

Nevada Parents Encouraging Parents (PEP) is Nevada's statewide PTI center for families who have children with disabilities. Based in Las Vegas, PEP offers information and referral, a statewide lending library, a quarterly newsletter, conflict resolution support, training workshops, individual assistance, and parent mentors and advocates.
Phone: (702) 388-8899 or (800) 216-5188
www.nvpep.org.

Matthew Schneider is an attorney in Las Vegas practicing special education law.

Phone: (702) 274-0854
E-mail: mschneider.esq@gmail.com.

UMC Attention Deficit Clinic in Las Vegas provides testing and treatment for children with ADHD. A case-management approach is emphasized, and the child's parents and teacher are closely involved.
Phone: (702) 383-3642
www.umc-cares.org/med_serv/lied/attention.asp.

Anne M. Vohl, Esquire, is an attorney in Reno, offering advocacy and legal services for LD children.
Phone: (775) 686-6068
E-mail: vohl@aol.com.

NEW HAMPSHIRE

The Disabilities Rights Center (DRC) is New Hampshire's designated P&A agency. DRC pursues legal, administrative, and other appropriate remedies on behalf of individuals with disabilities. Based in Concord.
Phone: (603) 228-0432 or (800) 834-1721
www.drcnh.org.

Education A Must is a nonprofit corporation providing advocate services for the child or youth with physical, emotional, behavioral, or learning disabilities. It serves New Hampshire, Massachusetts, and Rhode Island.
Phone: (603) 437-6286
www.education-a-must.com.

Hunter School is a private special education day and boarding school for children in kindergarten through eighth grade, ages 5 through 15, with ADHD and/or other coexisting conditions. Located in Rumney on 137 acres on the west slope of Stinson Mountain.
Phone: (603) 786-9427
www.hunterschool.org.

Theresa Kraft, Esquire, is an attorney practicing special education law in Concord.
Phone: (603) 225-7555
www.kraftlawnh.com.

Parent Information Center (PIC) is a TAC resource that promotes effective parent involvement in the special education process. It is located in Concord but provides services throughout New Hampshire.
Phone: (603) 224-7005 or (800) 947-7005
www.parentinformationcenter.org.

Jennifer Sawyer, Esquire, is an attorney practicing special education law at the law firm of Cooper, Deans, and Cargill in North Conway.

Phone: (603) 356-5439
E-mail: jsawyer@cdc-law.com.

SPED Solutions, LLC is an advocacy service operated by Angela Kouroyen. Based in Derry.
Phone: (603) 216-7685
E-mail: specialedsolutions@comcast.net.

New Jersey

ADHD Center of Northern New Jersey in Morristown offers coaching, counseling, and therapy to persons with learning disorders.
Phone: (973) 605-5000
www.feelgoodandfocused.com.

ADDvantages Learning Center in Cherry Hill offers coaching, therapy, and tutoring to persons with LDs.
Phone: (856) 482-0756
www.addvantages.com.

E. Jennifer Brown is a special education advocate in Lebanon.
Phone: (908) 832-6754
E-mail: jenn.bubb.brown@gmail.com.

Stacey Therese Cherry is an attorney who serves New Jersey and New York. She will travel throughout the state or country as time allows, but primarily serves Rockland and Orange County. Ms. Cherry provides telephone, e-mail, and in-person consultations, and may offer a free initial telephone consultation.
Phone: (201) 909-0404
www.edadvocacycenter.com.

Child and Adolescent ADHD Clinic at Fairleigh Dickinson University (Teaneck) offers assessment and intervention services for children with ADHD. Individual and family therapy and school-based consultation are available. Located in Hackensack.
Phone: (201) 692-2649
http://alpha.fdu.edu/ucoll/ps/children.html.

Mary Pat Correro, Ed.M., is an educational consultant in Mount Laurel, offering evaluation and advocacy services.
Phone: (856) 234-7337
www.bridgeslearning.com.

Lisa K. Eastwood, Esquire is an attorney practicing special education law in North Bergen.
Phone: (201) 867-0751
E-mail: lkeastwood@verizon.net.

Nancy Friedman-Cohen is a special education advocate in Lebanon.
Phone: (732) 220-0055
E-mail: nancyfcohen@yahoo.com.

Carole Ann Geronimo is an attorney practicing special education law in Ramsey.
Phone: (201) 512-4400
E-mail: cageronimolaw@optonline.net.

Stephanie Glaser is a special education advocate in Hightstown.
Phone: (609) 529-2524
E-mail: artmom@aol.com.

Elizabeth H. Hamlin is an attorney practicing special education law in Montclair with the firm of Garrity, Graham, Favetta, and Flinn, PC.
Phone: (973) 509-7500, ext 219
www.garritygraham.com.

Lauren Hirtes is a special education advocate in Morristown.
Phone: (973) 347-1976
E-mail: Lspan@optonline.net.

Lisa Krizman, Esquire, is an attorney practicing special education law in Cherry Hill.
Phone: (856) 751-4131
www.krizmanlaw.com.

Rachelle H. Milstein, Esquire, is an attorney practicing special education law in Watchung.
Phone: (908) 561-1977
www.milsteinlaw.com.

My Community Care Team is an advocacy service founded by Maria and Frank Tetto after their 12-year-old daughter Maria suffered a traumatic brain injury. They provide telephone, e-mail, and in-person consultations, and may render some services at no cost.
Phone: (973) 691-8619
www.mycommunitycareteam.com.

New Jersey P&A, Inc., is the designated P&A center for persons with disabilities in New Jersey. Based in Trenton.
Phone: (609) 292-9742 or (800) 922-7233
www.njpanda.org.

Personalized Educational Care in Lambertville offers coaching, counseling, and reading tutoring to persons with LDs.
Phone: (609) 397-6696
www.maesakharov.com.

Special Education Alliance is a network of special education advocates and other professionals serving families throughout the State of New Jersey. Founded by Ellen Smolko.
Phone: (973) 252-4541
www.nj-sped-advocate.com.

Shelley Lynn Stangler is an attorney practicing special education law in Springfield.
Phone: (973) 379-2500
www.stanglerlaw.com.

Statewide Parent Advocacy Network (SPAN) is a TAC resource that provides training, support, and advocacy to families in New Jersey.
Phone: (973) 642-8100
www.spannj.org.

Jerry Tanenbaum is an attorney practicing special education law at Schnader, Harrison, Segal, and Lewis LLP in Haddonfield.
Phone: (856) 482-5733
www.schnader.com.

Windsor School and Windsor Learning Center offers two programs in Pompton Lakes for students with ADHD. The Learning Center has grade kindergarten through 5, and the School has grades 6 through 8.
Phone: (973) 839-4050
www.windsorschools.com.

Renay Zamloot is a special education advocate in Annandale.
Phone: (908) 730-0080
E-mail: rzamloot@earthlink.net.

New Mexico

Abrazos Family Support Services is a CPRC, serving twenty-two American Indian Communities from its headquarters in Bernalillo. Covered areas include Bernalillo and Sandoval counties, and the Indian Pueblos of Santo Domingo, Cochiti, San Felipe, Santa Ana, Sandia, Zia, and Jemez.
Phone: (505) 867-3396
www.abrazosnm.org.

I. Michael J. Kaczor is a special education advocate in Glorieta.
Phone: (505) 575-6133
E-mail: kazeman@juno.com.

Native American Disability Law Center is a designated P&A center for Native Americans with disabilities. Based in Farmington.
Phone: (505) 566-5880 or (800) 862-7271
E-mail: tyanan@nadlc.org.

Parents Reaching Out is an Albuquerque-based nonprofit TAC resource serving the entire state. Parents Reaching Out develops educational opportunities, workshops, and materials for families, parents, educators, service providers, and other professionals.
Phone: (505) 247-0192 or (800) 524-5176
www.parentsreachingout.org.

Protection & Advocacy, Inc., is the designated P&A center for persons in New Mexico with disabilities. Based in Albuquerque.
Phone: (505) 256-3100 or (800) 432-4682
www.mnpanda.org.

New York

ADHD Center at Schneider Children's Hospital, Developmental and Behavioral Pediatrics Department, sees patients at Consultation Centers located in Commack, Hewlett, Flushing, and West Islip.
Phone: (516) 802-6100
www.schneiderchildrenshospital.org/sch_pat_dev_behave.html.

ADHD Center of Mount Sinai School of Medicine in New York offers assessment, treatment, and research for ADHD in children.
Phone: (212) 241-5420
www.mssm.edu/psychiatry/adhd/child_clinical.

The Advocacy Center is a nonprofit TAC resource that educates, supports, and advocates for people who have disabilities, their families, and circles of support. Their area of service is the entire state except for New York City.
Phone: (585) 546-1700 or (800) 650-4967
www.advocacycenter.com.

Advocates for Children of New York (AFC) is a TAC resource providing a full range of services: free individual case advocacy, technical assistance, and training for parents, students, and professionals about children's educational entitlements and due process rights in New York City.
Phone: (212) 947-9779
www.advocatesforchildren.org.

Rachel Asher, Esquire is an attorney practicing special education law in Katonah.
Phone: (914) 232-1150
E-mail: rachelsasher@aol.com.

Lauren A. Baum, Esquire is an attorney practicing special education law in New York City.
Phone: (212) 201-5426
E-mail: Lbaum@nyspecialedlaw.com.

Sarah Bronson, Ph.D., is a neuropsychologist in Bronxville with offices in New York City and Bayside. Dr. Bronson offers assessments with full recommendations for interventions and learning strategies.
Phone: (914) 961-1469
E-mail: sarahbronson@earthlink.net.

The Children's Advisory Group, Inc. (TCAG) is a team of special education advocates and attorneys in New York City.
Phone: (212) 769-4644
www.childadvisors.com.

Larry A. Cohen, CPRP, is a special education advocate in Beacon.
Phone: (914) 474-9624
E-mail: Larry@TheFamilyCohen.com.

Dr. Jayne Cohodas is a psychologist in New York City, offering services for behavior issues and helping develop learning strategies.
Phone: (917) 328-7318
E-mail: jaynedr@aol.com.

James A. Costello, Esquire, is an attorney practicing special education law in Smithtown.
Phone: (631) 979-4300
E-mail: costello239@hotmail.com.

Andrew Cuddy is an attorney practicing special education law in Auburn.
Phone: (716) 868-9103
E-mail: akcuddy132@aol.com.

Linda Marie Dardis, Esquire, is an attorney practicing special education law in Brooklyn.
Phone: (718) 377-0600 or (516) 384-5838
ww.kaplandardis.com.

Barbara J. Ebenstein, Esquire, is an attorney practicing special education law in Scarsdale.
Phone: (914) 725-2257
E-mail: bjeslaw@aol.com.

EBL Coaching in New York City offers coaching and tutoring in reading, writing, reading comprehension, math, and other skill areas.
Phone: (646) 342-9380
www.eblcoaching.com.

Educational Consulting Services, Inc., in City Island offers coaching and educational consulting for persons with LDs.
Phone: (718) 885-1150
E-mail: edconsultschool@aol.com.

Jospeh M. Fein, Esquire, is an attorney practicing special education law in Hewlett. Serving Nassau, Suffolk, Brooklyn, and Queens.

Phone: (516) 792-9119
www.educationalesq.com.

FPI Attention Disorders Clinic in Endicott is directed by Vincent J. Monastra, Ph.D., and offers ADHD assessment, parenting classes, social skills groups, educational advocacy, EEG biofeedback, cognitive behavioral therapy, family and marital therapy.
Phone: (607) 785-0400
www.theADHDdoc.com

Gary Mayerson & Associates is a law firm based in New York City. Mr. Mayerson is the author of *How to Compromise with Your School District without Compromising Your Child.* The firm primarily serves New York, New Jersey, Connecticut, and Pennsylvania, although they have represented families in approximately twenty-six states, as far away as Alaska.
Phone: (212) 265-7200
www.mayerslaw.com.

Dr. Larry E. Hess is a neuropsychologist in New York City, offering individual assessment, consultation, and treatment for persons with LDs.
Phone: (212) 462-9251
www.drlarryhess.com.

Peter D. Hoffman, Esquire, is an attorney practicing special education law in Katonah.
Phone: (914) 232-2242
www.lawofficeofpdhoffman.com.

Camp Huntington is a co-ed, residential, 7-week program for children and young adults with various LDs. Located in High Falls in the Catskill Mountain region.
Phone: (845) 687-7840
www.camphuntington.com.

Bernadine Jacobs, Esquire, is an attorney practicing special education law in Scarsdale.
Phone: (914) 725-5568
E-mail: brjesquire@hotmail.com.

Julie Michaels Keegan, Esquire, is an attorney in Albany offering educational program design, IEP assistance, and legal services for persons with LDs.
Phone: (518) 435-8068
attorneyforspecialneeds.com.

Michele Kule-Korgood, Esquire, is an attorney practicing special education law in Forest Hills.
Phone: (718) 261-0181
E-mail: mkulespecialed@aol.com.

Legal Services of the Hudson Valley (LSHV) provides civil legal services to low-income people. LSHV takes calls between the hours of 9:00 A.M. and

4:00 P.M., Monday through Thursday and between 1:00 and 3:00 P.M. on Friday. It is serving Westchester, Dutchess, Orange, Putnam, Rockland, Sullivan, and Ulster counties.
Phone: (877) 574-8529
www.lshv.org.

Literacy Leap, LLC, offers assessment and tutoring for person with LDs such as dyslexia. Located in Merrick.
Phone: (516) 771-3400
literacyleap.com.

Little Yellow Classroom in Huntington Station offers assessment of LDs and tutoring.
Phone: (631) 421-6888
E-mail: AbilitiesEduc8r@aol.com.

Nancy Marano-Silva is a special education advocate in Westbury.
Phone: (516) 338-7272
E-mail: educ8advoc8@aol.com.

John McGrath is an attorney practicing special education law in Mineola.
Phone: (516) 747-9779
E-mail: specialeducationlawyer@yahoo.com.

NY State Commission on Quality of Care & Advocacy for Persons with Disabilities is an independent state agency charged with P&A of the rights of New Yorkers with disabilities.
Phone: (800) 522-4369
www.cqcapd.state.ny.us.

NYU Child Study Center's Institute for Attention Deficit Hyperactivity and Behavior Disorders develops and investigates new interventions for ADHD, both pharmacological and psychosocial. It sponsors the NYU Summer Program for Kids with ADHD.
Phone: (212) 263-0760 or (516) 358-1811
www.aboutourkids.org/aboutus/programs/adhd.

Pediatric Speech Language and Literacy Services in Cross River specializes in speech and language delay, and reading, writing, and spelling.
Phone: (914) 763-3278
www.SpeechLanguageLiteracy.com.

Mary Petronella is a special education advocate in Bronxville.
Phone: (914) 771-5398
E-mail: mtpetronella@yahoo.com.

Resources for Children with Special Needs is an independent, not-for-profit TAC resource, providing information and referral, case management and support, advocacy, training, and information services to New York City's parents and caregivers of children with disabilities and special needs.

Phone: (212) 677-4650
www.resourcesnyc.org.

Sinergia operates two TAC PTI centers, the Metropolitan Parent Center (MPC) and the Long Island Parent Center (LIPC). Training includes a 5-week series in educational advocacy offered at least twice annually to assist parents become better advocates for their children. One-to-one assistance and advocacy is provided to parents experiencing difficulties with school issues.
Phone: (212) 643-2840 or (866) 867-9665
www.sinergiany.org.

Stepping Forward Parent Education Program in New York City offers training to parents of children with LDs.
Phone: (646) 479-4648
E-mail: lyuan427@gmail.com.

Upstate Attention Deficit Hyperactivity Disorders Program at SUNY Upstate Medical University offers assessment and treatment of ADHD. Located in Syracuse.
Phone: (315) 464-3188
www.upstate.edu/uh/psych/psychclinics/adhd.php.

Ronald Van Norstrand, Esquire, is an attorney practicing special education law in Syracuse.
Phone: (315) 422-3300
E-mail: ronvannorstrand@choiceonemail.com.

NORTH CAROLINA

ADHD Clinic at Wake Forest Medical Center provides assessment and treatment services for children and adolescents with ADHD.
Phone: (336) 716-2255 or (800) 446-2255
http://www1.wfubmc.edu/psychiatry/.

Stacey Bawtinhimer is an attorney practicing special education law in Ayden.
Phone: (252) 349-3273
E-mail: bawtinhimer@coastalnet.com.

Camp Timberwolf is an outdoor tent camping program in Hendersonville for boys and girls ages 6 through 12 with ADD, ADHD, LD, and similar behavioral challenges.
Phone: (828) 697-9379
www.camptimberwolf.com.

Cynthia Daniels-Hall is a special education advocate in Cary.
Phone: (919) 469-2684
danielshallc@aol.com.

Duke ADHD Program is part of the Child and Family Study Center in the Division of Child Psychiatry, Department of Psychiatry at Duke University

Medical Center in Durham. Services include assessment and treatment of ADHD.
Phone: (919) 416-2096
http://www2.mc.duke.edu/adhdprogram.

Exceptional Children's Assistance Center (ECAC) is a TAC PTI center based in Davidson, and is serving families throughout the entire state of North Carolina. ECAC may offer some services at no charge.
Phone: (704) 892-1321 or (800) 962-6817
www.ecac-parentcenter.org.

F.I.R.S.T. is a nonprofit TAC resource based in Asheville that serves Buncombe, Madison, Henderson, and Yancey counties. F.I.R.S.T. directs families to resources, and provides information and training on IEPs and other education issues.
Phone: (828) 277-1315 or (877) 633-3178
www.firstwnc.org.

Lisa Flowers is an attorney practicing special education law in Charlotte.
Phone: (704) 943-9475
E-mail: lflowers@childrenslaw.org.

Governor's Advocacy Council for Persons with Disabilities is the designated P&A center for persons with disabilities in North Carolina. Based in Raleigh.
Phone: (919) 733-9250 or (800) 821-6922
www.gacpd.com.

Olson Huff Center for Child Development provides medical and therapy services to children and adolescents with learning difficulties. Part of Mission Children's Hospital and located in Asheville.
Phone: (828) 213-1780
http://missionhospitals.org/huff-other.htm#adhd.

University of North Carolina Greensboro Psychology Clinic provides assessment and evaluation for ADHD in both children and adults.
Phone: (336) 334-5662
www.uncg.edu/psy/psychologyclinic/index.html.

NORTH DAKOTA

North Dakota Protection & Advocacy Project is the designated P&A center for persons with disabilities in North Dakota. Based in Bismark.
Phone: (701) 328-2950 or (800) 472-2670
www.ndpanda.org.

Pathfinder Parent Training and Information Center is a statewide nonprofit TAC resource, providing special education services for parents of

children and youth with all disabilities and professionals. It is centrally located in Minot.
Phone: (701) 837-7500 or (800) 245-5840
www.pathfinder.minot.com.

OHIO

Julie Bonasera is a special education advocate in Columbus.
Phone: (615) 451-9581
E-mail: julie@bonasera.org.

Anne Brigham is an attorney practicing special education law in Fairport Harbor.
Phone: (216) 513-7450
E-mail: brighamat@aol.com.

Cincinnati Children's Developmental Disabilities at Cincinnati Children's Hospital Medical Center provides diagnosis, evaluation, treatment, training, and education for infants, children, and adolescents with developmental disorders, including ADHD.
Phone: (513) 636-4200 or (800) 344-2462
www.cincinnatichildrens.org/svc/alpha/d/disabilities.

Cleveland Clinic's ADHD Center for Evaluation and Treatment (ACET) offers assessment and treatment designed to include recommendations for both home and school.
Phone: (216) 445-2066
http://cms.clevelandclinic.org/childrenshospita.

Hickman & Lowder is a law firm practicing special education law in Cleveland.
Phone: (216) 861-0360
www.hickman-lowder.com.

Legal Aid Society of Columbus (LASC) provides legal assistance in civil cases to low-income individuals. LASC also holds workshops on various subjects, including child advocacy.
Phone: (614) 224-8374
www.columbuslegalaid.org.

Judy L. Marks is a special education advocate in Canton.
Phone: (330) 265-7931
E-mail: marks815@aol.com.

Ellen Mavriplis is a special education advocate in Cincinatti.
Phone: (513) 543-7771
E-mail: emavriplis@cinci.rr.com.

Ohio Coalition for the Education of Children with Disabilities (OCECD) is a statewide nonprofit TAC resource based in Marion. OCECD provides

one-on-one consultation, parent training sessions, literature, and cooperative projects with local parent support organizations, including training on early childhood.
Phone: (740) 382-5452 or (800) 374-2806

Ohio Legal Rights Service is the designated P&A center for persons with disabilities in Ohio. Based in Columbus.
Phone: (614) 466-7264 or (800) 282-9181
http://olrs.ohio.gov.

Cindy L. Slavens is a special education advocate in Salem.
Phone: (330) 332-2860
www.geocities.com/cslavens2000/mypage.html.

Special Education Services is a TAC CPRC based in Cleveland.
Phone: (216) 289-4332
www.ocecd.org.

STARFISH Advocacy Association (SAA) is a nonprofit organization, providing support to families of children with neurological disorders. Based in Shaker Heights.
Phone: (216) 283-2377
www.starfishadvocacy.org.

Stark County Mental Health Foundation Child and Adolescent Service Center offers ADHD clinics for assessment and treatment of ADHD for children ages 6 through 18.
Phone:
Shipley office: (330) 454-7917 or (800) 791-7917
Belden office: (330) 649-7373
Alliance office: (330) 823-5335
www.casrv.org/adhd_clinic.htm.

Summer Treatment Program (STP) is a 7-week-long program for children with ADHD, sponsored by the Cleveland Clinic Foundation. Individually designed treatment plans are made with each family to address its child's behavioral, emotional, and learning difficulties. Ages 6 through 14.
Phone: (216) 445-2066
http://cms.clevelandclinic.org/childrenshospital.

Thomas J. Zraik, Esquire, is an attorney practicing special education law in Sylvania.
Phone: (419) 882-2559
E-mail: zraiklaw@buckeye-express.com.

OKLAHOMA

Melody Ruth Andrews is a special education advocate in Norman.
Phone: (405) 364-0270
www.parentadvocat.info.

Wanda Cassidy is a special education advocate in Clayton.
Phone: (918) 569-7571
E-mail: oldokie@pisp.net.

Child Study Center at the University of Oklahoma Health Sciences Center in
Oklahoma City provides an Autism clinic, speech/language screenings, physical
developmental screenings, and ADD/ADHD testing. Potential clients must
have a referral from their physician, social worker, SoonerStart, or other health
professional.
Phone: (405) 271-5700
www.pediatrics.ouhsc.edu.

George McCaffrey is a special education attorney in Oklahoma City.
Phone: (405) 767-3300
www.mccaffreylegal.com.

Neurocognitive & Behavioral Diagnostic Associates are educational specialists and neuropsychologists in Tulsa, offering LD assessment services with
recommendations for home and school.
Phone: (918) 488-6165
www.nbdaok.com.

Oklahoma Disability Law Center, Inc., (ODLC) is a federally funded P&A
center. ODLC provides legal services to eligible clients, as well as information,
education, and referrals to other agencies that might be able to help. Based in
Oklahoma City.
Phone: (405) 525-7755
www.oklahomadisabilitylaw.org.

Oklahoma PTI Project is a TAC resource providing training and information
to parents of special needs children.
Phone: (877) 533-4332.

Town & Country School is an accredited private school for children with
LDs in grades K through 12.
Phone: (918) 296-3113
www.tandcschool.org.

Paul E. Swain is an attorney practicing special education law in Tulsa.
Phone: (918) 599-0100
www.swainlawtulsa.com.

OREGON

Mary E. Broadhurst is an attorney practicing special education law in Eugene.
Phone: (541) 683-8530
www.marybroadhurst.com.

Oregon Advocacy Center is the designated P&A center for persons with
disabilities in Oregon. Based in Portland.

Phone: (503) 243-2081 or (800) 452-1694
www.oradvocacy.org.

Oregon Parent Training & Information Center (OR PTI) is based in Salem but has regional staff throughout the state. Services offered include a lending library of videos and books, training on a variety of topics related to children with disabilities, IEP training, information and referral, and a special education helpline.
Phone: (503) 581-8156 or (888) 505-2673
www.open.org/~orpti/.

Dana R. Taylor, Esquire, is an attorney practicing special education law in Portland.
Phone: (503) 226-1371
E-mail: dtaylor@duffykekel.com.

PENNSYLVANIA

ABC Consulting Services is an information and advocacy agency operated by Pam Cook in Pittsburg.
Phone: (412) 851-0252
www.abcadvocacy.net.

ADHD Program at Allentown's Sacred Heart Hospital provides evaluation and treatment planning services to Lehigh Valley families.
Phone: 610-776-5456
www.shh.org/programs/adhd.asp.

Maryann Amici is a parent mentor at the Chester County Intermediate Unit (CCIU).
Phone: (484) 237-5000
E-mail: MaryannA@cciu.org.

The ARC of Lehigh and Northampton Counties provides advocacy services to persons with developmental disabilities. Based in Bethlehem.
Ph: (610) 849-8076.

AVID Learning Center in New Kensington offers diagnosis, therapy, and educational advocacy for persons with LDs.
Phone: (724) 594-1090
www.avidlearning.org.

Stepheni Trott Batipps is a special education advocate in Philadelphia.
Phone: (215) 732-7277.

Karen Brenneman is an advocate with Parents Involved Network (PIN) of Pennsylvania in Chester County.
Phone: (610) 932-8864
www.PINofPa.org.

John and Jeana Brooks are special education advocates in Chambersburg.
Phone: (717) 264-6169
E-mail:
John: horses305@yahoo.com
Jeana: quicknana1@yahoo.com.

Camp Lee Mar is a private residential camp in Lackawaxen for children and young adults with mild-to-moderate learning and developmental challenges.
Phone:
Summer phone: (570) 685-7188
Winter phone: (215) 658-1708
www.leemar.com.

Center for Management of ADHD at the Children's Hospital of Philadelphia diagnoses and treats attention and learning problems in children and adolescents. Specialty Care Centers operate in Bucks County, Exton, King of Prussia, Princeton, Voorhees, and the Atlantic region.
Phone: (877) 827-2343
www.chop.edu.

Richard Chamovitz is an attorney practicing special education law in Wayne.
Phone: (610) 687-0703
E-mail: Rchamovitz@comcast.net.

Dr. Robyn Forbes Druckker is a special education advocate in Paoli.
Phone: (610) 296-9828
E-mail: rforbesdrucker@gmail.com.

Education Law Advocates, **PC**, is a law firm practicing special education law in West Chester.
Phone: (610) 696-5006
www.educationlawadvocates.com.

Trudy Fulmer is a special education advocate in Sellersville, focusing on evaluations, educational consulting, teacher/parent training, Down's syndrome, mental retardation, diabetes, and ADHD.
Phone: (215) 258-3377
E-mail: rfulmer@comcast.net.

Kathy Gingerich is a special education advocate with the Arc of Lebanon County.
Phone: (717) 920-2727
E-mail: kgingerich@arcofdc.org.

Good Shepherd's Pediatric Rehabilitation Program at Dornsife Pediatric Center in Allentown provides diagnostic, evaluative treatment and referral services for children up to 18 years old with ADHD.
Phone: 610-776-3100 or (888) 447-3422
www.goodshepherdrehab.org/pediatric-rehab.

Nova Harris is an advocate with the Mental Health Association of Berks (MHA). Nova focuses on autism, writing, IEPs, behavior, and discipline.
Phone: (610) 775-3000.

Carol Hemingway is a special education advocate in Philadelphia.
Phone: (215) 551-5729
E-mail: Carol1725@msn.com.

Hispanics United for Exceptional Children (HUNE) is a nonprofit TAC CPRC based in Philadelphia. HUNE provides training, support, and limited individual assistance for parents of children with disabilities.
Phone: (215) 425-6203
www.huneinc.org.

Linda Holgate is an educational advocate based in Wyoming County. Ms. Holgate will consider travel to the Poconos, Philadelphia, and the New York border.
Phone: (570) 945-3402
E-mail: LJH3402@aol.com.

Learning Styles & Solutions, LLC, is based in Aston and provides individualized educational therapy to families in Bergen and Delaware counties.
Phone: (610) 459-8878
E-mail: moiraprager@comcast.net.

Dennis C. McAndrews, Esquire, is an attorney practicing special education law in Berwyn.
Phone: (610) 648-9300
www.mcandrewslaw.com.

Deirdre McDermott is a special education advocate in Havertown.
Phone: (610) 446-0237
E-mail: mcdermottclan5@verizon.net.

Oni McMullen is a special education advocate in Philadelphia.
Phone: (215) 923-3349.

Sheri Mearhoff, M.Ed., is a special education advocate in Douglasville.
Phone: (610) 689-9330
E-mail: sheritm@dejazzd.com.

The Mentor Parent Program is a TAC CPRC based in Pittsfield and is serving rural northwest Pennsylvania.
Phone: (814) 563-3470 or (888) 447-1431
www.mentorparent.org.

Amber Mintz is a special education advocate in Wernersville, focusing on autism, IEPs, parent training, elementary age students, and positive behavioral interventions.
Phone: (610) 927-9904
E-mail: amintz@ptd.net.

Connie Mohn is an advocate at the ARC of Chester County in West Chester.
Phone: (610) 696-8090, ext 220
www.arcofchestercounty.org.

Janice Nathan, M.S., CCC-SLP, is a special education advocate in Pittsburg.
Phone: (412) 363-8388
E-mail: janaz5@aol.com.

Robyn L. Oplinger is a special education advocate in Wescosville.
Phone: (610) 398-7862
E-mail: rloplinger@rcn.com.

Parent Education and Advocacy Leadership Center is a TAC resource in Pittsburg that serves western and central Pennsylvania. The Peal Center provides training and information for parents and friends of children with disabilities, as well as their educators and advocates.
Phone: (412) 422-1040 or (866) 950-1040
www.pealcenter.org.

Parent Education Network is a statewide TAC PTI center based in York.
Phone: (717) 600-0100 or (800) 522-5827
www.parentednet.org.

Pennsylvania P&A, Inc., is a nonprofit organization serving as the P&A center for persons with disabilities in Pennsylvania. Based in Harrisburg.

James Peters is an attorney practicing special education law in Newton.
Phone: (610) 353-8531
www.educationlawservices.com.

Catherine Merion Reisman is an attorney practicing special education law in Philadelphia.
Phone: (215) 772-1500
www.mmwr.com.

Round Lake Camp in Lakewood is for children between the ages of 7 and 19 with ADHD and/or mild social skill disorders. Jewish Shabbat services are provided.
Phone:
Winter phone: (973) 575-3333, ext 145
Summer phone: (570) 798-2551
http://roundlakecamp.org.

Debra Schafer, B.A., is a special education consultant in Newton.
Phone: (215) 497-9738
E-mail: ASPEDAdvocate@aol.com.

Summit Camp in Honesdale serves special needs boys and girls ages 8–17, including those with ADHD.
Phone: (212) 689-3880 or (800) 323-9908
www.summitcamp.com.

Bill Whitecavage is a special education advocate in Ringtown.
Phone: (570) 889-5571
E-mail: wwhitecavage@accessservices.org.

Young Law Office in Doyletown offers advocacy and IEP services, as well as legal services for persons with LDs.
Phone: (215) 348-5448
www.ileneyoung.com.

Puerto Rico

APNI is a TAC resource protecting the rights and services of special needs children and their families. APNI is based in San Juan, but provides services throughout Puerto Rico.
Phone: (787) 763-4665 or (800) 981-8492
www.apnipr.org.

Ombudsman for Persons with Disabilities is the designated P&A center for Puerto Ricans with disabilities. Based in San Juan.
Phone: (787) 725-2333 or (800) 981-4125
www.oppi.gobierno.pr.

Rhode Island

Mary Norton Bobrowski, Esquire, is an attorney practicing special education law in Providence.
Phone: (401) 223-1400
E-mail: mbobrowski@mtmlaw.us.

Merrill Friedmann, Esquire, is an attorney practicing special education law in East Greenwich.
Phone: (401) 884-4737
E-mail: mjf417@cox.net.

Shelly Greene, M.Ed., is a special education advocate and consultant in Providence.
Phone: (401) 454-4682
E-mail: shellygreene@cox.net.

Learning, Attention and Behavior (LAB) Program at the Child Neurodevelopment Center at Rhode Island Hospital in Providence offers assessment, treatment, and medication management for children in the preschool through junior high school years who have ADHD or other related school and behavioral problems.
Phone: (401) 444-2345
www.lifespan.org/hch/services/.

Rhode Island Disability Law Center (RIDLC) provides free legal assistance to persons with disabilities, acting as the state's designated P&A center. Based in Providence.

Phone: (401) 831-3150 or (800) 733-5332
www.ridlc.org.

Rhode Island Parent Information Network (RIPIN) is a charitable TAC resource. It is located in Pawtucket but provides assistance throughout the state.
Phone: (401) 727-4144 or (800) 464-3399
www.ripin.org.

Amy R. Tabor, Esquire, is an attorney practicing special education law in Pawtucket.
Phone: (401) 727-1616
E-mail: htcamy@yahoo.com.

South Carolina

Family Resource Center for Disabilities and Special Needs is a nonprofit TAC resource located in Charleston, and is providing information services throughout the Low Country.
Phone: (843) 266-1318
www.frcdsn.org.

Demal I Mattson, Jr., is an attorney practicing special education law in Mt. Pleasant.
Phone: (843) 881-2334
E-mail: ymattson@aol.com.

Parents Reaching Out to Parents of South Carolina is a private, nonprofit TAC resource based in Columbia, and is providing services throughout the state. PRO-Parents provide information and training to families of children with all types of disabilities. Telephone counseling, workshops, and written material are available.
Phone: (803) 772-5688 or (800) 759-4776
www.proparents.org.

Protection and Advocacy for People with Disabilities, Inc. (P&A) is the designated P&A center for persons with disabilities in South Carolina. Based in Columbia.
Phone: (803) 782-0639 or (866) 275-7273
www.protectionandadvocacy-sc.org.

South Dakota

South Dakota Advocacy Services (SDAS) is an independent nonprofit corporation designated by the Governor to assist in providing P&A services to South Dakotans with disabilities. Based in Pierre.
Phone: (605) 224-8294 or (800) 658-4782
www.sdadvocacy.com.

South Dakota Parent Connection is a PTI center based in Sioux Falls. SD Parent Connection provides information and training to parents of children with disabilities or special health care needs throughout the state.
Phone: (605) 361-3171 or (800) 640-4553
www.sdparent.org.

Tennessee

William Allen, Esquire, practices special education law with the firm of Mostoller, Stulberg, and Whitfield in Oak Ridge.
Phone: (865) 482-4466
www.msw-law.com.

Disability Law & Advocacy Center of Tennessee (DLAC) is a nonprofit organization designated as the P&A center for Tennesseans with disabilities. Based in Nashville.
Phone: (615) 298-1080 or (800) 342-1660
www.dlactn.org.

Barbara H. Dyer, Esquire, is an attorney practicing special education law in Johnson City.
Phone: (423) 534-9827
E-mail: bhdyer1@netscape.net.

Jennifer C. Parker, Esquire, is an attorney practicing special education law with the firm of Kramer, Horne, Wells, and Strong in Memphis.
Phone: (901) 524-0200
E-mail: jparker@kramerhorne.com.

Support and Training for Exceptional Parents (STEP) is a statewide family-to-family TAC resource based in Greeneville. STEP provides free information, advocacy training, and support services, and may render some services at no cost.
Phone: (423) 639-0125 or (800) 280-7837
www.tnstep.org.

Texas

ADD Treatment and Research Center provides psychological services, evaluation, and counseling for children and adults with ADHD and LDs.
Phone: (972) 980-7488
www.addtesting.com.

Advocacy, Inc., is the federally funded and authorized P&A system for Texans with disabilities. Education and referral services are available to everyone; advocacy services may be available for eligible individuals.
Phone:
Austin office: (512) 454-4816, (800) 252-9108, or (800) 315-3876
Beaumont office: (409) 832-4872 or (800) 880-0821

Corpus Christi office: (361) 883-3623
Dallas office: (214) 630-0916 or (800) 880-2884
El Paso office: (915) 542-0585 or (800) 948-1824
Ft. Worth office: (817) 336-0075
Houston office: (713) 974-7691 or (800) 880-0821
Laredo office: (956) 722-7581
Longview office: (903) 758-8888 or (866) 758-5888
Lubbock office: (806) 765-7794
McAllen office: (956) 630-3013 or (800) 880-8401
Nacogdoches office: (936) 560-1455
San Antonio office: (210) 737-0499 or (800) 880-8401
Wichita Falls office: (940) 761-1199
www.advocacyinc.org.

ARC of Texas is a nonprofit volunteer organization for people with mental retardation and other developmental disabilities. The ARC supports families, advances public policies, provides training programs, and refers families to a statewide network of advocates. It has more than thirty-five local chapters throughout the state.
Phone: (713) 734-5355, (713) 643-6291, or (800) 252-9729
www.thearcoftexas.org.

Kathy Bennett is a special education advocate in Dallas with Advocating Solutions for Kids (ASK). Spanish bilingual services are available.
Phone: (214) 793-6352
www.askadvocate.org.

Briarwood School is an independent, nonprofit, co-educational day school for children with learning differences in grades K through 12.
Phone: (281) 493-1070
www.briarwoodschool.org.

Martin J. Cirkel, Esquire, is an attorney practicing special education law in Round Rock with Cirkiel and Associates, O.C.
Phone: (512) 244-6658
www.cirkielaw.com.

Rose Marie Cruz is a volunteer special education advocate in Laredo.
Phone: (956) 728-9907
www.rosemariecruz.com.

Matthew L. Finch is an attorney practicing special education law in San Antonio.
Phone: (210) 223-1123
www.mfinchlaw.com.

FOCUS Initiative is a consulting firm offering social coaching sessions, student advocacy services, educational consultations, and conference presentations. Based in Sugar Land.

Phone: (281) 240-0663
www.asdfocus.com.

Susan Feller Heiligental is an attorney practicing education law in Austin.
Phone: (512) 585-1576
E-mail: studentslawyer@sbcglobal.net.

Legal Aid of Northwest Texas is a legal aid regional office with lawyers who take some special education cases for families who meet their income requirements. They have several branch offices in northwest Texas.
Phone: (888) 529-5277; Monday–Friday 9–12 A.M.
www.lanwt.org.

Lolalee E. Livingston is a special education advocate in Plano.
Phone: (972) 758-9123
www.advocacyedu.org.

Lone Star Legal Aid provides a full range of legal services to a significant number of low-income clients and the client community in seventy-two counties in the east region of Texas and four counties in southwest Arkansas. Offices are located in Angleton, Beaumont, Bellville, Belton, Bryan, Conroe, Galveston, Houston, Longview, Nacogdoches, Paris, Texarkana, Tyler, and Waco.
Phone: (936) 560-2012
www.lonestarlegal.org.

National ARD/IEP Advocates, or NARDA, is a professional child advocacy service based out of Sugar Land and founded by Louis H. Geigerman. NARDA primarily serves Texas but considers cases out of state. Telephone consultations are considered on a case-by-case basis.
Phone: (281) 265-1506
www.narda.org.

Partners Resource Network or PRN is a TAC PTI center. The Beaumont office serves the Dallas, Fort Worth, Austin, Wichita Falls, southeast Texas, and east Texas areas. The Lubbock office serves the Amarillo, Lubbock, Abilene, San Angelo, and El Paso areas. The Houston office serves the San Antonio, Houston, and Lower Rio Grande Valley areas.
Phone:
Beaumont office: (409) 898-4684 or (800) 866-4726
Lubbock office: (806) 762-1434 or (877) 762-1435
Houston office: (713) 524-2147 or (877) 832-8945
www.PartnersTX.org.

Parents Supporting Parents Network, or PSPN, is a TAC resource in Weslaco that serves families of children ages 0–26 with the full range of disabilities in the Rio Grande Valley, including Hidalgo, Willacy, Star, and Cameron counties. PSPN services include local and regional workshops and

conferences, information and referral, a lending library, support groups, local advocacy, and assistance with the special education process. PSPN may provide many services at no cost.
Phone: (956) 447-8408 or (888) 857-8688
www.pspofrgv.org.

River Oaks Academy in Houston has a specialized summer camp for children ages 5–15 with ADHD or conduct disorder.
Phone: (713) 783-7200
www.riveroaksacademy.com.

Dr. William Robb is a special education advocate in Carrollton.
Phone: (214) 390-1749
E-mail: newfoundinc@aol.com.

Special Kids, Inc. (SKI) is a TAC resource located in Houston, and is serving the Houston south, south central, and central independent school districts.
Phone: (713) 734-5355
www.specialkidsinc.org.

Texas Children's Learning Support Center is part of Texas Children's Hospital in Houston. The staff evaluates each child to identify specific learning obstacles and develop a customized intervention program. Other services include individual, group, and family therapy.
Phone: (832) 825-4164
www.texaschildrenshospital.org/CareCenters/LearningSupport.

Texas Legal Services Center in Austin assists lower income clients. It can refer qualified persons to legal aid centers across the state.
Phone: (800) 622-2520
www.tlsc.org.

Texas Rio Grande Legal Aid Texas provides free legal services to indigent residents of south and west Texas, and to migrant and seasonal farm workers throughout Texas, Alabama, Arkansas, Kentucky, Louisiana, Mississippi, and Tennessee.
Phone: (888) 988-9996
www.trla.org.

The Winston School (Dallas) is an accredited nonpublic school for children whose minds learn differently. Grades 1 through 12.
Phone: (214) 691-6950
www.winston-school.org.

Winston School San Antonio is an accredited nonpublic school for children whose minds learn differently. Grades 1 through 12.
Phone: (210) 615-6544
www.winston-sa.org.

Mary Lou Wright is a special education advocate in Wichita Falls.
Phone: (940) 723-2818
E-mail: mjwrightMJ@netscape.net.

UTAH

The Disability Law Center (DLC) is a private, nonprofit organization designated as the P&A agency for persons with disabilities in the State of Utah.
Phone: (801) 363-1347 or (800) 662-9080
www.disabilitylawcenter.org.

Utah Parent Center is a nonprofit TAC resource based in Salt Lake and designated as the PTI center for the State of Utah.
Phone: (801) 272-1051 or (800) 468-1160
www.utahparentcenter.org.

VERMONT

Brice Palmer is an attorney practicing special education law in Fair Haven.
Phone: (802) 537-3022
E-mail: askotis@shoreham.net.

Vermont Parent Information Center (VPIC) is a statewide network of support and information for families who have a child with special needs or disabilities, and the professionals who work with them. VPIC is a TAC resource and may provide some or all services at no cost.
Phone: (802) 876-5315 or (800) 639-7170
www.vtpic.com.

Vermont Protection & Advocacy (P&A) is a nonprofit organization, working to ensure the rights of persons with disabilities in Vermont. Based in Montpelier.
Phone: (802) 229-1355 or (800) 834-7890
www.vtpa.org.

VIRGIN ISLANDS

Disability Rights Center of Virgin Islands is the designated P&A center for Virgin Islanders with disabilities. Based in St. Croix.
Phone: (340) 772-1200
www.drcvi.org.

Virgin Islands Family Information Network on Disabilities, or VIFIND, has TAC PTI centers in St. Thomas, St. Croix, and St. John.
Phone: (340) 774-1662
www.taalliance.org/ptis/vifind/.

VIRGINIA

A Balanced Child of Northern Virginia offers dyslexia assessment, individualized academic recommendations, learning strategies, and referrals to experienced professionals. It is located in Catlett but provides services in Prince William, Fauquier, Loudoun, Fairfax, Culpepper, Rappahannock, Stafford, Orange and Madison counties, and the surrounding areas.
Phone: (540) 349-4253
http://abalancedchild.com.

Advocating 4 Education is a special education advocacy service operated by Sharon Tropf in Ashburn.
Phone: (703) 309-4805
E-mail: stropf@adelphia.net.

William Brownley is an attorney practicing special education law in Reston.
Phone: (703) 758-5562
www.brownleylaw.com.

Children's Hospital of Richmond Developmental Program offers a treatment for ADHD or LDs based on each child's individual developmental needs.
Phone: (804) 228-5818
http://childrenshosp-richmond.org/services/developmental_pgm.htm.

Counseling Center of Fairfax offers testing, counseling, and advocacy for persons with LDs.
Phone: (703) 385-7575
www.ccf-web.com.

Ruth Heitin is a special education advocate in Alexandria.
Phone: (703) 519-7181
E-mail: highten@aol.com.

Colleen Henkle is a special education advocate in Leesburg.
Phone: (703) 669-6959
E-mail: irishcakid@aol.com.

Charles Henter, Esquire, is an attorney practicing special education law at Davidson and Kitzmann, PLC, in Charlottesville.
Phone: (434) 972-9600
www.wklawyers.com.

Hyperactivity, Attention and Learning Programs Clinic (HALP) at Children's National Medical Center in Fairfax serves children and adolescents who present difficulties with inattention, hyperactivity, impulsivity, behavioral issues, academic underachievement, and developmental delays, such as ADHD.
Phone: (571) 226-8393
www.cnmc.org/dcchildrens.

Learning Resource Center in Virginia Beach specializes in one-on-one tutoring for students with ADHD. Parent advocacy services are also available.
Phone: (757) 428-3367
www.learningresourcecenter.net.

People with Attentional and Developmental Disabilities (PADDA) is a TAC resource located in Newport News, and is providing services throughout southeastern Virginia.
Phone: (888) 337-2332
www.padda.org.

Beth T. Sigall is an attorney practicing special education law in Arlington.
Phone: (571) 215-3435
E-mail: bethsigall@bethsigall.com.

Virginia Office for Protection and Advocacy serves to help protect the rights of Virginians with disabilities. Based in Richmond.
Phone: (804) 225-2042 or (800) 552-3962
www.vopa.state.va.us.

WASHINGTON

Parent to Parent POWER is a nonprofit CPRC with offices in Tacoma and Seattle. It serves Asian families of children with disabilities, providing transportation, translation and interpretation assistance, educational workshops, community activities, and social events.
Phone: (253) 531-2022
www.p2ppower.org.

Rural Outreach is a CPRC based in Pullman, and is serving eastern Washington.
Phone: (509) 595-5440.

Jeffrey A. Trelka, M.Ed., is a special education advocate in Algona.
Phone: (253) 833-3617
E-mail: pratamedmig@msn.com.

Washington Protection and Advocacy System (WPAS) is a nonprofit organization, protecting the rights of people with disabilities in the State of Washington. WPAS is part of the federally funded P&A system. Based in Seattle.
Phone: (206) 957-0728 or (800) 562-2702
www.wpas-rights.org.

Washington State Parent Information and Training Center is a Tacoma-based nonprofit organization, serving children and adults with disabilities. PAVE offers help in understanding the available education programs for preschoolers and school-age children, and refers parents to resources in the community.
Phone: (253) 565-2266 or (800) 572-7368
www.washingtonpave.org.

Jan Zager, Esquire, is an attorney practicing special education law from his offices on Mercer Island.
Phone: (206) 232-8237
E-mail: jgzager@comcast.net.

WEST VIRGINIA

ADHD Treatment Clinic at West Virginia University offers individualized diagnosis and treatment for children, adolescents, and adults with inattentiveness, impulsivity, noncompliance, troubled peer relations, learning difficulties, and hyperactivity.
Phone: (304) 598-4214
www.hsc.wvu.edu/som/bmed/clinicalServiceSpecialityADHA.asp.

West Virginia Advocates, Inc., is the designated P&A center, protecting the rights of West Virginians with disabilities. Based in Charleston.
Phone: (304) 346-0847 or (800) 950-5250
www.wvadvocates.org.

West Virginia Parent Training and Information (WVPTI) is a statewide nonprofit group located in Clarksburg. It is a TAC resource and may provide some or all services at no cost.
Phone: (304) 624-1436 or (800) 281-1436
www.wvpti.org.

WISCONSIN

Patricia N. Engel, Esquire, is an attorney practicing special education law with the firm of Schott, Bublitz, and Engel in Brookfield.
Phone: (262) 827-1668
www.sbe-law.com.

Native American Family Empowerment Center is a TAC resource in Lac du Flambeau operated by the Great Lakes Intertribal Council.
Phone: (715) 588-3324 or (800) 472-7207.

Walbridge School in Madison offers an elementary school and middle school program for children in grades 1 through 8 of normal or higher intelligence with LDs, such as dyslexia and ADHD.
Phone: (608) 833-1338
www.walbridgeschool.org.

Wisconsin Coalition for Advocacy (WCA) is a nonprofit agency chosen by Wisconsin's Governor to provide protection and advocacy for people with disabilities throughout the state.
Phone:
Madison office: (608) 267-0214 or (800) 928-8778
Milwaukee office: (414) 773-4646 or (800) 708-3034

Rice Lake office: (715) 736-1232 or (877) 338-3724
www.w-c-a.org.

Wisconsin Family Assistance Center for Education, Training & Support
(FACETS) is a nonprofit TAC resource based in Milwaukee. The PTI center
serves statewide, while the CPRC serves the City of Milwaukee.
Phone: (414) 374-4645 or (877) 374-4677
www.wifacets.org.

WYOMING

Parent Information Center (PIC), a project of Parents Helping Parents of
Wyoming, Inc., is a nonprofit PTI center funded by the U.S. Department of
Education. Among other services, PIC maintains a database of parents who
have volunteered to provide support to other parents. Based in Buffalo.
Phone: (307) 684-2277 or (800) 660-9742
www.wpic.org.

Wyoming Protection & Advocacy System, Inc. (P&A) is the official nonprofit
organization designated to provide protection and advocacy services to persons
with disabilities in Wyoming.
Phone:
Cheyenne office: (307) 632-3496
Evanston office: (307) 789-3035
Launder office: (307) 332-8268
http://wypanda.vcn.com.

14

ONLINE AND PRINT RESOURCES

A listing of a group or organization or a link to a Web site does not imply the author's or publisher's agreement with or endorsement of the listed service or provider.

INFORMATIVE WEB SITES

www.add.org. The Attention Deficit Disorder Association (ADDA) provides information, resources, and networking about attention deficit hyperactivity disorder (ADHD).

www.addinfonetwork.com. The Attention Deficit Information Network offers support and information to families of children with attention deficit disorder (ADD), adults with ADD and professionals through a network of attention deficit information (AD-IN) chapters. Parent and adult support group chapters can be found throughout the country.

www.cec.sped.org. The Council for Exceptional Children (CEC) is a large international organization dedicated to improving the education of exceptional children, including gifted students and those with disabilities. Many local chapters exist throughout the nation.

www.chadd.org. Children and Adults with Attention Deficit Hyperactivity Disorder (CHADD) is a group with 20,000 members nationwide and 200 support groups across America.

www.copaa.org. The Council of Parent Attorneys and Advocates (COPAA) is a nonprofit organization of attorneys, advocates, and parents, promoting collaboration among parents and educators of children with learning disabilities. COPAA administers the federally funded special education advocate training (SEAT) project, a uniform training program to produce competent special education advocates.

www.4-adhd.com. This Web site offers articles, a listing of online resources, and a directory of persons and organizations providing services to families with ADHD children.

www.ideallives.com. It provides information and resources for parents of children with autism, attention deficit disorder, Down's syndrome, cerebral palsy, developmental delays, spina bifida, dyslexia, a vision or hearing impairment, traumatic brain injury, speech impairment, and mental health concerns.

www.ldanatl.org. The Learning Disabilities Association of America (LDA) provides support to parents and teachers of children with learning disabilities. LDA has more than 200 state and local affiliates in 42 states and Puerto Rico.

www.ldonline.org. LD OnLine is an extensive Web site, containing articles, expert columns, essays, children's writing and artwork, a resource guide, bulletin boards, and a yellow pages referral directory of professionals, schools, and products. The Web site is an educational service of public television station WETA in Washington, DC.

www.ldresources.org. It is a collection of more than 1,000 entries, relating to learning disabilities (LDs) with hundreds of comments from community members. Topics include LD news, books, education, schools and colleges for LD persons, support sites, and assistive technology.

www.ncld.org. The National Center for Learning Disabilities (NCLD) provides essential information to parents, professionals, and individuals with learning disabilities, promotes research and programs to foster effective learning, and supports policies to protect and strengthen educational rights and opportunities.

www.nimh.nih.gov/publicat/adhd.cfm. It is the National Institute of Mental Health's home page for ADHD information.

www.schwablearning.org. It is a nonprofit organization dedicated to providing reliable, parent-friendly information about learning disorders from experts and parents.

www.studentswholearn.fawco.org. From the Federation of American Women's Clubs Overseas, this site defines common learning differences, such as dyslexia and ADHD, and provides suggestions and information on schools, teaching methods, and support groups for Americans living overseas.

www.theadhddoc.com. Dr. Vincent J. Monastra, "the ADHD doc," is a nationally recognized specialist in the treatment of children, teens, and adults with ADHD. Dr. Monastra provides parenting tips on a wide range of topics, including nutrition and behavior issues.

www.wrightslaw.com. It provides information about special education law, education law, and advocacy for children with disabilities. Wrights Law has thousands of articles and other free resources about dozens of topics.

HOMESCHOOL INTERNET RESOURCES

www.americanhomeschoolassociation.org. The American Homeschool Association is a service organization sponsored in part by the publishers of *Home Education* magazine. It offers a variety of resources, including e-mail discussion list and free newsletter.

http://californiahomeschool.net. The California Homeschool Network is a statewide grassroots organization dedicated to protecting the fundamental right of parents to educate their children. Its Web site explains current state and federal legislation affecting homeschooling families, and it links families to local support groups throughout California.

http://eho.org. It is a Web site operated by the Eclectic Homeschool Association, a nonprofit corporation. Many Christian resources are listed.

http://groups.yahoo.com/group/ADHD_Homeschool. A Yahoo Group dedicated to parents who homeschool their children with ADHD. Many members are openly

Christian, although secular homeschoolers are not excluded. Membership is required, and it may be given at the discretion of the group leader.

http://home-educate.com/DE/. This Web site offers information specifically to homeschoolers living in the state of Delaware.

www.home-school.com. This is an official site of *Practical Homeschooling* magazine, providing free articles on homeschooling, a listing of organizations, access to homeschooling experts, and an online homeschool forum.

www.homeschool.com. This popular site offers a free "Getting Started e-Kit," access to local homeschool support groups, a free newsletter, community message boards, and links to a number of other resources.

www.homeschoolacademy.com. Bridgeway Academy has been delivering accredited homeschool education since 1989. Its self-paced curriculum makes it possible for some children to graduate early.

www.homeschoolarts.com. Raymond Bohac, Jr., operates this free Web site giving online art lessons in several different media, including pencil, watercolor, pastel, and acrylic paints.

www.homeschoolcentral.com. This Web site offers advice to new homeschoolers, referrals to national organizations and local support groups, and links to curriculum providers.

www.homeschoolchristian.com. This site is a source for information and support for Christian homeschoolers, offering homeschooling information, message boards, and regularly scheduled chats.

www.homeschoolclassifieds.com. The Homeschool Classifieds is a large Web site for buying and selling new and used homeschool materials. It also helps connect and support homeschooling families by announcing homeschool support groups, activities, and events.

www.homeschoolfriendlycolleges.com. This site maintains a large list of private and public colleges and universities that accept homeschool students and homeschoolers. Colleges are listed alphabetically and by region.

http://homeschooling.gomilpitas.com. It is an expansive and popular Web site providing information, resources, and communities for homeschool families, including a large area of articles on special needs of children.

www.homeschoollearning.com. The Home School Learning Network Web site contains many free resources, as well as a dynamic online K-12 curriculum service available with a subscription.

www.homeschoolmath.net. HomeschoolMath.net is a math resource site for homeschooling parents and teachers, offering free worksheets, interactive tutorials and quizzes, extensive links to games, curriculum guides, teaching tips, and math e-books.

www.homeschoolportal.com/directory. The Homeschool and Education Information Directory lists educational resources, Web sites, and businesses that provide support to the homeschooling community.

www.homeschoolreviews.com. Homeschooling parents or students (ages 13+) who become a member of this site may submit reviews of curricula they have used, giving their perspective to other homeschoolers who are facing curriculum choices. The site also contains a member's forum and online "swap meet."

www.homeschoolzone.com. This Web site has many links to books and resources on homeschooling.

www.hsc.org. The Homeschool Association of California, a nonprofit volunteer-driven support organization, operates this Web site. Even homeschoolers outside of California will benefit from much of the advice and information found here.

www.hslda.org. The Home School Legal Defense Association (HSLDA) is a non-profit advocacy organization established to defend and advance the constitutional right of homeschooling parents. HSLDA offers legal consultation by letter and phone, negotiations with local officials, and representation in court proceedings. HSLDA also lobbies for homeschool-friendly legislation at both the federal and state levels.

www.internethomeschool.com. The Internet Home School is an accredited K-12 online school, offering math, English, science, social science, health, computer science, foreign languages, and art history.

www.k12.com. The K-12 curriculum is secular, and it includes six subjects: language arts/English, math, science, history, art, and music. It may also be possible for your child to enroll in a K-12 virtual academy or distance learning program, subject to availability in your area.

www.letshomeschool.com. Let's Homeschool provides free resources and curriculum information for homeschooling, including a blog, news, books, curriculum guide, ideas for socialization, homeschool laws, and links to support groups.

www.mathgoodies.com/homeschool. Homeschool Helper's Web site offers free math lessons, worksheets, puzzles, books, links, and other resources.

www.midnightbeach.com/hs. It is a popular noncommercial site operated by a home-schooling father, offering free handbooks, interviews, essays, mailing lists, news-groups, discussion boards, and a Web directory that includes a list of private homeschooling pages sorted by zip code.

www.nheri.org. It is National Home Education Research Institute's Web site, detailing its mission to provide statistics, facts, and other findings on home-based education.

www.nhen.org. It is a site operated by the National Home Education Network (NHEN), a diverse network providing homeschool information, support group listings, news, and related resources.

www.oklahomahomeschool.com. This site includes links to local resources and support groups in Oklahoma, as well as information about Oklahoma laws that affect homeschoolers.

www.thehomeschoolmom.com. It is a Web site operated by Mary Ann Kelley, a mother who began homeschooling in 2000. Local support groups, co-ops, classes and conventions, free Spanish lessons, planners, lesson plans, software downloads, activity pages, homeschool articles, discussion boards, and other resources are available.

www.thsc.org. The Texas Home School Coalition, publishers of the *Handbook for Texas Home Schoolers*, maintains this Web site.

www.washhomeschool.org. The Washington Homeschool Organization (WHO) is a statewide, nonprofit organization supporting homeschoolers across the state.

BOOKS ON PARENTING

Attention, Please! A Comprehensive Guide for Successfully Parenting Children with Attention Deficit Disorders and Hyperactivity. Edna Copeland and Valerie Love. Plantation, FL. Specialty Press.

Dr. Larry Silver's Advice to Parents on ADHD (Second Edition, 1999). Larry Silver. New York. Three Rivers Press.

From Chaos to Calm: Effective Parenting of Challenging Children with ADHD and Other Behavioral Problems (2001). Janet E. Heininger and Sharon Weiss. New York, NY. Perigee Books.

How to Handle a Hard-To-Handle Kid: A Parents' Guide to Understanding and Changing Problem Behaviors (1999). C. Drew Edwards. Minneapolis, MN. Free Spirit Publishing.

1-2-3 Magic: Training Your Child to Do What You Want! (Third Edition, 2003). Thomas Phelan. Ellyn, IL. ParentMagic Inc.

Parents and Adolescents Living Together, Part 1: The Basics (2005). Gerald R. Forgatch and Marion S. Forgatch. Champaign, IL. Research Press.

Parents and Adolescents Living Together, Part 2: Family Problem Solving (2005). Gerald R. Forgatch and Marion S. Forgatch. Champaign, IL. Research Press.

Parenting Children with ADHD: 10 Lessons That Medicine Cannot Teach (2004). Vincent Monastra. Washington, DC. Magination Press.

Power Parenting for Children with ADD/ADHD: A Practical Parent's Guide for Managing Difficult Behaviors (1996). Grad Flick. San Francisco, CA. Jossey-Bass.

Preventive Parenting with Love, Encouragement, and Limits: The Preschool Years (1996). Thomas J. Dishion and Scot G. Patterson. Eugene, OR. Castalia Publishing Co.

Raising Resilient Children: Fostering Strength, Hope, and Optimism in Your Child (2001). Robert Brooks and Sam Goldstein. Lincolnwood, IL. Contemporary Books.

Taking Charge of ADHD: The Complete Authoritative Guide for Parents (Revised Edition, 2000). Russell Barkley. New York. Guilford Press.

The ADD Hyperactivity Workbook for Parents, Teachers, and Kids (Third Edition, 1999). Harvey Parker. Harvey Plantation, FL. Specialty Press.

BOOKS ON CHILDREN'S SOCIAL SKILLS

Good Friends Are Hard to Find: Helping Your Child Find, Make and Keep Friends (1996). Fred Frankel. Glendale, CA. Perspective Publishing.

How to Raise Your Child's Social IQ: Stepping Stones to People Skills for Kids (2000). Cathi Cohen. Washington, DC. Advantage Books.

Why Don't They Like Me? Helping Your Child Make and Keep Friends (1998). Susan Sheridan. Longmont, CO. Sopris West.

BOOKS ON EDUCATION

ADHD Handbook for Families: A Guide to Communicating with Professionals (1999). Paul L. Weingartner. Washington, DC. Child and Family Press.

Attention Deficit Disorder and the Law (Second Edition, 1997). Peter Latham and Patricia Latham. Washington, DC. JKL Publications.

How to Compromise with Your School District Without Compromising Your Child (2004). Gary Mayerson. New York. DRL Books.

Making the System Work for Your Child with ADHD (2004). Peter S. Jensen. New York. Guilford Press.

Negotiating the Special Education Maze: A Guide for Parents and Teachers (Third Edition, 1997). Winifred Anderson, Stephen Chitwood, and Deidre Hayden. Bethesda, MD. Woodbine House.

BOOKS ON ADHD AND COMORBID CONDITIONS

ADHD with Comorbid Disorders: Clinical Assessment and Management (2001). Steven R. Pliszka, Caryn Leigh Carlson, and James M. Swanson. New York. Guilford Press.

Kids in the Syndrome Mix of ADHD, LD, Asperger's, Tourette's, Bipolar, and More!: The One Stop Guide for Parents, Teachers, and Other Professionals (2005). L. Martin, M.D. Kutscher, Tony Attwood, and Robert R. Wolff. London. Jessica Kingsley Publishers.

HELPING FATHERS BECOME INVOLVED

At-Home Dad. This quarterly newsletter promotes the home-based father. It is available at www.parentsplace.com/family/dads.

www.babycenter.com. This site is for new and expectant fathers, with information on preconception, pregnancy, babies, and toddlers.

Bay Area Male Involvement Network. The network is a partnership of Bay Area child services agency workers to increase the involvement of fathers in the lives of their children. It has a male involvement curriculum for training teachers in early childhood education. It is available at www.bamin.org.

www.childtrends.org. Child Trend's Web site includes reports, papers, and other resources in several critical social areas.

Daddy's Home. This is an online resource for primary caregiving fathers. It is available at www.daddyshome.com.

D.A.D.S. (Directing All Dads to Success). This site provides support, education, and varied resources to help dads, along with a discussion forum. It is available at www.dadsinc.com.

FamilyEducation Network. This site brings local, state, and national educational resources together in one place. Its goals include helping parents to be more involved with schools and education. It is available at www.familyeducation.com.

www.fathering.org. This site works to increase awareness of the essential role of fatherhood.

Fathers' Forum Online. This site is dedicated primarily to expectant and new fathers with children up to the age of 2. It is available at www.fathersforum.com.

Fathers' Network. This site serves fathers of children with special needs, namely chronic illness and developmental disability. It is available at www.fathersnetwork.org.

FatherWork. This site contains personal stories from fathers and children, as well as ideas to promote good fathering under various challenging circumstances. It is available at www.fatherwork.byu.edu.

"Father to Father" Initiative. Minnesota was the first state to launch this initiative, and this site has an abundance of state links and resource information. It is available at www.cyfc.umn.edu/Fathernet.

Fedstats. More than seventy agencies of the federal government produce statistics of interest (including fathering) to the public and this site provides access to the full range of them. It is available at www.fedstats.gov.

Kidsource OnLine. This is an online community sharing values and goals in raising, educating, and providing for children. Its goal is to find and deliver the best of health care and education information. It is available at www.kidsource.com.

National Campaign to Prevent Teen Pregnancy. This site seeks to prevent teen pregnancy by supporting values and stimulating actions that are consistent with a pregnancy-free adolescence. It is available at www.teenpregnancy.org.

National Center for Fathering. This site conducts research and distributes data on fathers and fathering. Practical resources are available for dads in nearly every fathering situation. It is available at www.fathers.com.

National Center for Strategic Non-profit Planning and Community Leadership. This site provides details about National Center for Strategic Non-profit Planning and Community Leadership (NPCL)'s public and customized workshop series to help community-based organizations and public agencies better serve young, low-income single fathers, and fragile families. It is available at www.npcl.org.

National Center on Fathers and Families. Its goal is to improve the life chances of children and the efficacy of families. It conducts and disseminates research that advances the involvement of fathers. It is available at www.ncoff.gse.upenn.edu.

National Fatherhood Initiative. This site highlights the importance of dads to the well-being of their children and the entire community. It organizes coalitions and promotes a profathering message to dads. It is available at www.fatherhood.org.

National Head Start Association. The "father-friendly assessment and planning tool" provides checklists for programs to assess their readiness to serve fathers and to develop a father-friendly action plan. It is available at www.nhsa.org/partner/fatherhood/ffanp.htm.

National Latino Fatherhood and Family Institute. This site highlights programs serving Latino fathers and families. It is available at www.nlffi.org.

Zero to Three. This organization promotes the healthy development of babies and young children by promoting good child development practices for mothers, fathers, and providers of childcare. It is available at www.zerotothree.org.

NOTES

INTRODUCTION

1. President's Commission on Excellence in Special Education, *A New Era: Revitalizing Special Education for Children and Their Families*, Executive Summary (Washington, DC: U.S. Department of Education, July 1, 2002).

CHAPTER 1

1. Frank Lewis Dyer and Thomas Commerford Martin, *Edison—His Life and Inventions* (New York: Harper Brothers, 1910), 12.

2. Jonathan Williams and Eric Taylor, "The Evolution of Hyperactivity, Impulsivity and Cognitive Diversity." *Journal of the Royal Society*, October 2005.

CHAPTER 3

1. Gabrielle Weiss and Lily Trockenberg Hechtman, *Hyperactive Children Grown Up: ADHD in Children, Adolescents, and Adults*, Second Edition (New York: The Guilford Press, May 14, 1993).

2. A.T. Henderson and N. Berla, *A New Generation of Evidence: The Family Is Critical to Student Achievement* (Washington, DC: Center for Law & Education, June 1994).

3. "100 Ways for Parents to be Involved in their Child's Education," reprinted with permission from National PTA, www.pta.org. Last accessed September 16, 2004.

CHAPTER 4

1. National Council on Disability, "Discipline of Students with Disabilities; A Position Statement," May 1998. Available at www.ncd.gov/newsrooms/publications/1998/discipline.htm.

2. Office of Special Education and Rehabilitative Services, "A Guide to the Individualized Education Program" (Washington, DC: U.S. Department of Education, May 30, 2006). Available at http://www.ed.gov/offices/OSERS.

CHAPTER 6

1. Marlene Bumgarner, "A Conversation with John Holt," 1980. Available at http://www.naturalchild.com/guest/marlene_bumgarner.html.

2. National Center for Education Statistics, "1.1 Million Home Schooled Students in the United States in 2003," Issue Brief (Washington, DC: Department of Education, July 2004).

3. National Center for Education Statistics, "National Household Education Surveys Program; Parent and Family Involvement in Education Survey" (Washington, DC: Department of Education, 2003).

4. Brian D. Ray, "Strengths of Their Own—Home Schoolers across America: Academic Achievement, Family Characteristics, and Longitudinal Traits" (Salem, OR: National Home Education Research Institute, 1997).

5. Scripps National Spelling Bee, 2005. Available at http://www.spellingbee.com/spellerindex2005.shtml.

6. Office of Special Education and Rehabilitative Services, Office of Special Education Programs, "Home Schooling Children with ADHD Tendencies: Instructional Strategies and Practices" (Washington, DC: Department of Education, 2004). Available at http://www.ed.gov/teachers/needs/speced/adhd/adhd-resource-pt2.pdf.

CHAPTER 7

1. Roy F. Baumeister, Jennifer D. Campbell, Joachim I. Hrueger, and Kethleen Dabis, "Exploding the Self-esteem Myth." *Scientific American Mind*, December 2005, 50–51.

2. David Dunning, Chip Heath, and Jerry M. Suls, "Picture Imperfect." *Scientific American Mind*, December 2005, 22.

3. Roy F. Baumeister, Jennifer D. Campbell, Joachim I. Hrueger, and Kethleen Dabis, "Exploding the Self-esteem Myth." *Scientific American Mind*, December 2005, 51–57.

4. Office of Special Education and Rehabilitative Services, "A New Era: Revitalizing Special Education for Children and Their Families" (Washington, DC: U.S. Department of Education, 2002), 7.

5. Emmy Werner, *The Children of Kauai: A Longitudinal Study from the Prenatal Period to Age Ten* (Honolulu: University of Hawaii Press, 1971).

6. Department of Health and Human Services, "Feeling Good About Yourself," March 2006. Available at http://www.girlshealth.gov/mind/feelinggood.htm.

7. Daniel M. Landers, "The Influence of Exercise on Mental Health." Available at http://www.fitness.gov/mentalhealth.htm. Last accessed January 29, 2007.

8. President's Council on Physical Fitness and Sports Report, "Physical Activity & Sport in the Lives of Girls" (Washington, DC: U.S. Department of Health and Human Services, Spring 1997). Available at http://www.fitness.gov/girlssports.pdf.

9. U.S. Department of Health and Humana Services, "Bullying." Available at http://www.stopbullyingnow.hrsa.gov/HHS_PSA/pdfs/SBN_Tip_24.pdf. Last accessed January 29, 2007.

10. Norma V. Cantu and Judith E. Heumann, "Dear Colleauge," Letter, July 25 2000, Available at http://www.ed.gov/PressReleases/07–2000/Policy Disabilityharassment.doc.

11. U.S. Department of Health and Humana Services, "Tips on Stopping Bullying." Available at http://www.stopbullyingnow.hrsa.gov/HHS_PSA/pdfs/SBN_Tip_21.pdf. Last accessed August 21, 2006.

CHAPTER 8

1. Frank Lewis Dyer and Thomas Commerford Martin, *Edison—His Life and Inventions* (New York: Harper Brothers, 1910), 9.

2. Office of Communications and Outreach, "Helping Your Child Become a Reader," Foreword (Washington, DC: U.S. Department of Education, 2005.).

3. Office of Intergovernmental and Interagency Affairs, Educational Partnerships and Family Involvement Unit, "Reading Tips for Parents" (Washington, DC: U.S. Department of Education, 2003).

4. Frank Lewis Dyer and Thomas Commerford Martin, *Edison—His Life and Inventions* (New York: Harper Brothers, 1910), 97.

5. Ibid., p. 8.

6. Ibid., p. 41.

7. Peggy Soari and Stephen Allison, *Scientists: The Lives and Works of 150 Scientists, Vol. I* (New York: U•X•L publishing, an imprint of Gale, 1996).

CHAPTER 9

1. American Academy of Pediatrics, "Corporal Punishment in Schools," *Pediatrics*, Vol. 106, No. 2, August 2000, 343.

2. American Academy of Pediatrics, "Statement of Reaffirmation," September 1, 2006. Available at http://aappolicy.aappublications.org/cgi/content/full/pediatrics;118/3/1266.

3. Karen M. Carlson, M.Ed., "Early Childhood Education" (University of Minnesota Center for Early Education and Development). Available at http://education.umn.edu/ceed/publications/questionsaboutkids/discipline.htm. Last accessed January 29, 2007.

CHAPTER 10

1. National Center on Birth Defects and Developmental Disabilities, "2003 National Survey of Children's Health" (Washington, DC: Centers for Disease Control). Available at http://www.cdc.gov/ncbddd/adhd/adhdmedicated.htm. Last accessed January 29, 2007.

2. NIMH—The MTA Cooperative Group, "A 14-Month Randomized Clinical Trial of Treatment Strategies for Attention-Deficit Hyperactivity Disorder (ADHD)." *Archives of General Psychiatry*, 1999, 1073–1086.

3. National Institutes of Mental Health, "Attention Deficit Hyperactivity Disorder," 2003. Available at http://www.nimh.nih.gov/publicat/adhd.cfm#treat.

4. Food and Drug Administration, "Public Health Advisory for Adderall® and Adderall® XR," 2005. Available at http://www.fda.gov/cder/drug/advisory/adderall.htm.

5. Food and Drug Administration, "Daytrana®," 2006. Available at http://www.fda.gov/bbs/topics/NEWS/2006/NEW01352.html.

6. National Institutes of Mental Health, "ADHD Drugs Can Stunt Growth," May 2, 2006. Available at http://www.forbes.com/forbeslife/health/feeds/hscout/2006/05/02/hscout532460.html.

7. National Institutes of Mental Health, "Attention Deficit Hyperactivity Disorder," 2003. Available at http://www.nimh.nih.gov/publicat/adhd.cfm#treat.

8. Benjamin W. Van Voorhees, *Medical Encyclopedia: Hyperactivity and Sugar*, January 24, 2006. Available at http://www.nlm.nih.gov/medlineplus/ency/article/002426.htm.

9. National Institutes of Health Consensus Development Panel, "Defined Diets and Childhood Hyperactivity," Volume 4, Number 3, Summary (Washington, DC: National Institutes of Health, 1982).

10. D.W. Hoover and R. Milich, "Effects of Sugar Ingestion Expectancies on Mother-child Interaction," *Journal of Abnormal Child Psychology*, 1994, 501–515.

11. M. Wolraich, R. Milich, P. Stumbo, and F. Schultz, "The Effects of Sucrose Ingestion on the Behavior of Hyperactive Boys," *Pediatrics*, 1985, 657–682.

CHAPTER 11

1. National Center on Birth Defects and Developmental Disabilities, "Other Conditions Associated with ADHD," September 20, 2005. Available at http://www.cdc.gov/ncbddd/adhd/otherconditions.htm.

2. U.S. National Library of Medicine, "Conduct Disorder," *Medline Plus*, December 9, 2004. Available at http://www.nlm.nih.gov/medlineplus/ency/article/000919.htm.

3. Substance Abuse and Mental Health Services Administration, "Children's Mental Health Facts, Children and Adolescents with Conduct Disorder," April 2004. Available at http://www.mentalhealth.samhsa.gov/publications/allpubs/CA-0010.

4. U.S. National Library of Medicine, "Oppositional Defiant Disorder," *Medline Plus*, May 17, 2006. Available at http://www.nlm.nih.gov/medlineplus/ency/article/001537.htm.

5. National Center on Birth Defects and Developmental Disabilities, "ADHD and Risk of Injuries," September 20, 2005. Available at http://www.cdc.gov/ncbddd/adhd/injury.htm.

6. National Center for Injury Prevention and Control, "Playground Injuries: Fact Sheet," September 7, 2006. Available at http://www.cdc.gov/ncipc/factsheets/playgr.htm.

7. National Center on Birth Defects and Developmental Disabilities, "Peer Relationships and ADHD," September 20, 2005. Available at http://www.cdc.gov/ncbddd/adhd/peer.htm.

8. Office of Communications and Public Liaison, National Institute of Neurological Disorders and Stroke, "NINDS Dyslexia Information Page," February 7, 2006. Available at http://www.ninds.nih.gov/disorders/dyslexia/dyslexia.htm.

9. National Institute of Child Health and Human Development, "Children's Reading Disability Attributed to Brain Impairment," August 2, 2002. Available at http://www.nichd.nih.gov/new/releases/disability.cfm.

10. Office of Communications and Public Liaison, National Institute of Neurological Disorders and Stroke, "Tourette Syndrome Fact Sheet," September 25, 2006. Available at http://www.ninds.nih.gov/disorders/tourette/detail_tourette.htm.

11. National Institute of Mental Health, "Obsessive-Compulsive Disorder," October 11, 2006. Available at http://www.nimh.nih.gov/HealthInformation/ocdmenu.cfm.

12. National Institute of Mental Health, "Obsessive-Compulsive Disorder," July 24, 2006. Available at http://intramural.nimh.nih.gov/pocd/pocd-faqs.htm.

13. National Institute of Mental Health, "What Is PANDAS—Pediatric Autoimmune Neuropsychiatric Disorders Associated with Streptococcal Infections?" July 24, 2006. Available at http://intramural.nimh.nih.gov/pocd/pocd-faqs.htm.

14. The National Institute of Mental Health, "Depression in Children and Adolescents," July 1, 2006. Available at http://www.nimh.nih.gov/healthinformation/depchildmenu.cfm.

15. Substance Abuse and Mental Health Services Administration, "Major Depression in Children and Adolescents," April 2003. Available at http://www.mentalhealth.samhsa.gov/publications/allpubs/CA-0011.

16. National Institute of Mental Health, "Child and Adolescent Bipolar Disorder," February 17, 2006. Available at http://www.nimh.nih.gov/publicat/bipolarupdate.cfm.

17. National Institute of Child Health and Human Development, "Autism and Autism Spectrum Disorders," September 1, 2006. Available at http://www.nichd.nih.gov/health/topics/autism_and_autism_spectrum_disorders.cfm.

18. Center for Disease Control and Prevention, "Can Developmental Screening Provide Early Detection?" October 29, 2004. Available at http://www.cdc.gov/ncbddd/autism/asd_devscreen.htm.

19. Office of Communications and Public LiaisonNational Institute of Neurological Disorders and Stroke, "NINDS Asperger Syndrome Information Page," July 17, 2006. Available at http://www.ninds.nih.gov/disorders/asperger/asperger.htm.

CHAPTER 12

1. Head Start Bureau, "Father Involvement—Building Strong Programs for Strong Families" (Washington, DC: Administration on Children, Youth and Families, Department of Health and Human Services, June 2004), 2.

2. Christine Winquist Nord, DeeAnn Brimhall, and Jerry West, "Fathers' Involvement in Their Children's Schools" (Washington, DC: U.S. Department of Education, National Center for Education Statistics, 1997), V.

3. Ibid., p. VI.

4. Ibid., p. VIII.

5. Ibid., p. IX.

6. Ibid., p. VII.

7. U.S. Department of Health and Human Services, "A Call to Commitment: Fathers' Involvement in Children's Learning" (Washington, DC: U.S. Department of Education, 2000), 4–5.

INDEX

About the Author

SCOTT TEEL is a freelance writer based in Texas. He holds a degree in nuclear technology and is also a certified employee benefits specialist. Teel is an adult who has been diagnosed with attention deficit hyperactivity disorder. As a child he was a "tangential thinker" who despite a high I.Q. struggled in the conventional school system.